Union Fleet

Ian Farquhar

NEW ZEALAND SHIP & MARINE SOCIETY (INC)

Endpapers: *A montage of Captain Angus Cameron and his ships*   DE MAUS
Title pages: *The Union Company bought the liner* **Tahiti** *in 1911
and ran her on the Pacific service until her loss in 1930*

First published 1968. Revised edition 1976. This edition 2001.

New Zealand Ship & Marine Society (Inc)
P.O. Box 5104
Wellington
www.nzshipmarine.com

ISBN: 0-9597834-7-4

Text © Ian Farquhar

The right of Ian Farquhar to be identified as the author of this work in terms of
section 96 of the Copyright Act 1994 is hereby asserted.

All rights reserved. No part of this publication may be reproduced, stored in a retrieval system
or transmitted in any form or by any means, electronic, mechanical, photocopying, recording or otherwise,
without the prior written consent of the publisher.

Designed by Afineline
Edited by Gavin McLean
Printed in Hong Kong by Kings Time Printing Press through
Bookprint Consultants Ltd, Wellington, New Zealand.

TAIERI
WAIHORA
MOANA
WAREATEA
PUKAKI
SP CO.
MAPOURIKA
WANAKA
MOURA
WHANGAPE
OVALAU

UNION FLEET

Contents

Preface	*vii*
Chronology	*xvii*
Notes to Fleet List	*xxviii*

PART ONE

Steamers and Motorships from 1875	*1*

PART TWO

Subsidiary and Associated Companies, Sailing Vessels and Hulks	*211*
Subsidiary and Associated Companies	*213*
Sailing Ships	*228*
Chartered, Part Owned and Managed Vessels	*231*
Coal and Oil Storage Hulks	*244*
Harbour Launches, Passenger Tenders	*249*

APPENDICES

Company Colour Scheme, Motto and Coat of Arms	*253*
Personalia	*255*
Acknowledgements	*258*
Reference Sources and Bibliography	*260*
Index	*263*

Preface

Ships of the Union Steam Ship Company of New Zealand Ltd have been sailing in and out of New Zealand and Australian ports for 125 years. Few, if any, corporate enterprises in New Zealand can match the remarkable record of this company. For over 75 years of its history, it was the largest employer, other than government, in New Zealand; it controlled the majority of the shipping services around the New Zealand coast, between Tasmania and mainland Australia, on the Tasman Sea and also had regular sailings to India, North America and islands in the Pacific. It moulded the fragmented early air services in New Zealand into Union Airways of New Zealand Ltd, which was the principal New Zealand commercial airline from 1936 to 1947. Union Airways was also the majority shareholder in Tasman Empire Airways, which commenced Trans Tasman air services in 1940. The company was also a shareholder in the Australian companies Holyman Air and Australian National Airways Ltd.

Although the company had its origins in Dunedin in 1875, the stage was set for its successful debut some years before. Gold had been discovered close to Dunedin in 1861 and the resultant rush of miners and general prosperity in the area that followed made Dunedin the largest city in New Zealand. Its port of Port Chalmers was the busiest in the country and the third largest in the South Pacific behind Sydney and Melbourne. At the time the most prominent businessman in the area was John Jones who had come to Otago in 1838 and established a whaling station at Waikouaiti, a few miles north of Dunedin. Born in Sydney in 1809, he began his career as a waterman and by 1830 he had an inter-

John Jones, *the mercurial entrepeneur whose enterprise guided the rise of the Harbour Steam Company and paved the way for the eventual establishment of the Union Steam Ship Company*   HOCKEN LIBRARY

est in three whaling ships operating around the New Zealand coast. Between 1835 and 1845 he owned eighteen sailing ships, all registered at Sydney. Establishing a trading store in Dunedin in 1848, he moved from Waikouaiti to Dunedin

vii

The young **James Mills** *who controlled every facet of the Union Company, from its establishment in 1875 until he retired as Managing Director in 1913. As Chairman from 1913 to 1936, his advice was widely sought by successive managements*

A partner in the Harbour Steam Company, **John Darling** *was an outstanding innovative engineer and later of considerable help to* **James Mills** *in the supervision of the flow of new ships from Scottish shipyards. He was the first Engineering Superintendent of the company*

in 1854 and was instrumental in taking shares in many new business enterprises. Some of these were successful and some were not. He was the major backer of the ferry services on Otago Harbour and gave every encouragement to shipmasters and shipowners wanting to develop trade with other New Zealand ports and Australia.

From 1863 the ferry services operated under the name of the Harbour Steam Company and it was this consortium of interests – John Jones, Captains James Malcolm, James Macfarlane and engineer John Darling – that put some strength and order into the early steam shipping services in Otago Harbour and to nearby South Island ports. In the latter part of 1868, Jones appointed a young 21-year-old, James Mills, as manager of the Harbour Steam consortium. Mills was the son of the Collector of Customs at Port Chalmers and had grown up in the port through the hustle and bustle of the gold rush period. His appointment, at such a young age, was reflective of the skill of Jones in picking talent and recognising ability. The confidence he expressed in Mills was fully understood a few months later when Jones died suddenly on 16 March 1869, leaving his eldest son, J.R. Jones, his son-in-law, William Isaac and James Mills, trustees of his estate.

Although the shipping enterprise was an established business, its main operating areas would soon be superseded by road and rail connections beyond the province of Otago and if it was to expand and grow, new ships were needed to extend its trading base well beyond Port Chalmers. The little 174-ton steamer *Maori* was purchased in 1869, and the *Beautiful Star* joined her in 1871. Two years later services extended north to Oamaru, Timaru and Lyttelton while the managed steamer *Pretty Jane* called at southern ports.

Although James Mills had become the leading

Merchant bankers Bright Bros. and Company of Liverpool provided bridging mortgage finance for the first few ships of the Union Company. Their only New Zealand office was in Dunedin and the manager, **James A. Walcott**, *was a close friend of* **James Mills**

Peter Denny, *a senior partner in the Dumbarton shipbuilding firm of Wm. Denny & Bros., provided financial support to* **James Mills** *in the building of the first few ships for the Union Company. He formed a sound rapport with* **Mills** *and remained a major shareholder in the company until his death in 1895*

shipping figure in Otago, he knew he had to expand the Harbour Steam Company business if the enterprise was going to survive. He approached a number of local businessmen for financial support and on 17 November 1873 issued his first prospectus for a Union Steam Ship Company of New Zealand Ltd. He sought capital to build three new steamers in Scotland and to absorb the assets of the Harbour Steam Company into the new company. Despite all his efforts in Otago, Canterbury, Wellington and Auckland, he failed to raise sufficient capital in the colony. He had already sent John Darling to Scotland in 1872 to supervise the building of the first new steamer. In March 1874 Mills decided to follow Darling, as he believed capital could be obtained from Scottish investors. He had also established that mortgage monies were readily obtainable through merchant bankers, Bright Bros and Company of Liverpool, which had its only New Zealand office in Dunedin, but he was reluctant to have too much debt at that early stage when the company would commence operations. Through his friendship with the Dunedin manager of Bright Bros., James A. Walcott, he had already secured a substantial loan to build the 335-ton steamer *Bruce* in 1874.

In Glasgow he met Peter Denny, senior partner in the famous Dumbarton shipbuilding firm, Wm. Denny & Bros. In order to secure continuity of business in their shipyard, Peter Denny occasionally took shares in some of the ships they built and following his meetings with Mills, he agreed to provide 37.5 % of the cost of building two steamers. For his part, Mills undertook to raise further capital from Scottish investors, as well as loans from Bright Bros. In a letter to Peter Denny he said "the loan monies will form a very heavy charge on our shares and in fact rather dishearten me". Denny was obviously impressed with the young man from Dunedin, and subsequently agreed to extend the repayments on his investment over a longer period and also suggested to Mills that he might consider "the convenience and propriety in every way of putting all your steamers built and the two proposed ones in Stock as a company. By the interest of our friends and yourselves we might thus be able to place a greater amount in this country than by 64ths [at that time ownership of individual vessels was in shares totaling 64 or in segments of 64 shares divided by 4] in individual ships and thus freeing you from expensive and disagreeable financing".

Mills heeded the advice and with the finance secured for the two new ships to be built by Wm. Denny & Bros., he returned to Dunedin to greet the new steamer *Bruce* of 335 tons, which arrived from Scotland after a 138-day passage. The first of the other two new ships, *Hawea*, arrived at Port Chalmers on 11 June 1875. At 721 tons gross, she was the largest ship on the New Zealand register. Her sister *Taupo* arrived on 3 July and both vessels commenced regular services from Port Chalmers to Manukau via Lyttelton, Wellington, Picton, Nelson, and Taranaki.

The dust was blown off the blueprints of the 1873 plan for the Union Steam Ship Company of N.Z. Ltd and the first meeting of the provisional directors took place in Dunedin on 31 May 1875. The company officially commenced business on 1 July 1875 with its two new steamers as well as three Harbour Steam Company ships – *Maori*, *Beautiful Star* and *Bruce*. The nominal capital of the company was £250,000 but paid up capital on commencement was only £83,580. Of this, the value of the Harbour Steam assets, plus shares from Otago interests totalled 53.1%. Scottish subscribers, including Peter Denny's 28.7%, contributed 39.7% of the capital, with the balance of 7.2% being provided by Canterbury and Wellington shareholders. Of the Otago interest, James Mills and his father held 26.9% of the capital. The long steady build up of customer support through the Harbour Steam Company was a significant factor in consolidating a strong company image with customers.

Within a year of establishment, the Union Company had absorbed its principal competitor on the New Zealand coast. It commenced Trans Tasman services in October 1876 and two years later purchased McMeckan, Blackwood and Company of Melbourne – the largest company operating on the Tasman. It just kept on growing and absorbing any opposition, as well as developing new services out of New Zealand, within Australia, the Pacific Islands and to North America. In 1885 it owned 28 ships; a decade later it had 51 ships.

The company was also a leader in ship design and technology. In 1879 its *Rotomahana* was the first ship in the world to be built of mild steel. She was also fitted with bilge keels to ease the rolling. *Manapouri* in 1882 was the first to be fitted throughout with incandescent electric light and the *Loongana* in 1904 was the first vessel with steam turbine propulsion to operate in Australasian waters. The *Aorangi* in 1924 was the largest (17,491 tons) and fastest (18 knots) motor liner in the world. The inter-island express steamer *Rangatira*, built in 1931, was the first turbo electric powered vessel in the fleet, with the capacity to operate at 21.5 knots, making her one of the fastest ferry steamers in the world. The record passage times of the *Awatea* in 1937, which was the largest (13,482 tons) passenger ship built by the company for the Trans Tasman service, stood for 24 years. In 1975 the Union Company took delivery of the first of four vessels powered by gas turbines. Burning 20% more fuel than diesel-powered vessels but with fewer moving parts requiring less maintenance, the unforseen world oil crisis undercut the benefits of gas turbine propulsion. Soaring fuel prices made the ships quite uneconomic and the first two vessels *Seaway Prince* and *Seaway Princess* remained in service only eight years while one of the two remaining gas turbine vessels (*Union Rotoiti*) was re-engined with diesel propulsion eleven years after entering service.

Throughout its history the company continued to develop the latest technology in ship design, propulsion systems and new concepts in cargo handling ranging from the traditional union purchase derricks, to shipboard cranes and eventually roll-on, roll-off, initially with stern ramps and later using quarter ramps for greater port call flexibility.

As a first step in reducing labour intensive handling of cargo, the Union Company introduced a 120 cubic foot container in 1959. The size was determined by the maximum weight that the union purchase derricks of the ships could lift. The introduction of the first roll-on, roll-off ships in the Bass Strait services in 1964 saw the development of a large steel pallet (14.5 feet x 8 feet) called a "Railroader". This unit could be handled by a heavy-duty forklift and was initially used for the carriage of rolls of newsprint. As further roll-on, roll-off services were developed in the New Zealand coastal trades from 1965 and across the Tasman from 1969, the company added collapsible sides to the pallet and renamed it the "Seafreighter". Shippers also had the option of stowing one Seafreighter on top of the other to gain freighting benefits while the company had the advantage of better space utilisation in the vessels. Empty Seafreighters could be collapsed and transported in groups of ten. At that time many warehouses did not have heavy lifting equipment and the Seafreighter proved a very successful unit until it was progressively superseded by the standard ISO container from the mid 1970s.

With the changing pace and style of business, particularly over the past 50 years, it is quite unusual, for any company to have survived as an entity under its original name and of the names of shipowners in *Lloyd's Register of Shipping* registers over a century ago compared to lists of British companies still operating as shipowners today, only P & O, Andrew Weir and Denholms remain. All the famous Australian-registered shipping companies established last century – Adelaide Steam, Australasian United Steam Navigation, Burns Philp, Howard Smith, Huddart Parker, McIlwraith McEacharn and Melbourne Steam are no longer cargo handling shipowners.

Over its lifetime, the Union Company owned over 300 vessels, had a financial interest in up to another 30 vessels, and has chartered several hundred more to supplement existing services. The gross tonnage of the first five ships totalled 2127 tons compared to the three ships the company owned in 1999 at 72,455 tons! The greatest number of ships owned at any one time was 81 in 1921 and from a fleet in 1923 with a total gross tonnage of 267,958 tons, there has been a steady decline ever since as particular trades and services have been dropped. With their bronze green hulls and red and black funnels the ships essentially retained the identity established in 1875.

The company also underwent some significant financial restructuring at various times throughout its history. It was renamed Union Shipping Group Ltd in 1980 and the Australian operations came under the control of a separate company from 1987. The importance of the Australian business was recognised in 1996 when the Chief Executive Officer of the company moved his office from Auckland to Sydney.

In terms of profitability, it still held its own despite a much smaller fleet and the extreme elements of competition the company had to contend with. Profits fluctuated depending on the trade restraints and economic conditions in New Zealand and Australia, competition and the ability to share space with other companies to achieve better port coverage and service frequency. In 1905 the company made a net profit of £66,678 and in 1916 the net profit was £156,000. If these figures are converted on consumer price indexes over the period they equate to present day figures of $6,667,800 and $12,000,000 respectively. Neither figure compares to the record net profit of $32,474,000 achieved in 1990.

How did the Union Company manage to survive all these years when so many other promising ventures have disappeared through bankruptcy, merger and changing business trends, particularly within the last 40 years when the pace of change in all areas of business has been so dramatic? The success formula for the Union Company has been no different to any other company – it lies with just a few key people who were around at the right time and who had the foresight and vision to lead the company into a new development phase. To be simplistic there have probably been only three entrepreneurial leaders throughout the history of the company – there have been many good managers but they essentially maintained the company structure that had been set out for them.

The first of these leaders was of course, James Mills, the company's founder. The build up of the company and its steady expansion is well documented by Dr Gavin McLean in his book *The Southern Octopus* (New Zealand Ship and Marine Society 1990). The level of expansion was not just luck and a dream ride on a period of colonial growth – it was essentially driven by Mills, whose management techniques and skills were remarkable. Nowadays it is customary for companies to be ISO qualified and audited. Total quality management is nothing new and the Union Company, under James Mills, was one of the best-run enterprises in Australasia.

The company had excellent documented systems both on shore and at sea – *The General Instructions for Captains and Officers* (Red book), *Instructions for Pursers* (Blue book), the monthly *Pocket Guide* setting out all the sailings and services of the fleet and the like were all based on experience, common sense and the measure of pride in that the Union Company was number one! The instruction booklets covered every conceivable situation – for example no short ropes were to be thrown overboard – any condemned rope was to be saved and put ashore when the ship next called at 'Headquarters' (Port Chalmers). There was a system of fines for non-compliance and the monies gained from offences were placed in a special fund for the benefit of the officers in the company. Every instruction issued was regularly updated and there were few circumstances that could not be found within the pages of directives that flowed from Head Office in Dunedin. The company policies were also quite firm and masters had a clear incentive to navigate skilfully. Although the company paid a 'safe navigation' bonus every six months, masters were given no second chance if they had a mishap and the finding of the Inquiry went against them. Even if vindicated, the Board of the company sometimes made its own judgement and the errant master was transferred from a high profile passenger ship to a lowly collier.

The other great attribute displayed by Mills was his ability to pick the right managers and to ensure those in key positions had the initiative and enthusiasm to be responsible for their particular role. It is interesting to reflect that the system of decentralised control developed by Mills from 1875 was a business style promoted 50 years later by Alfred P. Sloan who headed General Motors Corporation between 1923 and 1956 and made it the largest business enterprise in the world. Sloan's system of 'decentralisation with co-ordinated control' ensured that all outposts of the General Motors empire were working and moving forward to the betterment of the total enterprise. Mills could easily assess the abilities of his managers by their regular reporting of activities in their areas and whilst the Board of the company made all the policy decisions, branch managers were left to implement them. Writing to his great friend and engineering expert, John Darling, as early as February 1875, Mills wrote 'Of course, in my experience of other steam companies in New Zealand is that Directors' interference with anything in the shape of detail does more harm than good and that the more power in the hands of the Manager, if you know him, the better'. He also had the ability to lead and to earn the respect of the management and staff, both ashore and afloat. That was his forte.

The Union Company directors were content to give Mills his head and although the Board in Dunedin met two or three times a month, there was many an occasion when it decided that the matter would be left in the hands of the managing-director to resolve. In some cases these decisions related to the dismissal of masters and other company employees whom Mills had known for many years and were his long time friends.

With his confident, decisive style and the well-managed structure of the company, Mills commanded respect wherever he went. From his first meeting with Peter Denny of the Dumbarton shipbuilding firm, a rapport developed between the two men and Dennys subsequently went on to build 30 ships for the Union Company between 1875 and 1900. It was not until 1894 that the company's indebtedness to Dennys was finally paid off and the long-standing personal association between the two men ended with the death of Peter Denny the following year. In a letter from Peter Denny to Mills in 1875, he said he regarded Bills from either Mills or Cargills (Dunedin merchant house) to be as good as cash, but to anyone else in New Zealand the terms were 'cash down'! On Peter Denny's death he was still a substantial shareholder in the Union Company.

To ensure adequate supplies of coal bunkers were always available for their steamers and to protect the pricing, the company invested in coal mining and through a process of takeovers, mergers and amalgamations, virtually obtained a monopoly on coal supplies. Apart from owning the mines, its ships were the principal carriers of coal around New Zealand ports and they purchased old sailing ships for conversion to coal storage hulks and these were sited in the main ports of call. When oil fuel moved to replace coal, the company developed its own facilities for storing fuel oil and apart from the two tankers owned by the company in the 1920s many more were directly chartered to bring in its own oil supplies.

After the first 25 years of continuous expansion, the Union Company had a monopoly within most trades and particularly all those out of New Zealand. It became a management skill to convince the travelling public, the cargo shippers and the government, that elements of competition did exist and that the company did need their business support. Mills achieved this outlook to some extent by making secret trade share deals with other companies in New Zealand and Australia as well as investing in competitors through holding companies not directly linked to the Union Company. In this way the smaller localised and often family-owned companies carried on as usual, financially backed by the Union Company, but giving the impression to all, including the various waterfront and seafaring unions, that an element of competition did exist and these smaller companies were effectively competing against the red funnel colossus!

James Mills gradually eased out of day-to-day management from 1898 and left New Zealand to live in England from 1906. He was knighted in 1907 and awarded the K.C.M.G. in 1909 – the first such award to a native-born New Zealander. Whilst he served as member for the Waikouaiti constituency in the Otago Provincial Government between 1873 to 1875 and was later a Member of the House of Representatives from 1887 to 1893, Mills was always first and foremost, the Managing Director of the Union Company. Although he remained in this role until 1913 and was Chairman of the company until 1936, successive managements kept the company 'ticking over' but without the flair and entrepreneurial leadership so characteristic of his early days.

The directors were content to sell out to the British P & O group in 1917 and thereafter the Union Company was essentially run to conform with P & O requirements rather than the needs of its customers in the Southern Hemisphere. Expansion of services was largely denied as they would invariably come into competition with other P & O group services and capital expansion was tightly controlled by London.

It was not until the appointment of Norris Stephen Falla as Managing Director in 1934 that once more the company rose from its 'steady as she goes' style into a more positive growth pattern. Falla had joined the company in 1898, trained as an accountant and became General Traffic Manager in 1919. He had a distinguished army career during World War 1, being awarded the C.M.G., the D.S.O. and was mentioned in dispatches on three occasions. Like Mills, he had the ability to choose the right man for the job, rather than rely on seniority of service to be the promotional yardstick. Under Falla, the company built its finest Trans Tasman liner – *Awatea* – to compete against the subsidised American Matson liners; the white painted *Matua* made her debut on the Pacific Islands run and a new series of specialist cargo ships was ordered for the Trans Tasman services. Had war not intervened a new fast steamer express would have been built for the Lyttelton – Wellington service.

Falla's other major contribution was to put the Union Company into the air. Following his experience with the Royal Flying Corps in Europe during the latter stages of World War 1, he saw the potential for the carriage of passengers and cargo by air. He took an active interest in the

*Managing Director of the Union Company from 1934 to 1945, **Norris Stephen Falla**, presided over a remarkable period of expansion, including the development of the air services which saw Union Airways as the leading airline in the country – Union Company*

development of the New Zealand Air Force and this was recognised with his appointment as a Group Captain in the Territorial Air Force. The Union Company commenced an involvement with air services in New Zealand by buying shares in some of the fledgling air companies from 1934 and a year later formed Union Airways Limited as a wholly-owned subsidiary. In 1936, Union Airways commenced the first regular air service in New Zealand between Palmerston North and Dunedin and later that year, the Union Company became a 20% shareholder in Australian National Airways. It also had an involvement with Tasmanian-based Holyman Airways.

It was Norrie Falla's initiative that saw him approach the British Imperial Airways to provide a Trans Tasman service that would connect with the Australia/London flights of Imperial Airways. Frustrated by interference from the governments of Great Britain, Australia and New Zealand, Falla ordered the first three flying boats for the service in the name of the Union Company! This action got results and in the setting up of Tasman Empire Airways Limited, New Zealand secured a majority shareholding of 39%. His strong approach ensured an advantage for New Zealand which in the long term provided the catalyst for Air New Zealand to gain dominance in the Trans Tasman commercial aviation services in later years. TEAL commenced its flying boat services in 1940.

Falla's enthusiasm and knowledge of the commercial aviation business made him a world authority on civil aviation and placed the Union Company in a dominant position in this field. He succeeded Sir James Mills as Chairman in 1936 and in 1944 he was appointed a director of the parent P & O company – an honour in recognition of his ability. He was the only Union Company director ever to serve on the P & O parent board.

He died suddenly in 1945 but there was no one to grasp the nettle to protect the new investments. The Labour Government of the day obviously did not want the Union Company to monopolize the air as it had done with the sea over the past 70 years, so nationalised the airline industry. Union Airways, including its investment in TEAL, was acquired by the New Zealand Government from 1 April 1947 on behalf of New Zealand National Airways Corporation. Falla was aware of this prior to his death and he was very disheartened after the efforts he and the company had made to the development of commercial aviation within New Zealand and across the Tasman. The Union Company's pioneering involvement was effectively nipped in the bud. While the government did subsidize some of the Union Airways services around the country, the amounts of the subsidy were much less than the tax paid by Union Airways.

In ten years from 1936 to 1946, Union Airways carried 309,708 passengers and travelled nearly 52 million passenger miles on 31,475 flights. Although there was a later opportunity to buy back the airline investment from the government, the Union Company management of the day contended that it was overcommitted with the purchase of new ships and passed over the chance to once again secure supremacy in commercial aviation.

The Union Company continued under another series of caretaker managing directors until a third entrepreneur arrived in the form of Sir Peter Abeles. In 1970, three years after he had established one of the largest transport groups in Australia – Thomas Nationwide Transport Ltd – better known as T.N.T., Peter Abeles made overtures to P & O to buy the Union Company. E.H.P. Abeles was born in Vienna and had come to Australia as a migrant from Hungary in 1949. He had steadily built his transport empire by the purchase of a number of smaller transport firms. It took 18 months to conclude the deal and from 1 January 1972, the ownership of the Union Company passed from P & O to Tasman Union Limited – a company jointly owned by T.N.T. and New Zealand shareholders as the New Zealand Government had ensured 50% New Zealand ownership by providing guarantees for the purchase of shares. For the first time since the late 1870s, New Zealanders again owned at least 50% of the Union Company.

Had Abeles and T.N.T. not arrived on the scene when they did, there is little doubt that some other fate would have overtaken the Union Company. The successive managements were trying to hold the empire together but there was continual erosion from the lack of financial control, greater industrial problems with the maritime unions and the remoteness of P & O in London from the changing scene in New Zealand did not help. P & O was becoming very disenchanted with the meagre financial returns being obtained from its Antipodean investment.

Abeles, like Mills and Falla, ignored the hierarchy of tradition and seniority and appointed senior managers on ability. Financial planning and control became the priority and it is significant that he consulted with the senior company auditor for answers, rather than the company management. In fact that auditor – John Keegan – became the Executive Director of Finance and Administration in the new management team after the takeover by T.N.T. from 1972 to 1975. He was then sent to New York to gain a greater understanding of the TNT group and the freighting business in general. Changing the attitudes of almost a century of tradition was no mean

Following the takeover by Thomas Nationwide Transport (TNT) in 1972, the subsequent recovery of the financial fortunes of the Union Company were led by **Sir Peter Abeles**, *the entrepeneur who had created TNT into one of the largest transport groups in Australia – Union Company*

challenge and many of the older hands within the company were extremely critical of the TNT management style. However, there is little doubt that if such positive steps had not been taken, the Union Company would not have survived, as in the years since the end of World War 2, its traditional services had been steadily eroded and at the time of the TNT takeover, the trans-Tasman trade was the only significant service left.

After a century of total control of the Tasman, reinforced by the long standing accord between the maritime unions that only vessels manned by Australian or New Zealand crews could carry cargo on the Tasman Sea, the Union Company was facing competition from a number of companies. It had to trim off the fat and become more competitive if it was going to stay in the business. When TNT took over in 1972, the Union Company had 47 ships and a staff of 3345. Ten years later there were 13 ships and 1619 staff. When Peter Abeles stepped down as Chairman in 1988 there were 9 ships and 835 people employed with a total turnover in excess of $285,000,000.

Under the influence of Abeles as Chief Executive and Chairman of the new consortium, the company moved out of its loss-making mode and in 1973 returned a net profit in excess of $2,000,000 and thereafter results progressively improved although there were some massive losses when the trade between New Zealand and Australia dropped off for varying political or economic reasons. The Union Company also had a significant loss in 1988 following the costs associated with moving away from permanent staffing in its terminals and also a change from the use of the smaller Seafreighter containers to greater use of standard 20ft ISO containers. A $26,000,000 profit in 1989 and $32,000,000 in 1990 were the highest net profits ever achieved by the company.

Although Abeles remained a director until 1992, he relinquished his role as Chief Executive in 1979 in favour of the young auditor he had taken into the TNT group after the takeover in 1972. John Keegan returned to New Zealand as Managing Director of the Union Company from 1979 to 1990 and maintained an aggressive TNT management style. Abeles also brought into the company key financial and marketing personnel from within the TNT group. He was knighted in 1972 and his 'rags to riches' career made him one of Australia's great business leaders of the 20th century.

Over the years the various divisions within the company were re-structured to suit the latest corporate style and in some cases, to make them easier to sell off, with Union Travel and N.Z. Stevedoring being examples of divisional sales of this nature. The 50 or so New Zealand companies that took shares in the Union Company in 1971 to protect its entity as a New Zealand registered company progressively sold their shares and from 1986 to 1996, Brierley Investments Limited was the sole owner of the 50% New Zealand share. In 1996, T.N.T. itself was the subject of a takeover and Brierleys acquired the total ownership of the Union Company. It sold the Union Company Australian interests and services to Holyman Ltd effective from 3 September 1997. Afterwards, it purchased through its Australian subsidiary, Australian Consolidated Industries Ltd, 50% of the Australian and New Zealand Direct Line (ANZDL) running an eight-ship container service between Australia, Auckland and the West Coast of North America. In turn ANZDL purchased 50% of the Union Company's trans-Tasman business. These two interests were both sold to CP Ships of Canada in 1998. At the beginning of 1999, the Union Company was the owner of two roll-on, roll-off vessels (*Union Rotoiti* and *Union Rotoma*), a coastal tanker (*Taiko*), as well as some residual interests in property and subsidiary companies. Since then, these ships have been disposed of, along with most of the subsidiary interests. As this book went to press, the once-proud company, which had dominated New Zealand shipping for a century and a quarter, looked certain to soon be but a memory within New Zealand's maritime history.

Many histories have been written over the years about the Union Company, its ships and its people. This book, which covers brief histories of all the ships of the company since its inception, details of subsidiary concerns, chartered ships, coal hulks and other smaller craft as well as providing a chronology of significant dates in its history, is designed as a book of reference. In upgrading and revising the information from the two previous editions of *Union Fleet* published in 1968 and 1976, the opportunity has been taken to enhance the presentation by providing illustrations of most of the vessels owned by the company. The material has been upgraded to July 2000.

Ian Farquhar
Dunedin
2000

Chronology

A chronology covering some of the significant dates in the history of the Union Company.

1875-1879

31/05/1875   First meeting of provisional directors at Dunedin.

01/07/1875   Union Steam Ship Company of N.Z. Limited (James Mills, Managing Director) commenced operations by taking over Harbour Steam Company steamers (*Maori*, *Beautiful Star* and *Bruce*), together with *Hawea* and *Taupo* which were built for the company. The company also operated the paddle steamer *Samson*, owned by the Harbour Steam Company.

Initial Services

Hawea, *Taupo*	Fortnightly service from Port Chalmers to Manukau (Onehunga) and return via Lyttelton, Wellington, Picton, Nelson and Taranaki (New Plymouth).
Bruce, *Beautiful Star*	Weekly service from Port Chalmers to Lyttelton and return via Timaru and Akaroa.
Samson	Twice weekly service from Port Chalmers/Dunedin to Oamaru and return.
Maori	Monthly voyage around the South Island – Port Chalmers, Bluff, Martin's Bay, Jackson's Bay, Hokitika, Greymouth, Westport, Nelson, Picton, Lyttelton with each alternate voyage in reverse order of ports.

12/07/1875   Certificate of Incorporation issued. Initial nominal Capital was £250,000 but paid up Capital on commencement was £83,580.

23/06/1876   Purchased New Zealand Steam Shipping Co. Ltd., Wellington (vessels *Phoebe*, *Ladybird*, *Taranaki* and *Wellington*).

31/07/1876   Acquired coastal trade of Albion Shipping Company, Glasgow (*Taiaroa*).

04/10/1876   *Wakatipu* (under Union Company management) sailed Port Chalmers for Sydney via Wellington and inaugurated Trans Tasman service of the Union Company.

10/01/1877   *Rotorua* sailed Port Chalmers for Sydney via Manukau (Onehunga) commencing the first Trans Tasman voyage by a company-owned vessel.

19/01/1877   *Wanaka* sailed Port Chalmers on excursion around the South Island, including the West Coast Sounds – the first summer cruise run by the company.

10/02/1877   *Wanaka* sailed Port Chalmers for Auckland and inaugurated a three weekly service via East Coast ports (Akaroa, Lyttelton, Wellington, Napier, Poverty Bay and Tauranga).

21/08/1877   *Taiaroa* commenced mail service from Sydney to Noumea under contract to Government of New Caledonia (25/01/1878 – contract was transferred to Australasian Steam Navigation Co., Sydney).

08/09/1878   Union Company appointed agents throughout New Zealand for the Orient Line, London.

19/11/1878   Purchased Melbourne–New Zealand service of McMeckan, Blackwood and Co.,

	Melbourne, and took over *Albion, Arawata, Ringarooma* and *Tararua* as well as the coal hulks *Sampson* and *Sir Harry Smith*.
05/06/1879	*Rotomahana* launched – first ocean going steamer in the world to be built of mild steel and fitted with bilge keels.
30/06/1879	Purchased remaining interests in Oamaru and Dunedin Steam Co. Ltd., Dunedin (*Waitaki*).
15/09/1879	Nominal Capital increased to £500,000 and agreed to establish London Board of Directors.

1880–1889

11/10/1880	Purchased Trans-Tasman service of Grice, Sumner and Company, Melbourne, together with steamer *Hero*.
19/04/1881	Sold *Wellington* together with Auckland to Whangarei, Tauranga and Russell trades to Captain Alexander McGregor and partners of Auckland (integrated into Northern Steam Ship Co. Ltd., Auckland, when it was formed 11/5/1881).
17/09/1881	Purchased Auckland Steam Ship Co. Ltd., (*Southern Cross*) together with goodwill of New Zealand–Fiji trade and Government subsidy for the service. (*Southern Cross* left Auckland 26/09/1881 and arrived Levuka 01/10/1881).
20/12/1881	*Manapouri* launched – first merchant ship in the world to be fitted throughout with incandescent electric light.
19/01/1882	Acquired Margaret Street Wharf, Sydney together with stores and other buildings from Australasian Steam Navigation Company, Sydney.
13/12/1882	Purchased the goodwill of Melbourne–Fiji service of J. McEwan & Co., Melbourne, together with *Suva*.
19/11/1883	Commenced first steamer express service in Australasia by running *Takapuna* on regular passenger schedule from Lyttelton to Onehunga via Wellington and New Plymouth.
04/06/1885	*Wairarapa* left Auckland on first cruise by the company to the South Sea Islands.
01/08/1885	Took over Black Diamond Line (Captain W.R. Williams), Wellington, together with Koranui coal mine, steamers *Grafton, Koranui, Maitai, Manawatu, Mawhera*, sailing ships and coal hulks.
04/12/1885	*Mararoa* sailed Sydney for San Francisco via Auckland on first Trans Pacific voyage under a joint contract (signed 15/10/1885) between Union Company and Oceanic Steamship Company, San Francisco with the New South Wales and New Zealand Governments for the carriage of the U.S. mails.
06/09/1886	Weekly service (in lieu fortnightly) to Sydney via Auckland commenced.
07/02/1887	Sold Koranui coal mine to Westport Coal Co. Ltd., Dunedin, and took over Westport Coal colliers *Kawatiri, Orowaiti* and *Wareatea*.
08/10/1887	*Tekapo* sailed Wellington for Calcutta. First Indian voyage of the Union Company. Service terminated 1970 but re-commenced for short period 1973 with joint service in conjunction with Royal Interocean Lines to South East Asian ports only.
11/08/1888	Acquired Brunner Coal Company Ltd., Greymouth (Martin Kennedy) and the three mines involved – Wallsend, Coalpitheath and Brunner, together with the steamers *Maori, Brunner* and *St Kilda* (converted to hulk). On 23/8/1888 the Tyneside coal mine owned by James Kilgour was also purchased along with the steamer *Oreti*. The ships were transferred directly into the Union Company fleet but the mining interests were merged into a new company called Grey Valley Coal Co. Ltd. – the Union Company and the Westport Coal Co. Ltd., being joint owners.
03/04/1889	*Mawhera* sailed Auckland inaugurating an Auckland – Tonga – Samoa service.

1890–1899

25/03/1890	Acquired Peninsula and Akaroa Steam Navigation Co. Ltd., Lyttelton (*Banks Peninsula*).

09/08/1890	*Bundhara* arrived Port Chalmers from Calcutta. First British India Steam Navigation Co. Ltd., vessel to New Zealand under agency of Union Company (agency transferred to P & O (N.Z.) Ltd., Wellington 10/1971).
06/09/1890	*Taviuni* arrived Melbourne direct from Greenock via Cape of Good Hope – the longest continuous steaming time to that date. (12,400 nautical miles at 10.5 knots – 48 days, 17 hours and 40 minutes).
23/09/1890	Nominal Capital increased to £1,000,000.
24/03/1891	Tasmanian Steam Navigation Co. Ltd., Hobart, to be taken over by Union Company effective from 01/04/1891 (*Corinna, Flinders, Flora, Mangana, Moreton, Oonah, Pateena* and *Talune*). A local Board established at Hobart.
01/04/1895	*Penguin* commenced at least two round trips per week between Wellington and Lyttelton becoming the first ship to be used exclusively on the inter-island passenger service.
01/05/1896	Union Company entered Auckland–Rarotonga–Tahiti trade with *Taupo* making first voyage.
01/09/1896	Purchased T. A. Reynolds and Co. Hobart – West Coast Tasmanian services (*Glenelg, Bellinger* and *Banks Peninsula* – the latter re-sold directly to Northern Steam Ship Co. Ltd., Auckland).
02/11/1896	Thrice-weekly service commenced between Wellington and Lyttelton, each way, with *Penguin*. From 01/11/1900 a daily service was run each way excluding Sunday, and the winter months, but from 1905 an all year round daily service, except Sundays, was instituted.
01/12/1896	Company acquired goodwill of Donald and Edenborough, Auckland service to Rarotonga and Tahiti and took over *Richmond*.
01/01/1897	Tahitian Government voted subsidy for Inter-Island service.
04/03/1897	Sold wharf and interest in Blenheim trade to Fell Bros and Captain Thomas Eckford.
12/09/1897	Union Company tender to extend Tahiti Inter Island service to the Marquesa Group accepted.
28/09/1897	Union Company interest in Wellington–Wanganui trade sold to Wellington Steam Packet Co. Ltd., Wellington, together with *Oreti* and *Moa*.

1900–1909

28/10/1900	*Moana* arrived Sydney and terminated direct San Francisco service commenced in 1885.
01/01/1901	Acquired half share in Canadian Australian Royal Mail Line, Melbourne, running service from Sydney to Vancouver and took over management of the line effective with the sailing of *Aorangi* from Sydney to Vancouver 25/03/1901. The remaining 50% interest was purchased 1910.
11/07/1901	*Orowaiti* commenced first regular Union Line service in North West Tasmania between Launceston, Stanley, Burnie and Devonport.
14/05/1903	Mail contract Melbourne–Launceston accepted.
02/06/1904	*Loongana* launched – first ship in the fleet and also first in Australasian waters to have steam turbine propulsion.
25/05/1905	Deed signed for Superannuation Scheme for office staff.
20/07/1905	First issue of the monthly journal *The Red Funnel*. (Ceased publication 1/7/1907).
07/10/1905	Actual commencement of a daily Wellington-Lyttelton steamer express service with *Rotomahana* and *Pateena* – *Mararoa* replaced *Pateena* 20/10/1905.
28/03/1907	Formed Wairau Steam Ship Company Ltd., Wellington with Johnson and Co. Ltd., Wellington to work the Blenheim/Wellington trade.
04/04/1907	Union Company acquired 25% interest in Invercargill Shipping Co. Ltd., Dunedin (Captain C.F. Sundstrum).

28/06/1907   James Mills made Knight Batchelor (Kt). (K.C.M.G. conferred 1909).

21/11/1907   Decision taken to purchase Wellington Patent Slip. Wellington Harbour Board proposed Bill providing compulsory sale to the Board but agreed that Union Company remain in possession for 25 years and thereafter the slip was leased from the Board. The Wellington Patent Slip Co. Ltd., was renamed Wellington Marine Repair Works Ltd. from 10/02/1970 and the works were finally closed 31/07/1980.

01/01/1908   *Koonya* sailed Lyttelton towing *Nimrod* (Shackleton Antarctic Expedition ship) and became the first steel vessel to cross the Antarctic Circle.

03/12/1908   First group of cadets joined *Dartford*, the company's sail training ship.

03/01/1909   *Manapouri* recommenced service from New Zealand to San Francisco by trans-shipping cargo and passengers at Tahiti to vessels of the Oceanic Steamship Company of San Francisco.

10/06/1909   Arranged with Northern Steam Ship Co. Ltd., Auckland to run its vessel *Rarawa* on joint account in the Onehunga–New Plymouth trade, withdrawing the Union Company *Rotoiti*. This arrangement terminated 09/06/1930.

1910–1919

19/10/1910   *Aorangi* sailed Wellington, commencing again, a direct service from Wellington to San Francisco via Rarotonga and Papeete.

19/10/1911   Steam laundry, workshops and stores built for Union Line at Evan's Bay, Wellington. The workshop building when completed was the largest steel frame structure in New Zealand. (The steam laundry ceased operations 31/7/1974).

11/12/1911   *Tahiti* sailed Sydney for San Francisco via Wellington, Rarotonga and Papeete, thus extending the San Francisco service to Sydney.

11/07/1912   Union Company acquired from New Zealand Shipping Co. Ltd., London, the former Australian/New Zealand/United Kingdom service of Houlder Bros Ltd. of London and took over the steamers *Limerick, Roscommon, Tyrone* and *Westmeath*.

03/10/1912   Sold *Squall* to Richardson & Co. Ltd., Napier together with Auckland-East Coast-Hawkes Bay trade. (Union Company acquired 25% interest in Richardson & Co. Ltd., at this time).

01/12/1912   Acquired financial interest in Opouri Shipping Co. Ltd., Christchurch (*Opouri*).

00/04/1913   Completion Grand Pacific Hotel, Suva, Fiji (Sold 1959).

31/08/1913   Chartered steamer *Canada Cape* (later renamed *Waihemo*) left Newcastle, N.S.W. and inaugurated regular Union Company purely cargo service between North Pacific coast ports, Australia and New Zealand ports and return. (Sailed San Francisco 27/10/1913 and arrived Wellington 28/11/1913).

01/10/1913   Original Union Steam Ship Company of N.Z. Ltd. wound up (30/09/1913) and a new company identically named was incorporated with a nominal capital of £3,000,000. (2,000,000 Ordinary shares, 1,000,000 cumulative preference shares)

00/12/1913   Local Board established at Sydney.

19/05/1915   Purchased remaining 50% interest in Maoriland Steamship Co. Ltd., Wellington, with steamers *Kahika, Karu* and *Kokiri*.

28/11/1917   Peninsular and Oriental Steam Navigation Company, London (P & O) purchased all the ordinary shares in Union Line.

1920–1929

22/06/1920   *Niagara* berthed Balls Head, Sydney and pumped first cargo of oil into the newly established Balls Head Oil Depot in which Union Company had a substantial interest. The first oil depot in New Zealand – the converted coal hulk *Adderley* – received initial oil delivery 20/08/1920.

19/01/1921	Decision taken to allot names beginning with "K" to single deck cargo ships and "W" to tween deck vessels.
25/08/1921	*Hauraki* launched – first motor ship in the fleet.
22/12/1921	Tasmanian Steamers Pty. Ltd., Melbourne incorporated (See page 224).
01/01/1922	Head Office and management transferred from Dunedin to Wellington although the Registered office of the company remained in Dunedin until 6/1945.
01/04/1922	Union Company took over the carriage of coal for the Blackball Coal Co. Ltd., of London, purchasing four coal hulks and taking the Blackball colliers *Ngahere, Ngakuta* and *Ngatoro* on charter (*Ngakuta* and *Ngatoro* being purchased 31/01/1942).
00/05/1923	Purchased property at Miramar, Wellington, with two oil tanks thereon and first delivery of 7600 tons taken on 28/06/1923 when *Orowaiti* commenced pumping ashore. Three more tanks on this site were completed 4/1925. (The Miramar tank farm and floating plant at Auckland and Wellington were sold to B.P. New Zealand Ltd., Wellington 01/01/1975 but management of Wellington harbour tug *Taioma* was vested in Union Company).
17/06/1924	*Aorangi* launched – largest (17,491 tons gross) and fastest (18 knots) motor liner in the world.
08/04/1925	Tasmanian Government steamers purchased (*Poolta* and *Melbourne* – with the latter being sold for conversion to a hulk).
00/12/1927	The Trans Pacific Passenger Agency Ltd., was formed in London to carry on the business of the company's West End passenger office. (It was renamed Pacific and World Travel Ltd. from 01/01/1974).
01/05/1929	Indo-Pacific Shipping Co. Ltd. (wholly owned subsidiary) formed in London (see page 215).

1930–1939

19/02/1930	Purchased remaining interest in fleet of R.S. Lamb & Co. Ltd., Sydney, and took over steamers *Gabriella, Kalingo, Omana* and *Kini* (building). (The interest in this concern initially acquired 21/10/1909).
16/04/1931	*Rangatira* launched – first turbo-electric powered vessel in fleet.
02/07/1931	Canadian Australasian Line incorporated (see page 214).
15/04/1935	First commercial air service in New Zealand established between Napier and Gisborne by East Coast Airways Limited, Gisborne. Union Company had acquired a major interest in this company 02/08/1934 and was appointed agent throughout New Zealand 5/1935. This service extended to Palmerston North 30/10/1937 and to Wanganui on 10/1/1938.
30/04/1935	Union Airways of New Zealand Ltd., formed as wholly-owned subsidiary of Union Company.
30/12/1935	Cook Strait Airways Ltd., Nelson, in which Union Company had majority interest commenced inaugural flight between Wellington, Blenheim and Nelson.
16/01/1936	Union Airways commenced first regular daily commercial New Zealand air service between Palmerston North and Dunedin.
23/01/1936	Death of Sir James Mills, K.C.M.G. in England (Managing Director 1875–1913, Chairman of Directors 1913–1936).
25/02/1936	*Awatea* launched – largest (13,482 tons gross) and fastest (23 knots) ship specially built by the Union Company for the Trans Tasman service – Sydney to Auckland and Wellington.
01/07/1936	Australian National Airways Ltd., Melbourne incorporated – Union Company having 20% shareholding as well as holding an indirect interest through the 20% shareholding held by Wm. Holyman & Sons Pty. Ltd.

> **UNION STEAM SHIP COMPANY OF N.Z., LTD.**
>
> Wellington – 13th October, 1937.
>
> FROM
> ASST SUPERINTENDING ENGINEER
>
> To GENERAL MANAGER.
>
> T.S.S. "AWATEA"
>
> The following is an extract from a letter from the Chief Engineer of the above vessel dated Wellington, 11th October, 1937.
>
> "I have pleasure in reporting that we made a record crossing for the Tasman from Auckland to Sydney. We left Auckland 5 p.m. 1st October and arrived anchorage Watsons Bay 11.5 p.m. October 3rd, time being 55 hours 28 minutes, average speed 23.1 knots.
>
> "Our highest revolutions were 129.3, average revs. for voyage 128.4, highest power developed 24,187 H.P.
>
> "Everything went well with us no trouble of any nature occurring.
>
> "Daily runs and averages were:-
>
> | | Time | Screw | Ship | Slip | Knots | Revs. | Fuel. |
> |---|---|---|---|---|---|---|---|
> | Oct. 1st | 19-03 | 469 | 443 | 5.5 | 23.2 | 127.9 | 137 |
> | Oct. 2nd | 24-40 | 611 | 576 | 5.7 | 23.3 | 128.8 | 170 |
> | Oct. 3rd | 11-45 | 290 | 262 | 9.6 | 22.4 | 128.5 | 85 |
> | Totals | 55-28 | 1370 | 1281 | 6.5 | 23.1 | 128.4 | 392 |
>
> You will note the above speed is calculated on the distance wharf to wharf but for record purposes the distance should be taken from Heads to Heads, thus making the average speed 22.89 knots.

12/12/1936	Union Royal Mail Line San Francisco/Australia/New Zealand passenger service operated by Union Company 1885–1900 and 1910–1936 terminated on *Makura*'s arrival in Sydney.
03/10/1937	*Awatea* arrived Sydney from Auckland making fastest passage between the two ports – 55 hours and 28 minutes (22.89 knots average speed).
23/10/1937	Union Company appointed New Zealand agents for Lloyd Triestino Line of Trieste.
24/11/1937	Union Company received agency appointment for Imperial Airways, London.
27/12/1937	*Awatea* arrived Wellington after making fastest passage Sydney to Wellington in 55 hours 47 minutes at 22.19 knots average speed.
01/04/1938	Union Company purchased remaining interest in East Coast Airways Ltd., Gisborne.
06/04/1939	*Rangatira* made fastest passage in Inter-Island Express Service – 8 hours 8 minutes between Lyttelton and Wellington at an average speed of 21.4 knots.

1940–1949

26/04/1940	Tasman Empire Airways Ltd. (TEAL) registered in Wellington to operate Trans Tasman air service (38% shareholding by Imperial Airways Ltd., London, 23% by QANTAS

	Airways of Australia and 39% held by Union Airways, but 20% of this taken by New Zealand Government). Management of Tasman Empire Airways Ltd. vested in Union Airways Ltd.
30/04/1940	Tasman Empire Airways Ltd. inaugural commercial flight from Sydney to Auckland by flying boat *Aotearoa* ZK-AMA.
28/04/1944	Maritime officers superannuation fund inaugurated. (A previous attempt to establish a fund in 1909 was rejected by some officers and engineers).
07/03/1945	Superannuation fund established for permanent regular weekly employees (foremen, tally clerks, women etc).
00/11/1946	Union Company acquired 25% shareholding in Eastern and Australian Steamship Co. Ltd., London as part of a P & O parent company reconstruction. (This holding taken over by P & O on 26/9/1966).
29/01/1947	Canadian Union Line Limited formed in Vancouver.
31/03/1947	Union Airways Ltd. went into liquidation, its services being taken over by New Zealand National Airways Corporation on 01/04/1947 in accordance with New Zealand Government Bill passed 11/1945. Union Airways Ltd. shareholding in Tasman Empire Airways Ltd. was also nationalised by the same Act of Parliament.
05/12/1947	Completed purchase of remaining shipping interests held by Captain A.F. Watchlin of Auckland. (*Port Tauranga* and *Port Waikato*).
00/06/1949	Union Company appointed General Agents in New Zealand, Australia and Fiji for Canadian Pacific Airlines, with its *Empress of Sydney* inaugurating its Vancouver/Honolulu/Canton Island/Nandi/Auckland/Sydney service 10/07/1949.

1950–1959

08/06/1953	*Aorangi* arrived Sydney terminating Canadian Australasian Line's passenger service from Vancouver to Australia and New Zealand.
31/08/1955	Nominal capital increased to £5,000,000.

1960–1969

31/05/1960	*Monowai* arrived Auckland from Sydney, terminating the Union Company Trans-Tasman passenger service commenced in 1876.
24/08/1960	Nominal capital increased to £7,000,000.
23/01/1962	*Ngakuta* launched – first ship in fleet to be entirely equipped with electric cranes for cargo handling.
02/08/1962	Under Union Company management, rail ferry *Aramoana* (owned by New Zealand Railways), left Wellington for Picton on trial voyage with the commercial service commencing on 11/08/1962.
11/08/1962	Union Company's Picton–Wellington passenger ferry service ceased on arrival of *Tamahine* at Wellington.
19/11/1963	*Seaway Queen* launched – First roll-on, roll-off ship for Union Company. (*Seaway Queen* commenced service Melbourne to Hobart 13/06/1964 and her sister ship *Seaway King* inaugurated a Sydney to Hobart service 01/09/1964).
14/12/1965	Trial run of converted *Maori* in Inter-Island service – first roll-on, roll-off passage in Wellington–Lyttelton Steamer Express service. (*Maori* commenced regular roll-on, roll-off service on 16/12/1965 and *Wahine* commenced regular service on same run 01/08/1966).
15/04/1967	*Waitemata* arrived Dunedin and terminated regular cargo service between North Pacific Coast ports, Australia and New Zealand, commenced by Union Company in 1913.
11/11/1967	*Hawea* sailed Auckland for Dunedin via Lyttelton inaugurating weekly roll-on, roll-off container/palletised cargo service between the three ports. (Service ceased on withdrawal of *Wanaka* 28/6/1973).

27/05/1969 *Maheno* sailed Auckland for Sydney via Wellington and Lyttelton and inaugurated the first Trans-Tasman roll-on, roll-off service by the Union Company. Sister ship *Marama* initiated Auckland to Melbourne via Wellington service 23/09/1969.

19/12/1969 *Wanaka* launched – first ship in fleet fitted with bulbous bow.

1970–1979

04/03/1970 *Wainui* sailed Auckland for Singapore on final voyage of a Union Company vessel on the India/East Asia service commenced with *Tekapo* in 1887. (Union Company made a brief return to this trade when in conjunction with Royal Interocean Lines of Amsterdam, *Union Aotearoa* made four round voyages between 6/1973 and 5/1974).

04/09/1970 First public announcement that Thomas Nationwide Transport Ltd., Sydney (T.N.T.) was negotiating with Peninsular and Oriental Steam Navigation Co (P & O) to acquire the ordinary shares of the Union Company.

04/02/1971 P & O announced that it had agreed, subject to New Zealand Government approval, to sell the Union Company to Thomas Nationwide Transport Ltd.

06/04/1971 New Zealand Government announced its agreement in principle to the acquisition of the Union Company by a company to be formed by T.N.T. and New Zealand interests – each to hold 50% of the shares.

01/01/1972 P & O ownership of Union Company transferred to Tasman Union Ltd. – a company jointly owned by N.Z. Maritime Holdings Ltd. and T.N.T. Shipping (N.Z.) Ltd.

28/03/1972 *Rangatira* – largest ship ever built for the Inter-Island Express service made inaugural voyage Wellington to Lyttelton.

01/09/1972 Union Company offices in Australia integrated with those of Associated Steamships Pty. Ltd., Melbourne, as Union Bulkships Pty. Ltd.

21/09/1974 *Seaway Prince* launched – first vessel in fleet with gas turbine propulsion.

25/03/1975 Nominal capital increased to $25,000,000.

16/01/1976 *Union Rotorua* launched – first roll-on, roll-off vessel in fleet with stern quarter ramp (as well as bow ramp).

15/09/1976 *Rangatira* arrived Wellington from Lyttelton, terminating the regular Union Company Steamer Express passenger service between the two ports initially commenced 02/11/1896.

25/08/1977 New Zealand Offshore Services Ltd. registered with a capital of $50,000. Union Company held 60% of the capital and Australian Offshore Services (a division of P & O Australia Pty. Ltd.) held the remaining 40%. (The P & O interest was acquired 7/1991).

20/12/1977 Executive Printing (1977) Ltd., Auckland, formed. Capital $10,000 wholly-owned by Union Company. Formed to handle all company printing. Sold 1982.

27/06/1979 Australian Seaway services operations transferred to Union Steam Ship Company of Australia Pty. Ltd., Melbourne, wholly-owned subsidiary of Union Steam Ship Company of N.Z. Ltd.

1980–1989

28/03/1980 Tasman Union Limited, the holding company for the Australian and New Zealand owners of the Union Company, was renamed Union Shipping Group Limited. Authorised and paid up Capital was $24,000,000.

01/04/1980 Company corporate structure organised into four separate divisions :

Union Steam Ship Company of N.Z. Ltd. (including Union Steam Ship Company of Australia Pty Ltd., Union Bulkships partnerships and New Zealand Offshore Services Ltd).

Fleet operations and management including provision of equipment.

Union Maritime Services Ltd. – Incorporated 24/12/1979.

Responsible for terminals, branches and agents as well as stevedoring. An associate company Union Stevedoring Services Ltd. formed 24/06/1981 to operate joint stevedoring venture with Nelson Waterside Workers' Union (Union Line holding 66% of the capital)

Union Travel Limited – Incorporated 16/01/1976 as Saturday Sunny Swingaway Holidays Ltd. but renamed Union Travel Ltd. 21/12/1979.

Handling all travel and tour activities but Union Citco Travel Ltd., which was formed in 1973 as a joint venture with the Cook Islands Trading Corp. Ltd. (Union Company held 51% of the capital) continued to operate separately.

Union Engineering Ltd. – Incorporated 11/01/1980

Responsible for company's engineering workshops and the subsidiary companies:
Diver Services International Ltd. (Renamed Conifor Consultants Ltd. 30/11/1988).
Union Industrial and Marine Ltd.
Union Merchants Ltd.

30/04/1981	1,000,000 Preference shares of $2 each in the Capital of the company redeemed and authorised Capital reduced to $23,000,000 (and to $17,000,000 from 05/11/1987).
01/11/1982	Union Travel Ltd. merged with Thos Cook Pty. Ltd. to form Thos Cook New Zealand Ltd. (51% Thos Cook, 49% Union Travel).
26/11/1982	Waitaki Container Line, managed by Maritime Carriers New Zealand Ltd., announced its withdrawal from the Trans Tasman service with Union Company taking over the service and charters of two vessels, *Totara* and *Waitaki*. *Totara* taken over 12/12/1982 and then laid up Auckland until she left for Singapore where she was re-delivered to her owners 01/10/1983. *Waitaki* taken over 1/1983 remained on charter work until 25/04/1984 when she was laid up Wellington. Sailed Wellington 14/01/1985 and re-delivered Malalag Bay, Philippines, 31/01/1985.
01/04/1983	Union Bulkships Pty. Ltd., Sydney (50% each Union Company and T.N.T.) became partnership under nomenclature of Union Bulkships.
16/06/1983	Union Company acquired 25% interest in Pacifica Shipping Co. Ltd., Christchurch, (through nominee company South Seas Shipping Ltd. incorporated 06/05/1983) which operated roll-on, roll-off cargo service between Lyttelton and Wellington. Controlling interest secured 21/08/1984 and the company subsequently sold to Skeggs Foods Ltd., Dunedin, effective from 07/11/1985.
15/12/1983	Union Company Head Office moved from 36 Customhouse Quay, Wellington to 36 Quay Street Auckland into new 12 storey building built for the company.
01/10/1984	Inter-Island Express Ltd., Auckland formed with a capital of $10,000 as a wholly-owned subsidiary company (Subsequently renamed Timaru Stevedoring Co. Ltd. 18/12/1987).
17/09/1985	Union Engineering Ltd. renamed Union Industries Ltd. to reflect more diverse nature of activities.
00/08/1986	Brierley Investments Ltd. completed purchase of all residual share holdings in N.Z. Maritime Holdings Ltd. Union Shipping Group then each owned 50% by Brierley Investments Ltd., New Zealand and T.N.T. Ltd., Australia.
01/11/1986	Union Maritime Services Ltd., and Seaport Operations Ltd. merge their stevedoring interests to form N.Z. Stevedoring and Wharfingering Co. Ltd. (Name changed to N.Z. Stevedoring Co. Ltd. 26/05/1989).
01/01/1987	Union Shipping, Australian National Line (A.N.L.) and the Shipping Corporation of N.Z. Ltd. rationalise their Trans Tasman sailing schedules and introduce space sharing arrangements. (The arrangement was terminated 04/07/1991).
01/12/1987	Union Shipping Group Ltd. finalise restructuring into independent and autonomous management divisions as follows:

Union Shipping New Zealand Ltd.

Union Steam Ship Company of Australia Pty Ltd. (consolidating under a single management – Seaway Sea Cargo services, Australian terminals and Bulkships partnership)

Union Maritime Services Ltd.

N.Z. Stevedoring and Wharfingering Co. Ltd.

31/03/1988 Management contract dating from 1976 with Tasman Pulp and Paper Co. Ltd., for their two specialised newsprint and timber carriers – *Tasman Enterprise* and *Tasman Venture* was terminated.

30/11/1988 Conifor Consultants Ltd. formed as forestry stevedoring consultancy company as subsidiary of N.Z. Stevedoring and Wharfingering Co. Ltd.

28/04/1989 Union Maritime Services Ltd. sells Fiji agency business with branches at Suva and Lautoka to Pacific Forum Line, the transaction effective from that date.

01/10/1989 N.Z. Stevedoring Co. Ltd. and related joint venture stevedoring companies take over direct employment of 626 waterside workers previously employed by the quasi-government agency – the Waterfront Industry Commission. From early 1992 the company was restructured into twelve stand-alone stevedoring companies operating on a port-by-port basis.

1990–1999

01/04/1990 Union Bulkships Pty. Ltd. appointed General Agents in Australia for Mitsui-O.S.K. Lines of Tokyo. (This role reduced to port agencies only from 01/04/1995).

30/06/1990 Union Maritime Services Ltd. became a subsidiary of Union Shipping New Zealand Ltd. and reverted to ownership of Union Shipping Group Ltd. on 01/07/1994.

01/01/1991 Union Shipping Group again re-structured. A dormant company – South Pacific Passenger Services Ltd. – acquired the existing main operating subsidiaries (with the exception of Union Shipping Australia Pty. Ltd.) from Union Shipping Group Ltd. which in turn was acquired from the shareholders – N.Z. Maritime Holdings Ltd. and T.N.T. Shipping (N.Z.) Ltd. – by South Pacific Passenger Services Ltd. This company was then renamed Union Shipping Group Ltd., while the former Union Shipping Group Ltd. changed its name to Union Corporate Services Ltd. The purpose of the latter company was to provide a corporate service function for the new group and to retain Union Shipping Australia Pty. Ltd. The share capital of the restructured Union Shipping Group Ltd. was $1,000,000.

02/04/1992 Union Shipping Group Ltd. agrees to sell 49% share in Thos Cook (N.Z) Ltd. to Thos Cook Holdings (N.Z.) Ltd., effective from 31/12/1992.

12/04/1992 Union Shipping Australia Pty. Ltd. and Australian National Line (A.N.L. Searoad Holdings Pty. Ltd., Melbourne) establish joint venture company – Coastal Express Line Pty. Ltd. – to rationalise their respective interests in the cargo shipping services between Tasmanian ports, Melbourne and Sydney effective from 12/04/1992.

03/05/1992 Union Shipping, Tasman Express Line (T.E.L.), Australian National Line (A.N.L.) and New Zealand Line (P & O Containers New Zealand Ltd.) commence new space-sharing arrangement for their Trans-Tasman services.

01/01/1993 Australasian Shipping – Joint management group established in Auckland by Union Shipping New Zealand and Australian National Line (A.N.L.) to rationalise management of Trans Tasman trade became operational. (Arrangement dissolved from 01/10/1994).

01/07/1993 N.Z. Stevedoring Co. Ltd. (including Conifor Consultants Ltd.) sold to Stevedoring Services of America International Inc., Seattle (S.S. & A.) effective from 01/07/1993, but operationally from 13/09/1993.

15/11/1994 Howard Smith (N.Z.) Ltd., Wellington (subsidiary of Howard Smith Industries Ltd.,

	Sydney) took over management of coastal oil tankers *Kotuku, Kuaka* and *Taiko*, from Union Shipping, with the latter retaining port agencies.
31/01/1996	Union Shipping Australia Pty. Ltd. acquired full ownership of Coastal Express Line (operating cargo services between Australian mainland and Tasmania) by purchasing the 50% share held by Australian National Line (A.N.L.), Melbourne – the company having been established 12/04/1992.
01/07/1996	The Chief Executive Officer, J.E. Bryant, commenced operating out of Sydney instead of Auckland, reflecting the increasing importance of the Group's Australian operations.
03/12/1996	It was announced that following the acquisition of T.N.T. by Dutch Group, Koninklijke Ptt Nederland N.V. (K.P.N.) in October 1996, Brierley Investments Ltd., exercised their pre-emptive rights and purchased the 50% T.N.T. share in the Union Shipping Group, effective from 05/03/1997.
07/01/1997	Brierley Investments Ltd., owner of the Union Shipping Group and Groupe Bollore Technologies of Paris, majority shareholder of A.N.Z.D.L. – Australian New Zealand Direct Line between Australia and New Zealand to West Coast of North America, agreed to form a new company which would see Brierley Investments Ltd. acquire 50% of A.N.Z.D.L. and Groupe Bollore Technologies 50% of Union Shipping's Trans Tasman liner services.
01/03/1997	Union Direct Line time charters *Union Rotoiti, Union Rotoma* and *Union Rotorua* and commenced an integrated Trans Tasman liner service incorporating the three Union Line vessels with the seven A.N.Z.D.L. container ships. At the same time Union Company withdrew from the previous space sharing agreement with P & O and Tasman Express Line.
16/03/1997	Ocean Bulk Limited, Auckland (a joint venture between Union Shipping New Zealand Ltd. and Ocean Towing and Salvage (Cook Island) Ltd.) established to export coal to Port Kembla in Australia directly from Westport, utilising a large barge (*Ocean Bulk 1*) and tug *(Frederick Brown)*. The first delivery left Westport 9/7/1997 and arrived Port Kembla 18/7/1997. The contract for the coal carriage terminated 24/6/2000.
10/06/1997	Announcement that Holyman Ltd. would buy the Australian operations of Union Company for A$58,300,000, the transaction covering Coastal Express Line (and the chartered vessels *Searoad Mersey* and *Searoad Tamar*), Union Stevedoring Services at Melbourne, Hobart and Devonport and shipping agency Union Bulkships Pty. Ltd. – the deal being concluded 3/9/1997.
15/09/1997	Union Shipping Group Ltd., acquires former TNT freight forwarding companies – TNT International (N.Z.) Ltd. (Auckland), and TNT International Pty. Ltd. (Sydney) and companies renamed Crossocean Forwarding Services (N.Z.) Ltd and Crossocean Forwarding Services Pty. Ltd. 24/4/1999. Both companies sold to the Owens Group Ltd. with the sale effective from 1/11/1999.
22/09/1998	CP Ships (a division of Canadian Pacific) announce the acquisition of ANZDL, including the subsidiary, Union Direct Line, from the joint owners – Bollore Technologies, Paris and Brierley Investments Ltd., Australian subsidiary – Australian Consolidated Industries Ltd., Sydney. The contract effective from 18/12/1998.
13/10/1998	Union Shipping Bulk Limited registered for the purpose of assuming the assets of Ocean Bulk Limited which became a wholly owned subsidiary of Union Shipping New Zealand Ltd. on 9/7/1998.
30/10/1998	Union Maritime Services Ltd. ceased business and the offices at all New Zealand ports closed, with McKay Shipping Limited, Auckland buying the goodwill of the name effective from 25/11/1998.
30/09/1999	With the sale of *Union Rotoma*, operated by Union Direct Line, the Union Company 123 year association with Trans Tasman shipping, came to an end.

Notes on Fleet List format

In the presentation of details of the ships listed, the following points should be noted:

TONNAGE — The gross tonnage of most ships varied throughout the life of the vessel and the procedure adopted in recording tonnage has been to take the gross tonnage figure applicable when the vessel concerned entered Union Company service.

OWNERSHIP — In a number of instances ships were bought and sold to individuals, who for the most part were acting as agents or brokers and in such cases temporary ownerships registered to agents have not been recorded. Wherever possible ownerships have been noted in the name of the company applicable, even though the register of the ship may have only recorded the name of the owner or manager. In most instances managers have been included as well as the name of the registered owner. Where vessels were converted to hulks etc and no new owner is specified, it may be assumed the vessels were still under Union Company ownership. The term Union Company is used throughout rather than specify the full name of the company or in some cases an associate or subsidiary company.

DATES — Where dates of loss etc have differed from previously published information mainly due to time zone differences, the date used in the list has been based on the date and local time at the place in question. In some cases the date of sale and or purchase may not agree with that shown in the register particulars. This is because it has been known from Company or other records that the actual sale or purchase was concluded some time prior to the register entry being changed. The period of the delivery voyage may also account for a difference between date of build and first ownership being registered.

FATES — Unless the fate of a ship is specifically recorded it can be presumed that she is still in service and is so listed in current Classification Society registers. Many vessels completed active service with the Union Company some years before they were sold out of the fleet and in order to give a more accurate indication of active service within the Company, a final 'lay up' date has been included where appropriate.

PART ONE

Steamers and Motorships from 1875

2 *Union Fleet*

The first Union Company steamer was the **Maori**, *which arrived at Port Chalmers in August 1869 for the Harbour Steam Company and ran a coastal service including trips right around the South Island, prior to transferring to the Union Company in 1875*   DE MAUS

Beautiful Star, *the second vessel of the Union Company, was built in 1862 and was employed by the Harbour Steam Company in the coastal trade between 1871–75*
DE MAUS

No photograph exists of the steamer **Bruce**, *which was the first ship specially built in Scotland for the Harbour Steam Company. She was wrecked within four months of the Union Company being formed. She was an exact sister ship of the* **Euro** *(pictured here) which was built for South Australian owners*

MAORI 174 GRT IN FLEET 1875–1884 & 1888–1902

BUILT: 1868 by Blackwood & Gordon, Port Glasgow.

PREVIOUS OWNERS: Built for Captain J. Orkney, Glasgow, who held quarter share 1868–69. Remaining three quarters share held by Blackwood and Gordon 1868–69. Harbour Steam Company, Dunedin, 1869–75 (James Mills, Mgr).

SUBSEQUENT HISTORY: Sold to Martin Kennedy, Greymouth (Brunner Coal Co.) 1884–1888 and resold Union Company 1888. Laid up Port Chalmers, 20/1/1900. Sold Captain E.F. Allen, Samoa, 1902–07. Transferred to Samoa Shipping and Trading Co. Ltd., Auckland, 1907–10, Sydney, 1910–13 (E.F. Allen, Mgr). (Although owned by Captain Allen 1902–07, financial control of the ship was registered to George Dunnet and J.L. Young, Auckland – partners in Henderson & Macfarlane Ltd.) Sank at her moorings at Saluafata, Samoa, 1913, raised and later scuttled. Sunken hull bombed during Second World War by USAF in mistake for Japanese submarine.

BEAUTIFUL STAR 177 GRT IN FLEET 1875–1899

BUILT: 1862 by J. Wigham Richardson, Low Walker, Northumberland.

PREVIOUS OWNERS: R. Whitaker, Sydney, 1862. W.H. Eldred and Partners, Sydney, 1862–1867. W.R. Roberts, Hokitika 1867. Mary Greer, Dunedin, 1867–69. E.P. Houghton, Dunedin, 1869–71. Harbour Steam Company, Dunedin, 1871–75 (James Mills, Mgr).

SUBSEQUENT HISTORY: Sold Thos Nichols, Hobart, 1899. Transferred to Huon Channel and Peninsula S.S. Co. Ltd., Hobart, (Thos Nichols, Mgr) 1904–07. Total loss after being burnt out at Hobart, 25/2/1907. Hulk towed to New Town Bay and broken up.

BRUCE 335 GRT IN FLEET 1875–1875

BUILT: 1874 by A. Stephen and Sons, Glasgow.

PREVIOUS OWNERS: Harbour Steam Company, Dunedin (James Mills, Mgr), 1874–75.

SUBSEQUENT HISTORY: Wrecked Taiaroa Head, Otago Harbour entrance, 16/10/1875, on passage Timaru to Dunedin.

The 721 ton steamer **Hawea** *was the first ship specially built by Wm. Denny & Bros for the Union Company. As the illustration shows, it was customary for early steamships to use sail power to save coal*

Sister ship to the **Hawea**, *the* **Taupo**, *built in 1875 had a short life, being wrecked at Tauranga in 1879*   DE MAUS

Phoebe *was acquired from the N.Z. Steam Navigation Company in 1876 and was already 25 years old when acquired by the Union Company. She is pictured here in the colours of J. & A. Brown of Newcastle, in whose fleet she served for 23 years*   LIVERMORE

HAWEA — 721 GRT — IN FLEET 1875–1888

BUILT: 1875 by Wm. Denny and Bros., Dumbarton (Built for Union Company but financed and registered to H. Bright, Liverpool, P. Denny and W. Brock, Dumbarton 1875).

SUBSEQUENT HISTORY: Wrecked New Plymouth breakwater 12/6/1888 on passage from Auckland to New Plymouth. Remains removed during dredging of Newton King Wharf 1925/30.

TAUPO — 720 GRT — IN FLEET 1875–1879

BUILT: 1875 by Wm. Denny and Bros., Dumbarton. (Built for Union Company but financed and registered to P. Denny and W. Brock, Dumbarton, J. Darling, Glasgow, 1875).

SUBSEQUENT HISTORY: Wrecked Stony Point, Tauranga, 18/2/1879, later raised 2/3/1881 but foundered 29/4/1881 off Mayor Island on passage Tauranga to Auckland.

PHOEBE — 613 GRT — IN FLEET 1876–1878

BUILT: 1851 by A. Denny and Brother, Dumbarton.

PREVIOUS OWNERS: Preston and Co., Liverpool, 1851–56. Brenan and Company, Waterford 1856–58. Union Steam Ship Company, Southampton, 1858–61. Z.C. Pearson, London, 1861–62. Geo. Fleming, London, 1862. Intercolonial Royal Mail Steam Packet Co., London, 1862–64. Panama, New Zealand and Australian Royal Mail Co. Ltd., London, 1864–69. Thos Henderson, Auckland, 1869–70. J. Martin, Wellington 1870–71. New Zealand Steam Shipping Co. Ltd., Wellington, 1871–76.

SUBSEQUENT HISTORY: Sold J. & A. Brown, Newcastle, 1878–1901. Sold Einerson & Jorgensen, Sydney 1901–04. (Converted to hulk 1901). Broken up at Sydney 1904.

Taranaki, *at Port Chalmers in N. Z. Steam colours, just prior to being taken over by the Union Company in 1876* DE MAUS

Wellington, *a sister ship to the **Taranaki**, lies at Port Chalmers, against a background of masts of sailing ships and steamers* DE MAUS

*The smart little steamer **Wanaka**, pictured here at Port Chalmers, was the first Union Company vessel to go alongside the breakwater at New Plymouth (24 March 1884)*

TARANAKI — 415 GRT — IN FLEET 1876–1878

BUILT: 1865 by Blackwood & Gordon, Port Glasgow.

PREVIOUS OWNERS: New Zealand Steam Navigation Co. Ltd., Wellington, 1865–68. Wreck Recovery Ltd, Wellington, 1869–71. New Zealand Steam Shipping Co. Ltd., Wellington, 1871–76. (Vessel foundered on Boat Harbour Rock, Tory Channel, 12 miles from Picton, 19/8/1868 but raised during 9/1869, towed to Wellington 1/10/1869 and later refitted for service).

SUBSEQUENT HISTORY: Wrecked Karewa Island near Tauranga 29/11/1878 on passage Auckland to Tauranga.

WELLINGTON — 429 GRT — IN FLEET 1876–1881

BUILT: 1863 by Blackwood & Gordon, Port Glasgow.

PREVIOUS OWNERS: New Zealand Steam Navigation Co. Ltd., Wellington, 1863–71. New Zealand Steam Shipping Co. Ltd., Wellington, 1871–76.

SUBSEQUENT HISTORY: Sold A. McGregor, Auckland, 1881. Sold Northern Steam Ship Co. Ltd., Auckland, 1881–1909. Sold G.T. Niccol, Auckland, 1909 and converted to hulk. Finally sunk as breakwater at Moehau, Coromandel 13/3/1913.

LADYBIRD — 421 GRT — IN FLEET 1876–1881

BUILT: 1851 by Wm. Denny & Bros, Dumbarton.

PREVIOUS OWNERS: H.P. Maples, London, 1851–53. Jas Cowie & Partners, Geelong, 1853–55. J. Crookes & Partners, Launceston, 1855–56. Green & Cleveland, Launceston, 1856. S.G. Henty, Melbourne, 1856–63. New Zealand Steam Navigation Co. Ltd., Wellington, 1863–70. J. Dransfield, Wellington, 1870–72, and converted to sailing schooner 1870–72. New Zealand Steam Shipping Co. Ltd., Wellington 1872–76.

SUBSEQUENT HISTORY: Sold Westport Coal Co. Ltd., Dunedin, 1881–1905. Converted to hulk 1883. Condemned 1905 and hull sunk as target practice for HMS *Challenger* in Cook Strait 20/5/1905.

WANAKA — 493 GRT — IN FLEET 1876–1891

BUILT: 1876 by T. Wingate & Co., Whiteinch.

SUBSEQUENT HISTORY: Wrecked Puketapu Reef, near Waitara, New Plymouth 2/4/1891 on passage Manukau to New Plymouth.

8 Union Fleet

The Union Company introduced cruises to the West Coast sounds between 1877 and 1910. **Rotorua** *is pictured here in Milford Sound* BURTON BROS.

Taiaroa *was sent to Otago in 1875 by the Albion Shipping Company of Glasgow to act as a coastal feeder vessel for its larger sailing ships. She joined the Union Company fleet in 1876 and is pictured laid up at Port Chalmers* DE MAUS

ROTORUA   926 GRT   IN FLEET 1876–1903

BUILT: 1876 by Wm. Denny & Bros., Dumbarton.

SUBSEQUENT HISTORY: Laid up Wellington 5/4/1902. Sold Koe Guan Co., Penang, 1903–07. Transferred to Eastern Shipping Co. Ltd., Penang, 1907–17. Sold Rotorua Steam Ship Co. Ltd., (Carroll Bros.) Hong Kong, 1917–18. T.W. Bowern, Shanghai, 1918–22. Sold San Peh Steam Navigation Co. Ltd., Shanghai and renamed *Shinlee* (China) 1922–32. Sold Tong Kong Steam Navigation Co., Shanghai and renamed *Tong Kong* (China) 1932–37. Broken up in China 1937.

Although the chartered **Wakatipu** *made the first Trans Tasman voyage for the Union Company,* **Rotorua** *was the first Union Company-owned vessel to enter the Trans Tasman service in 1877*   DE MAUS

TAIAROA   438 GRT   IN FLEET 1876–1886

BUILT: 1875 by A .& J. Inglis, Linthouse.

PREVIOUS OWNERS: Laid down for G. & J. Burns as *Jackal*. Launched as *Jackal* but sold on the stocks and renamed *Taiaroa* on completion. Albion Shipping Co., Glasgow. (James Galbraith, Mgr) 1875–76.

SUBSEQUENT HISTORY: Wrecked entrance to Clarence River, Waipapa Point, Kaikoura Coast 11/4/1886 on passage Wellington to Lyttelton.

Built by Denny Bros with ownership controlled by Captain Angus Cameron, the **Wakatipu**, *under Union Line management, initiated the first Trans Tasman voyage from Port Chalmers to Sydney via Wellington in October 1876*
DE MAUS

▲ **Ringarooma** *was the pride of the McMeckan Blackwood fleet when she entered its Trans Tasman service in 1875. Three years later the Union Company took over the McMeckan Blackwood service and its vessels*
DE MAUS

Arawata *was a sister ship to* **Ringarooma** *but had a chequered career with only 12 years' active service with the Union Company and then 30 years as a store ship/coal hulk in Wellington*

WAKATIPU   1797 GRT   IN FLEET 1878–1924

BUILT: 1876 by Wm. Denny & Bros., Dumbarton.

PREVIOUS OWNERS: (Built for Union Company service but financed and registered to P. Denny, Dumbarton, J. Darling, Glasgow, Capt. Angus Cameron, Oban and Dunedin, James Galbraith, Glasgow, 1876–78). (Union Company, Mgrs 1876–78).

SUBSEQUENT HISTORY: Laid up Sydney 26/9/1921. Sold to Wm. Waugh Ltd., Balmain, 1924 and dismantled at Sydney 1925. Hulk sold to Broken Hill Pty. Ltd. for use as tar storage reservoir at Port Waratah, 1925. Broken up by BHP 1930.

RINGAROOMA   1096 GRT   IN FLEET 1878–1901

BUILT: 1875 by Thos. Wingate & Co., Whiteinch.

PREVIOUS OWNERS: McMeckan, Blackwood & Co., Melbourne, 1875–78.

SUBSEQUENT HISTORY: Laid up Port Chalmers from 13/3/1890. Sold G. Kunst, Samoa, 1901 and renamed *Samoa* (Germany) 1901–03. Sold T. Hashimoto, Nagasaki & Osaka, 1903 and renamed *Geiho Maru* (Japan) 1903–12. Sold I. Hizume, Tarumi, 1912–14 (same name). Sold Hokuyo K.K., Tarumi, 1914–25 (same name). Broken up in Japan 1925.

ARAWATA   1098 GRT   IN FLEET 1878–1897

BUILT: 1875 by Thos. Wingate & Co., Whiteinch.

PREVIOUS OWNERS: McMeckan, Blackwood & Co., Melbourne, 1875–78.

SUBSEQUENT HISTORY: Laid up Auckland, 2/9/1890. Towed to Wellington by *Pukaki* 2/3/1897–6/3/1897. Used as storeship at Wellington from 1897 and later converted to coal hulk. Sunk at Kaiwharawhara, Wellington, 13/1/1927 after collision with S.S. *Devon*. Remains blown up 26/1/1928.

Another vessel acquired from McMeckan Blackwood in 1878, **Tararua** *was wrecked at Waipapa Point, Southland, in April 1881 with the tragic loss of 189 lives, including many women and children passengers.* W. FORSTER PAINTING

Albion, *shown here at Melbourne, was built in 1863 for the Otago Steam Ship Company and came into the Union Company fleet in 1878. She was its first two-funnelled ship*

Penguin *was built in 1864 for Glasgow owners and came to New Zealand 15 years later. She was the pioneer ship in the regular Wellington – Lyttelton inter-island service commenced in 1895 but had a tragic end when she was wrecked off Cape Terawhiti in February 1909 with the loss of 75 lives* DE MAUS

Steamers and Motorships

TARARUA — 828 GRT — IN FLEET 1878–1881

BUILT: 1864 by Gourlay Bros., Dundee

PREVIOUS OWNERS: (Built as speculation and launched un-named 21/4/1864, named *Grampian* (pro-tempore certificate) by builders until sold 7/1864 to Panama, New Zealand and Australian Royal Mail Co. Ltd., London, 1864–69. McMeckan, Blackwood & Co., Melbourne, 1869–78.

SUBSEQUENT HISTORY: Wrecked Waipapa Point, Southland, 29/4/1881 on passage Port Chalmers to Melbourne.

ALBION — 806 GRT — IN FLEET 1878–1883

BUILT: 1863 by Scott & Co., Greenock.

PREVIOUS OWNERS: Otago Steam Ship Co. Ltd., Dunedin, 1864–67. Cargills & McLean, Dunedin, 1867–68. A. McKinnon & C.J. Hoyt, Dunedin, 1868. C.J. Hoyt, New York, 1868–71. McMeckan, Blackwood & Co. Melbourne, 1871–78 (First two-funnelled ship in fleet).

SUBSEQUENT HISTORY: Sold J.C. Ellis and J.E. Mitchell, Sydney, 1883–87. Auctioned at Sydney to Captain T.R. Brown, Sydney, 1887 but repossessed by J.C. Ellis, Sydney, 1888. Renamed *Centennial* 1889 (Ellis Line). Foundered following collision with collier *Kanahooka* inside Sydney Harbour heads 23/8/1889.

PENGUIN — 749 GRT — IN FLEET 1879–1909

BUILT: 1864 by Tod & McGregor, Glasgow.

PREVIOUS OWNERS: G. & J. Burns, Glasgow, 1864–79 (Union Company intended to name ship *Tarawera*).

SUBSEQUENT HISTORY: Wrecked off Cape Terawhiti 12/2/1909 on passage Picton to Wellington.

Built for the Oamaru and Dunedin Steam Company in 1876, **Waitaki** *(pictured here at Timaru) was integrated into Union Company services from 1879* ALEXANDER TURNBULL LIBRARY

The graceful lines of the famous steamer **Rotomahana**, *as she appeared in her original rig. She was the first ocean going vessel in the world built of mild steel and through her speedy passages she was often called the "Greyhound of the Pacific"* DE MAUS

WAITAKI — 412 GRT — IN FLEET 1879–1883

BUILT: 1876 by Thos. Wingate & Co., Whiteinch.

PREVIOUS OWNERS: Oamaru & Dunedin Steam Co. Ltd., Dunedin, 1876–79 (James Mills, Mgr).

SUBSEQUENT HISTORY: Sold Kamo Colliery Co. Ltd., Auckland, 1883–87. Wrecked 24/4/1887 at Black Head, near Cape Palliser on passage Napier to Wellington.

ROTOMAHANA — 1727 GRT — IN FLEET 1879–1925

BUILT: 1879 by Wm. Denny & Bros. Dumbarton.

SUBSEQUENT HISTORY: Laid up Melbourne, 16/12/1920. Sold to Power and Davis, Melbourne shipbreakers, 4/1925. Hull sunk in Bass Strait 29/5/1928, 3.5 miles south west of Port Phillip.

In her later years, **Rotomahana** *was employed in the Bass Strait trade between Melbourne and Launceston. She was in active service for 41 years*

Te Anau was built as a sister ship to **Rotomahana.** *With her bluff bow she did not attract the same attention but was actively engaged in most services for 42 years. Her remains are still visible as a breakwater in the Wanganui River port area* DE MAUS

Prior to the Union Company acquiring the 17 year old **Hero** *in 1880, she had seen service between Hull and Gothenburg, as a blockade runner in the American Civil War, and trialing a mail service from Queensland to Batavia (Jakarta), as well as spending many years in the Trans Tasman trade* DICKSON GREGORY PAINTING

The Union Company entered the Auckland – Fiji trade through its purchase of the Auckland Steam Ship Company and its steamer **Southern Cross** *in 1881*

TE ANAU   1652 GRT   IN FLEET 1879–1924

BUILT: 1879 by Wm. Denny & Bros, Dumbarton.

SUBSEQUENT HISTORY: Laid up Port Chalmers, 12/3/1921. Sold to Todd & Borlase, Dunedin, dismantled at Port Chalmers, 6/1924 and hull towed to Wanganui by *Kaitoke* 1/8–4/8/1924 and placed as breakwater 23/8/1924.

HERO   985 GRT   IN FLEET 1880 – 1891

BUILT: 1861 by C. & W. Earle, Kingston-upon-Hull.

PREVIOUS OWNERS: Thos. Wilson, Sons & Co., Hull, 1861–62. Wm. Whitworth, Manchester, 1862–63. Black Ball Line, Liverpool, 1863 (James Baines & Joseph Greaves). T.J. Sumner, J. Benn, and R. Bright, Melbourne, 1873–78 (Bright Bros, Mgrs) with T.J. Sumner & J. Benn sole owners 1878–1880 (Grice, Sumner & Co, Mgrs).

SUBSEQUENT HISTORY: Sold 11/6/1886 to J.E. Mitchell, W. Taylor, P O'Connor & A. Irwin, Sydney but repossessed by Union Company 11/1886. Sold La Societe 'Le Nickel', Noumea 1891 and employed as hulk. Blown ashore and wrecked in hurricane at Kaouaouva, N.W. New Caledonia 22/1/1901. Salvaged and towed to Noumea, where her hull remained visible in Baie de la Moselle, until she was buried in reclamation in mid 1970s.

BOOJUM   38 GRT   IN FLEET 1880 – 1887

BUILT: 1880 by Wm. Denny & Bros., Dumbarton, in sections and assembled at Port Chalmers by Morgan & Cable Ltd., 1880.

SUBSEQUENT HISTORY: Driven ashore and wrecked during gale in Napier roadstead 11/5/1887 while taking crew off sailing ship *Northumberland*.

SOUTHERN CROSS   282 GRT   IN FLEET 1881–1906

BUILT: 1873 by J.T. Eltringham, South Shields.

PREVIOUS OWNERS: Built for Watt Bros. of Napier, but sold on arrival New Zealand to the Auckland Steam Packet Co. Ltd., Auckland, 1874–77 (in liquidation 1877). W.C. Daldy, Auckland, 1877–78 (as liquidator). Auckland Steam Ship Co. Ltd., Auckland, 1878–1881.

SUBSEQUENT HISTORY: Under charter to French Government at Papeete 1897–1900 and renamed *Croix du Sud* (French) for period of charter. Laid up Wellington 6/12/1900 and converted to hulk. Hull scuttled in Cook Strait 24/4/1906.

18   Union Fleet

*When the **Manapouri** entered Trans Tasman service for the Union Company in 1882 she was the first ship in the world to be fitted throughout with incandescent electric light*   BURTON BROS.

Mahinapua *in 1882 had the distinction of being the first twin screw ship in the Union Company fleet. Originally in the service to the West Coast, she spent her last eleven years in Tasmanian waters*

*The small tender **Waihi** was built in Scotland in sections in 1881. Transported to Otago in the sailing ship **Nelson** and re-assembled at Port Chalmers, she spent most of her life in the Wellington–Blenheim Trade*

MANAPOURI   1783 GRT   IN FLEET 1882–1915

BUILT: 1882 by Wm. Denny & Bros., Dumbarton.

SUBSEQUENT HISTORY: Laid up Port Chalmers, 22/10/1913. Sold Moller & Co., Shanghai, 1915–23 and renamed *Lindsay Moller* (Br) 1919–23. Sold Cheong On S.S. Co. Ltd., Shanghai and renamed *Fook Hong* (China) 1923–26. Sold Chin Sen Hong, Canton, 1926–27 (same name/registry). Sold Shun Cheong S.S. Co., Hong Kong, (K.T. Chung, Haiphong, Mgr) 1927–45. (Same name but transferred Kwang Chow Wan registry (French) 1931 and renamed *Tai Poo Sek* (French) 1935–45. (Requisitioned by French Government 1942–45). Sunk by US carrier-based aircraft in Mekong Estuary 12/1/1945.

MAHINAPUA   423 GRT   IN FLEET 1882–1910

BUILT: 1882 by Wm. Denny & Bros., Dumbarton.

SUBSEQUENT HISTORY: Laid up Hobart, 23/11/1909. Sold to Einerson Bros., Sydney, 1910 and converted to hulk 5/1910. Renamed *Sydney* (un-registered) and after capsizing at her moorings, Salamander Bay, Port Stephens, 7/10/1925, was scuttled at Duckhole, near Pindimar, northern shore of Port Stephens 1925.

WAIHI   92 GRT   IN FLEET 1882–1907

BUILT: 1881 by Wm. Denny & Bros., Dumbarton, in sections and assembled at Port Chalmers by Morgan & Cable in 1882 (originally intended to be named *Opotiki*).

SUBSEQUENT HISTORY: Laid up Gisborne 10/1905 and towed to Wellington by *Haupiri* 26/2/1906. Sold Wairau Steam Ship Co. Ltd., Wellington, 1907–26. Laid up Wellington 1914, dismantled at Evans Bay 1935/36 and remains removed by explosives 1943. (Register closed 1926)

Built for the West Coast coal trade, **Omapere** *in November 1883 loaded a record lifting of 650 tons of coal from Greymouth. On several occasions she had to jettison part of her coal cargo to clear the bars at both Westport and Greymouth*   DE MAUS

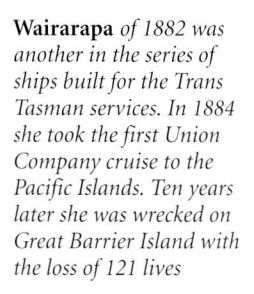

Wairarapa *of 1882 was another in the series of ships built for the Trans Tasman services. In 1884 she took the first Union Company cruise to the Pacific Islands. Ten years later she was wrecked on Great Barrier Island with the loss of 121 lives*

Hauroto *was yet another in the series of steamers built for the Trans Tasman passenger and cargo services. She arrived in Port Chalmers three months after* **Wairarapa** *in December 1882*   DE MAUS

OMAPERE — 601 GRT — IN FLEET 1882–1903

BUILT: 1882 by Wm. Denny & Bros., Dumbarton.

SUBSEQUENT HISTORY: Sold Koe Guan Co., Penang, 1903–07. Transferred Eastern Shipping Co. Ltd., Penang, 1907–21. Broken up 1921 at Penang.

WAIRARAPA — 1786 GRT — IN FLEET 1882–1894

BUILT: 1882 by Wm. Denny & Bros., Dumbarton.

SUBSEQUENT HISTORY: Wrecked 1 mile east of Miners Head, Great Barrier Island, 29/10/1894 on passage Sydney to Auckland.

HAUROTO — 1988 GRT — IN FLEET 1882–1915

BUILT: 1882 by Wm. Denny & Bros., Dumbarton.

SUBSEQUENT HISTORY: Laid up Auckland, 19/11/1912. Sold Hauroto Steamship Co. Ltd., Hong Kong, (Carmichael & Clarke, Mgrs) 1915–19. Went missing in typhoon in China Sea on passage Saigon (sailed 26/7/1919) to Hong Kong.

The little 30 ton **Snark** *was built in sections at Paisley in 1882 and re-assembled at Port Chalmers. She was employed as a tender servicing the Union Company passenger ships calling at Poverty Bay ports* ALEXANDER TURNBULL LIBRARY

Built in 1882, **Tarawera** *made her first voyage under the Union Company by taking the annual cruise to the West Coast sounds. She became the regular ship for the annual Sounds trips from 1882 to 1897, the eight-day excursions costing £12* BURTON BROS.

In 1882 the Union Company purchased the goodwill of the Melbourne-Suva service of J. McEwan & Company of Melbourne and its vessel **Suva**. *She had a short career with the company, being wrecked off Westport, only six years later* ALEXANDER TURNBULL LIBRARY

SNARK 30 GRT IN FLEET 1882–1905

BUILT: 1882 by Wm. Denny & Bros., Dumbarton, in sections and assembled by Morgan & Cable Ltd., Port Chalmers, 1882.

SUBSEQUENT HISTORY: Sold Karamea Steamship Co. Ltd., Wellington and renamed *Karamea* (N.Z.) 1905. Laid up Wellington 1906 and hull later beached for demolition, Kaiwharawhara, Wellington.

TARAWERA 2003 GRT IN FLEET 1882–1927

BUILT: 1882 by Wm. Denny & Bros., Dumbarton.

SUBSEQUENT HISTORY: Laid up Port Chalmers, 23/7/1921. Sold W. Borlase, Dunedin, for demolition. Later resold after partial stripping to Rosshavet Whaling Co., Sandefjord. Towed to Paterson's Inlet, Stewart Island, by tug *Southland* 19/12/1927, where she was employed as storeship for the Norwegian whaling fleet. On 21/8/1933 towed to Lowry's Beach, Stewart Island and grounded to form breakwater for small boats.

SUVA 293 GRT IN FLEET 1882–1888

BUILT: 1877 by Blackwood & Gordon, Port Glasgow.

PREVIOUS OWNERS: Wm. K. Thomson & Samuel Renwick, Melbourne, (Jas. McEwan & Co. Ltd.) 1877–1882.

SUBSEQUENT HISTORY: Wrecked 10/7/1888, 1 mile south west of Buller River breakwater, outward bound from Westport for Wellington.

Waihora *was the last of the series of 2000-ton passenger and cargo ships that Wm. Denny & Bros. built for the Union Company's Trans Tasman trade. She entered service in 1883. While on passage from Hobart to Melbourne on 17 February 1886 she struck Eddystone Point and had to be beached on Swan Island, Bass Strait to save her from sinking. Repairs required the renewal of 60 plates* DE MAUS

Specially built in 1883 for an express passenger and cargo service between Port Chalmers and Onehunga, the 930-ton steamer **Takapuna** *was the first Union Company vessel not to be built on the Clyde. For many years she was employed to carry the mails from Auckland to southern ports*

| **WAIHORA** | **2003 GRT** | **IN FLEET 1883–1903** |

BUILT: 1883 by Wm. Denny & Bros., Dumbarton.

SUBSEQUENT HISTORY: Sold Koe Guan & Co., Penang, 1903–06 (same name). Sold Diedrichsen, Jebsen & Co., Hamburg (later H. Diedrichsen & Co.) and renamed *Lysholt* (Germany). Broken up at Shanghai, 1911.

| **TAKAPUNA** | **930 GRT** | **IN FLEET 1883–1924** |

BUILT: 1883 by Barrow Shipbuilding Co., Barrow-in-Furness.

SUBSEQUENT HISTORY: Laid up Wellington 2/1/1917. Sold Wm. Borlase & James Todd, Dunedin, ship-breakers, 11/1924. Dismantled and hull scuttled in Cook Strait 18/6/1925.

| **OHAU** | **740 GRT** | **IN FLEET 1884–1899** |

BUILT: 1884 by Wm. Denny & Bros., Dumbarton.

SUBSEQUENT HISTORY: Foundered 13/5/1899 off Cape Campbell on passage Greymouth to Dunedin.

The 740 ton **Ohau** *was another smaller steamer built to carry coal from West Coast ports. She was one of the first vessels with insulated compartments for the carriage of frozen meat. She was lost with all crew (22 men) near Cape Campbell in 1899* DE MAUS

26   Union Fleet

*The **Tekapo** was built in 1881 solely as a cargo ship but in 1884 the Union Company acquired her and she was converted to a passenger and cargo ship for the Trans Tasman trade. In 1887 she made the first round voyage for the company from New Zealand to India and return. She was wrecked south of Sydney in 1899 and the illustration shows salvage operations under way*   WM. LIVERMORE

Mawhera *was acquired when the Union Company purchased the Black Diamond Line of W.R. Williams of Wellington in 1885. She ran ashore at Greymouth in October 1886 and was eventually refloated in January 1887 – an incident which saw repairs to 22 frames, 28 plates, the renewal of 36 feet of keel and a new stern post fitted. She was lost in the Pacific in 1902 while under charter to the French Government*   ALEXANDER TURNBULL LIBRARY

| TEKAPO | 2439 GRT | IN FLEET 1884–1899 |

BUILT: 1881 by R. Steele & Co., Greenock, as *Cape Clear*.

PREVIOUS OWNERS: Abram Lyle & Sons, Greenock, 1881–1884.

SUBSEQUENT HISTORY: Wrecked on reef, Maroubra Bay, 4 miles south of Coogee, Sydney, on 16/5/1899 on passage Sydney to Port Kembla.

| TAUPO | 737 GRT | IN FLEET 1884–1900 |

BUILT: 1884 by Wm. Denny & Bros., Dumbarton.

SUBSEQUENT HISTORY: Wrecked on breakwater, Greymouth, 16/7/1900 after breaking away from her moorings in strong wind and drifting down the Grey River. Remains blown up to clear channel 21/2/1901.

Built as a West Coast collier in 1884, the 737-ton **Taupo** *loaded a record 902 tons of coal from Greymouth in June 1885. The challenge of the river ports of Westport and Greymouth was lost in 1900 when was wrecked on the Greymouth breakwater after breaking away from her moorings* DE MAUS

| MAWHERA | 554 GRT | IN FLEET 1885–1902 |

BUILT: 1883 by H. McIntyre & Co., Paisley.

PREVIOUS OWNERS: Black Diamond Line, Wellington, (W.R.Williams) 1883–1885.

SUBSEQUENT HISTORY: Chartered to French Government, Papeete, 1901, for Marquesa group trade and while under charter known as *Croix du Sud*. Wrecked on reef Apatiki (Apataki) Island, Taumotu Group, 27/5/1902 on passage Fakarava to Kaukura.

Also purchased from the Black Diamond Line in 1885, **Koranui** *had a short life with the Union Company, being wrecked near French Pass four years later* BURTON BROS.

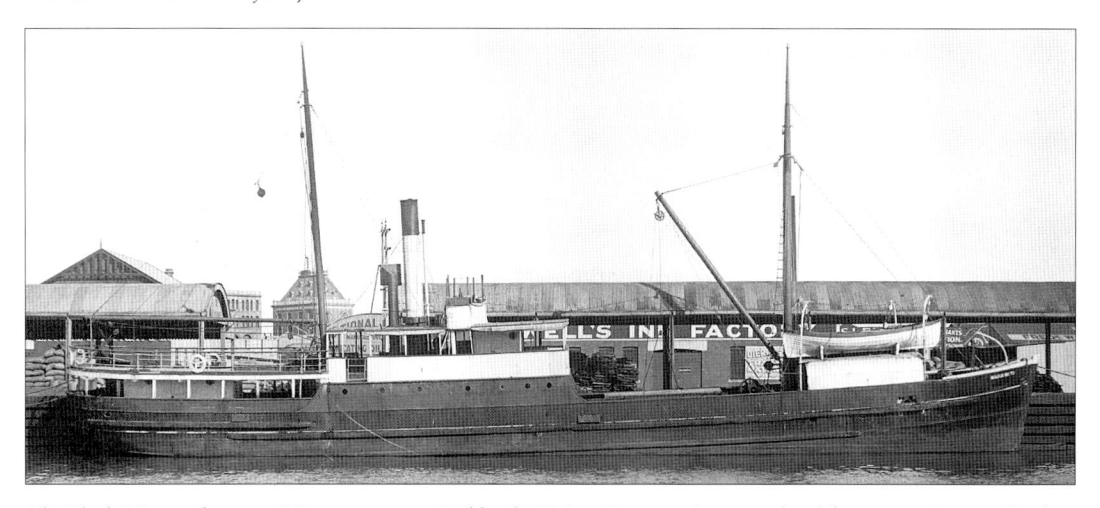

The Black Diamond steamer **Manawatu,** *acquired by the Union Company in 1885, dated from 1873. As a result of a collision in 1898 she was purchased by the owners of the other vessel and saw another 28 years of service around the Australian coast before being finally scrapped in 1929*

Another of the six steamers purchased from the Black Diamond Line, the 275-ton **Maitai** *had the distinction of being the largest iron steamer constructed in New Zealand when she was built in Wellington in 1885. She had a short life, being wrecked four years later. The illustration shows her aground at Greymouth 3 September 1887*

JAMES RING

| **KORANUI** | **488 GRT** | **IN FLEET 1885–1889** |

BUILT: 1883 by H. McIntyre & Co., Paisley.

PREVIOUS OWNERS: Black Diamond Line, Wellington, (W.R.Williams) 1883–1885.

SUBSEQUENT HISTORY: Wrecked Piege Rocks, Beef Barrels, Blind Bay near French Pass 27/9/1889 on passage Nelson to Wellington.

| **MANAWATU** | **183 GRT** | **IN FLEET 1885–1898** |

BUILT: 1873 by Henry Niccol, Auckland.

PREVIOUS OWNERS: New Zealand Steam Shipping Co. Ltd., Wellington, 1873–82. J. Martin, Wellington 1882. Black Diamond Line, Wellington (W.R.Williams), 1882–1885.

SUBSEQUENT HISTORY: Sunk 27/4/1898 in collision with S.S. *Edina* (380/1854) in Hobson's Bay, Melbourne. Raised 30/6/1898. Sold Wm. Howard Smith & Sons Ltd., Melbourne, 1898–1903. E. Mountjoy, Lorne, 1903–04. The Coastal Steamship Pty. Ltd., Melbourne, 1904–12. Gippsland Steamers Pty. Ltd., Melbourne, 1912–16. J.H. Edwards, Hobart, 1916 but later repossessed by Gippsland Steamers Pty. Ltd., under mortgage 1917. C.P. Preston, Melbourne, 1917–19. F.G. Wilson, Melbourne, 1919. Converted to hulk 1926. Sold Healey & Baxter, Melbourne and partially dismantled Williamstown 1929 with demolition completed by Weldcraft Pty. Ltd., 1939.

| **MAITAI** | **275 GRT** | **IN FLEET 1885–1889** |

BUILT: 1885 by S. Luke & Sons, Wellington.

PREVIOUS OWNERS: Black Diamond Line, Wellington, (W.R.Williams) 1885.

SUBSEQUENT HISTORY: Wrecked off Mercury Island, near Auckland, 2/6/1889 on passage East Coast ports to Auckland.

Grafton *was built at Birkenhead, in 1854 and was 31 years old when the Union Company took her over from the Black Diamond Line. She was lengthened by 28 feet in 1885 and had new bows fitted as well as other structural alterations in 1892. She was sent to Tasmania in 1896 and was lost on the notorious bar at the entrance to Macquarie Harbour two years later*

The 16 knot **Mararoa** *inaugurated the Union Company's Trans Pacific services in 1885 and was the first triple expansion powered steamer to enter San Francisco Bay. She was later employed on the Trans Tasman, inter-island and the Tasmanian trades before being withdrawn after 42 years of service with the company*

GRAFTON 548 GRT IN FLEET 1885–1898

BUILT: 1854 by Laird Bros., Birkenhead.

PREVIOUS OWNERS: Grafton Steam Navigation Co., Grafton, 1854–60. Clarence & Richmond River S.N. Co., Sydney, 1860–74. J. Edye Manning, Sydney, 1874–77. Black Diamond Line, Wellington, (W.R.Williams) 1877–85.

SUBSEQUENT HISTORY: Struck on bar, Macquarie Harbour entrance, Tasmania, 12/6/1898 on passage Melbourne to Strahan and sank 13/6/1898.

MARAROA 2466 GRT IN FLEET 1885–1931

BUILT: 1885 by Wm. Denny & Bros., Dumbarton.

SUBSEQUENT HISTORY: Laid up Wellington 4/6/1927. Dismantled and scuttled 16/2/1931 in Palliser Bay, Wellington, (41.28.25 S – 174. 58.75E).

Mararoa *with extended funnel and cross yards removed lying at Cross Wharf, Dunedin, in August 1901* S. RAWSON

32　*Union Fleet*

In 1895 the 459-ton **Australia** *was the first vessel over 400 tons to call at Gisborne. In May 1896 she became the first Union Company ship to enter Strahan, a port on the West Coast of Tasmania*

The 203-ton **Kanieri** *was built at Dumbarton in 1886 and took just on 119 days to sail out to Port Chalmers rigged as a fore and aft schooner. She was designed for the Wellington – Blenheim service and on the sale of that trade in 1897 she was sold to the Northern Steam Ship Company of Auckland*　ALEXANDER TURNBULL LIBRARY

In 1887 the Union Company took over three identical colliers owned by the Westport Coal Company and one of these was the **Kawatiri**. *She went to Tasmania in 1898 and was wrecked on the Strahan bar in 1907. She appears in Westport Coal colours in this photograph*
DE MAUS

AUSTRALIA — 459 GRT — IN FLEET 1886–1899

BUILT: 1884 by Burrell & Son, Dumbarton.

PREVIOUS OWNERS: John McFarlane, Loch Awe, Argyll, 1884–86.

SUBSEQUENT HISTORY: Wrecked south of West Point, Tasmania, 19/4/1899 on passage Launceston to Strahan.

KANIERI — 203 GRT — IN FLEET 1886–1893

BUILT: 1886 by Wm. Denny & Bros., Dumbarton.

SUBSEQUENT HISTORY: Sold Northern Steam Ship Co. Ltd., Auckland, 1893–1927. Dismantled by W. McKie, Auckland, 10/1922 and hull sunk in Western Reclamation, Auckland Harbour, 3/1927.

KAWATIRI — 453 GRT — IN FLEET 1887–1907

BUILT: 1882 by H. McIntyre & Co., Paisley.

PREVIOUS OWNERS: Westport Coal Co. Ltd., Dunedin, 1882–87. (Ownership registered to John McLean, Oamaru, 1886–87 as security for loan).

SUBSEQUENT HISTORY: Struck the breakwater at entrance Macquarie Harbour, Tasmania, 13/8/1907 and swung onto the North Spit, being totally wrecked on passage Hobart to Strahan.

Orowaiti *was another Westport Coal collier. Although built in 1882 and in the Union Company fleet from 1887 to 1903,* **Orowaiti** *continued in service in eastern waters under various names until 1941 – a career of 59 years* DE MAUS

The third Westport Coal collier taken over by the Union Company in 1887 was the **Wareatea** *and although she was sold out of the fleet in 1904, she remained in service for Tasmanian owners until 1945* DE MAUS

At the time of the Black Diamond Line takeover, a new vessel was building at Dumbarton for that company. The **Wainui** *(shown here at Hobart) was subsequently employed in the Fijian and Tongan trades, being the first ship to fly the Tongan ensign under a government-subsidized service. She was finally laid up in 1927 and her hull was scuttled at Whangaparaoa as a breakwater in 1929*
WILLIAMSON

OROWAITI 453 GRT IN FLEET 1887–1903

BUILT: 1882 by H. McIntyre & Co., Paisley.

PREVIOUS OWNERS: Westport Coal Co. Ltd., Dunedin, 1882–87.(Ownership registered to John McLean, Oamaru, 1886–87 as security for loan).

SUBSEQUENT HISTORY: Sold Huttenbach Bros., (A. Huttenbach, Mgr), Penang, 1903–06 and *renamed Pulo Riman* (Br). Sold Hakata K.K.K., Osaka and renamed *Kashi-i-Maru* (Japan) 1906–13. Sanriku K.K.K, Kamaishi, 1913–16. K. Yokoyama, Kamaishi 1916–19. Tanaka K.K.K., Kamaishi 1919–24. Kamaishi K.K.K. Kamaishi, 1924–26. Hokkai Yusen K.K., Kamaishi, 1926–32. Onishi Shinji, Kamaishi, 1932–33. Inui Yasajiro, Nemura, 1933–34. Ishimaru K.K.K. Kobe, 1934–36. I. Ishibashi, Tientsin, 1936–37. Ishibashi Masajiro, Tientsin, 1937. Tsutsumi Noboro, Tientsin, 1937–38.Tsutsumi Noboro, Dairen, 1938–39. Name altered to *Kasii Maru* (Japan) 1938–41. Sunk 1941.

WAREATEA 460 GRT IN FLEET 1887–1904

BUILT: 1883 by H. McIntyre & Co., Paisley.

PREVIOUS OWNERS: Westport Coal Co. Ltd., Dunedin, 1883–1887. (Ownership registered to John McLean, Oamaru, 1886–87 as security for loan).

SUBSEQUENT HISTORY: Sold Wm. Holyman & Sons Pty. Ltd., Launceston, 1904–45. Stripped Melbourne 1945 and remains scuttled off Barwon Heads 16/3/1945.

WAINUI 640 GRT IN FLEET 1887–1929

BUILT: 1886 by Murray Bros., Dumbarton.

PREVIOUS OWNERS: Built to the order of the Black Diamond Line, Wellington (J.H. Williams), 1886–87.

SUBSEQUENT HISTORY: Laid up Auckland, 5/6/1927. Sold to Borlase & McKay, Dunedin shipbreakers. Dismantled at Auckland, 10/1929 and hull sunk at Whangaparaoa to form breakwater 14/10/1929.

When the 1345-ton **Pukaki** *(pictured here in Adelaide River) arrived at Greymouth in November 1887 shortly after her delivery voyage she became the largest visitor to that port. Her Sunday arrival created so much interest that it was reported churches were deserted. Sold East in 1915, she was not broken up until 1937 – a career of 50 years*

Built in 1888 for Martin Kennedy to carry his Brunner Coal Company cargoes, **Brunner** *was taken over by the Union Company that year and served in the fleet until 1900*   W. FERRIER

The small 219-ton **Oreti** *saw only nine years' service with the Union Company before being sold to Wellington owners. She came into the fleet as a result of the coal company mergers of 1887*   ALEXANDER TURNBULL LIBRARY

PUKAKI 1345 GRT IN FLEET 1887–1915

BUILT: 1887 by Wm. Denny & Bros., Dumbarton.

SUBSEQUENT HISTORY: Sold Wm. Crosby & Co. Ltd., Melbourne, 1915–24. Sold Foo Chong S.S. Co. Ltd., Shanghai, 1924–26, renamed *Foo Kong* (China) 1924–26. Sold Wen Kee & Co. (Zung Wen Ping), Shanghai, 1926–33 (same name). Sold Kin Sing Li, Shanghai, 1933–34, renamed *Foo Nan* (China) 1933–34. Sold Foo Ning Steamship Co., Shanghai, 1934–37 (same name). Broken up China 1937.

BRUNNER 540 GRT IN FLEET 1888–1900

BUILT: 1888 by McArthur & Co., Paisley. Originally built for Martin Kennedy, Greymouth (Brunner Coal Company).

SUBSEQUENT HISTORY: Sold Wm. Laidley & Co. (Laidley, Gainford McLean), Sydney, 1900–04. Sold Loo Tom Fin, Sydney, 1904–13. Sold On Chong & Co., Sydney, 1913–15 (same name but Australian registry 1900–15). Wrecked Apamama (Abemama) Island, Gilbert Group 22/5/1915.

ORETI 219 GRT IN FLEET 1888–1897

BUILT: 1877 by Kincaid & McQueen, Dunedin.

PREVIOUS OWNERS: E.P. & H. Houghton & Partners, Dunedin, 1877–80. Henderson Law, Dunedin, 1880–81. F.H. King, Onehunga, 1881–82. F.H. King, Onehunga, J.W. Walker & E.N. Legge, Auckland, 1882–83. T.T. Masefield, Auckland, 1883–88. J. Kilgour, Greymouth, 1888.

SUBSEQUENT HISTORY: Sold Wellington Steam Packet Co., (C. Seagar & J. Joseph) Wellington, 1897–01. Sold Wellington & Wanganui Steam Packet Co. Ltd., Wellington, 1901–15. Converted to hulk 1911, later condemned and sunk Cook Strait 11/2/1915.

38   Union Fleet

▲ **Rosamond** *was under charter to the Brunner Coal Company when the Union Company took over its shipping services in 1888. She remained in the fleet for 36 years before being converted to an oil barge and spending a further 22 years in this role at both Wellington and Auckland*
HARRAWAY COLLECTION, HOCKEN LIBRARY

The 987-ton **Fijian** *was only in the fleet for a few months in 1889 before she was wrecked on Tanna Island in the New Hebrides*

An upsurge in trade saw the company purchase the steamer **Cairntoul** *on the stocks in 1889. She was subsequently renamed* **Taieri** *and remained in the fleet until 1908. Two years later she was lost at Greymouth as the* **Lauderdale**

ROSAMOND　　　721 GRT　　　IN FLEET 1888–1924

BUILT: 1884 by The Netherlands Steamboat Co., Rotterdam.

PREVIOUS OWNERS: R. Thomson, London, 1884–88. (On charter to Brunner Coal Co, Greymouth 1886–88).

SUBSEQUENT HISTORY: Laid up Wellington 18/5/1921. Converted to oil barge at Wellington 5/1924 and later towed to Auckland by *Kalingo* 7/1936. Hull towed to sea by *Maui Pomare* and sunk 200 miles from Auckland, 20/4/1946.

FIJIAN　　　987 GRT　　　IN FLEET 1889–1889

BUILT: 1886 by Palmers' Shipbuilding & Iron Co. Ltd., Jarrow.

PREVIOUS OWNERS: G.W. Nicoll, Sydney, 1886–89.

SUBSEQUENT HISTORY: Wrecked on reef, Tanna Island, New Hebrides, 13/5/1889 on passage Melbourne to New Hebrides.

TAIERI　　　1668 GRT　　　IN FLEET 1889–1908

BUILT: 1889 by Palmers' Shipbuilding & Iron Co. Ltd., Jarrow, as *Cairntoul*, R & D Cairns, Leith, 1889. (Not renamed *Taieri* until 1890).

SUBSEQUENT HISTORY: Sold Maoriland Steamship Co. Ltd., Wellington, 1908 and renamed *Lauderdale* 1908–10. On passage from Hokianga to Greymouth, touched Grey River bar, lost way, and became total wreck 27/6/1910.

The 640-ton steamer **Dingadee,** *which had been built for Australian owners in 1883 and given an Australian aboriginal name, was purchased by the company in 1890. The photograph shows her at Dunedin in the late 1890s*
DE MAUS

In 1890 the Union Company purchased the Peninsula & Akaroa Steam Navigation Company and its steamer **Banks Peninsula***. She was sold shortly afterwards to Tasmanian owners, who were acquired by the Union Company in 1896.* **Banks Peninsula** *was not required for any of its services and she was again sold. The photograph shows the vessel at Oamaru with two steam cranes alongside* ALEXANDER TURNBULL LIBRARY

Monowai *in 1890 was the largest steamer then built for the company. She was employed on the Trans Pacific service and in 1894 she made a record passage across the Pacific to deliver London mail in Auckland within 31 days*
WM. LIVERMORE

DINGADEE 640 GRT IN FLEET 1890 – 1900

BUILT: 1883 by Queenstown & Passage West Docks Co., Cork.

PREVIOUS OWNERS: Australasian Steam Nav. Co. Ltd., Sydney 1883–87. B.I. & Queensland Agency Co. Ltd., Brisbane, 1887. Australasian United Steam Nav. Co. Ltd., Sydney 1887–1890. (On charter to Union Company from 7/1889).

SUBSEQUENT HISTORY: Sold Blackball Coal Co. Ltd., Christchurch, 1900–03. Transferred to 'Dingadee' Steamship Co. Ltd., London, 1903–05 (Blackball Coal Company subsidiary but remained on charter to Blackball Coal Co). Sold C. Tanaka, Tokyo, (later Yokohama) 1905–19 and renamed *Chokyu Maru No 3* (Japan). Transferred Tanaka K.K.K. Uraga (later Shinagawa) 1919–22. Sold Taiwan Sotofuku, Shinagawa 1922–24 (same name). Sold Hayashi Kozo, Shinagawa, 1924–25 (same name). Broken up in Japan 1925.

BANKS PENINSULA 171 GRT IN FLEET 1890 – 1891

BUILT: 1889 by Grangemouth Dockyard Co., Grangemouth.

PREVIOUS OWNERS: Peninsula & Akaroa Steam Navigation Co. Ltd., Lyttelton, 1889–1890.

SUBSEQUENT HISTORY: Sold T.A. Reynolds & Co., (E.T. Miles, Mgr), Hobart, 1891–96. Sold Northern Steam Ship Co. Ltd., Auckland, 1896–1911, renamed *Waitangi* 1897–23. Sold Kauri Timber Co. Ltd., Auckland, 1911–19. Sold Patea Farmers Co-operative Freezing Co. Ltd., Patea, 1919. Stranded on Patea River bar 5/5/1923 and became total loss on passage Westport to Patea.

MONOWAI 3433 GRT IN FLEET 1890 – 1926

BUILT: 1890 by Wm. Denny & Bros., Dumbarton.

SUBSEQUENT HISTORY: Laid up Port Chalmers, 7/9/1920. Dismantled there and hulk sold to Gisborne Harbour Board for use as a breakwater at Whareongaonga. Towed to Gisborne by *Katoa* and sunk 16/12/1926.

The **Janet Nicoll** *gained her name from the original owners, G.W. Nicoll of Sydney and the name was not changed during the 13 years the vessel served in the Union Company fleet. The photograph shows her being towed, fully laden, out of Greymouth* JAMES RING

On her maiden voyage from Greenock to Melbourne, **Taviuni** *created a record for continuous steaming – 12,400 nautical miles in 48 days, 17 hours and 40 minutes. She is shown on trials over the Skelmorlie measured mile off the coast of Scotland* DE MAUS

| **JANET NICOLL** | **779 GRT** | **IN FLEET 1890 – 1903** |

BUILT: 1884 by Palmers' Shipbuilding & Iron Co. Ltd., Jarrow.

PREVIOUS OWNERS: G.W. Nicoll, Sydney, 1884–1890. Henderson & Macfarlane Ltd., Sydney, (H.W. Henderson) 1890.

SUBSEQUENT HISTORY: Sold Koe Guan & Co., Penang, 1903–07, transferred Eastern Shipping Co. Ltd., Penang, 1907–14. Wrecked at southern end of Kopah Inlet (Takuapa), Siam (Thailand) about 300 miles north of Penang, 10/5/1914 on passage Penang to Moulmein.

| **ROTOKINO** | **2004 GRT** | **IN FLEET 1890 – 1905** |

BUILT: 1890 by Wm. Denny & Bros., Dumbarton.

SUBSEQUENT HISTORY: Sold Ukon Gonzayemon, Kobe, (later Ukon Shoji K.K.) 1905–12 and renamed *Nanyetsu Maru No 2* (Japan). On passage to Taku, (Taiwan) vessel diverted to Taipanroku, (Taiwan) due to typhoon. Subsequently dragged anchor, stranded on rocks and became total wreck 16/9/1912.

Rotokino *was built by Wm. Denny & Bros, to the company's order but lasted only 15 years in the fleet before being sold to Japanese owners. Under charter to the New Zealand Shipping Company, she made one round trip to London with wool in 1893 and in 1901 she loaded 2437 tons of coal and 50 tons of timber at Westport – the largest cargo to leave the port to that date* DE MAUS

| **TAVIUNI** | **1465 GRT** | **IN FLEET 1890 – 1924** |

BUILT: 1890 by Wm. Denny & Bros., Dumbarton.

SUBSEQUENT HISTORY: Laid up Sydney 11/12/1921. Sold to W.Waugh Ltd., Balmain, and dismantled at Sydney 6/1924. Hull sunk off Sydney Heads 12/5/1931.

Purchased on the stocks in 1890, the **Poherua** *was mainly employed in the coal trade. In this photograph she is moving out of the Dunedin basin on 21 June 1906*

S. RAWSON

Ovalau *was built for the Pacific Island trades and entered service in 1891. She was sold in 1903 and a few months later was lost by fire at Lord Howe Island*

Mangana, *shown here at Hobart in Tasmanian Steam Navigation colours, was one of eight ships acquired from that company in 1891. Already 15 years old, she was sold in 1892*

POHERUA — 1175 GRT — IN FLEET 1890 – 1924

BUILT: 1890 by W. Harkess & Son, Middlesbrough, as *Croydon* 1890. W.F. Connor & Co., London, 1890.

SUBSEQUENT HISTORY: Laid up Wellington 9/7/1921, dismantled 9/1923. Towed to sea from Wellington and scuttled 9/2/1924 about 4 miles south, south east of Turakirae Heads, Cook Strait.

OVALAU — 1229 GRT — IN FLEET 1891–1903

BUILT: 1891 by Wm. Denny & Bros., Dumbarton.

SUBSEQUENT HISTORY: Sold Burns Philp & Co. Ltd., Sydney, 1903. Caught fire 18/10/1903 near Lord Howe Island on passage from Norfolk Island. After explosions in the hold, burnt out at Lord Howe Island 19/10/1903 and sank 20/10/1903.

MANGANA — 752 GRT — IN FLEET 1891–1892

BUILT: 1876 by D. & W. Henderson & Co., Partick, Glasgow.

PREVIOUS OWNERS: Tasmanian Steam Navigation Co. Ltd., Hobart, 1876–91.

SUBSEQUENT HISTORY: Sold Jouve & Co., Noumea, (Syndicat Caledonien) 1892–97. Sold E.F.A. Knoblauch, Sydney, 1897–00. Sold Huddart Parker Ltd., Melbourne, 1900 for conversion to hulk. Hulked Sydney 1901 and towed Adelaide. Hull beached at Port Adelaide 23/2/1931.

Another old Tasmanian Steam Navigation vessel was the **Flinders**. *She was also sold out of the Union Company fleet after three years for employment with other owners on the Australian coast*

The Tasmanian Steam Navigation Company vessel **Corinna**, *which was taken over by the Union Company in 1891, proved a very successful vessel, lasting 39 years in the company's fleet. From 1900 she was solely a cargo carrier* DE MAUS

Flora *was another successful acquisition from the Tasmanian Steam Navigation Company. She served from 1891 until 1925 and was then converted to an oil barge at Auckland in 1927, being finally dismantled in 1944*

FLINDERS 948 GRT IN FLEET 1891–1894

BUILT: 1878 by A. & J. Inglis, Glasgow.

PREVIOUS OWNERS: Tasmanian Steam Navigation Co. Ltd., Hobart, 1878–91 (On charter to McIlwraith, McEacharn Ltd., Melbourne for most of the period 1891–94).

SUBSEQUENT HISTORY: Sold John McIlwraith Snr, Melbourne, 1894–1901. Sold John McIlwraith Jnr, Melbourne, 1901–07. Sold Adelaide Steam Ship Co. Ltd., Adelaide, 1907–11. Caught fire in North Arm, Adelaide River, 28/1/1911 and subsequently converted to hulk. Sold Peninsula Traders Ltd., Adelaide, 1927 and broken up.

CORINNA 1319 GRT IN FLEET 1891–1930

BUILT: 1882 by D. & W. Henderson & Co., Partick, Glasgow.

PREVIOUS OWNERS: Tasmanian Steam Navigation Co. Ltd., Hobart, 1882–1891.

SUBSEQUENT HISTORY: Laid up Wellington 3/1/1930 and dismantled 9/1930. Hull sunk in Cook Strait, 5 miles south east of Turakirae Heads 8/11/1930 (41.29.5 S, 174.57.5 E).

FLORA 1283 GRT IN FLEET 1891–1927

BUILT: 1882 by Earle's Shipbuilding & Engineering Co., Hull.

PREVIOUS OWNERS: Bailey & Leetham, Hull, 1882–84. Tasmanian Steam Navigation Co. Ltd., Hobart, 1884–91.

SUBSEQUENT HISTORY: Laid up Auckland, 15/10/1925. Converted to oil barge at Auckland, 6/1927. Dismantled 1944 and hull scuttled off Great Barrier Island, Auckland, 1/12/1944.

The nine-year-old **Moreton** *had a short five-year life with the Union Company following the takeover of the Tasmanian Steam Navigation Company. She was an unlucky ship, as one year after she had been sold to Japanese buyers she was totally wrecked on the coast of Japan*

Despite a reputation as something of a roller, the **Pateena**, *which was acquired from the Tasmanian Steam Navigation Company in 1891, proved quite popular on inter-island ferry services in New Zealand. She served the Union Company until 1920*   ALLAN C. GREEN

One of the more modern Tasmanian Steam Navigation Company vessels was the **Oonah**, *built in 1888 and acquired in 1891. She remained on the mainland Australia services to Tasmania throughout her entire career, both under the Union Company and from 1921 under a joint company with Huddart Parker Ltd.*   ALLAN C. GREEN

MORETON — 581 GRT — IN FLEET 1891–1896

BUILT: 1882 by W. Walker & Co., Rotherhithe, London.

PREVIOUS OWNERS: Wm. Howard Smith & Sons Ltd., Melbourne, 1882–86. Tasmanian Steam Navigation Co. Ltd., Hobart, 1886–91.

SUBSEQUENT HISTORY: Sold Iwata Sadajiro, Fukuyama, 1896 and renamed *Iwai Maru* (Japan). After sailing Tateyama, Japan, 12/6/1897, ran into heavy fog. Struck rocks 15/6/1897 Kinkazan Island and sank within 10 minutes.

PATEENA — 1212 GRT — IN FLEET 1891–1924

BUILT: 1883 by A. & J. Inglis, Glasgow.

PREVIOUS OWNERS: Tasmanian Steam Navigation Co. Ltd., Hobart, 1883–91.

SUBSEQUENT HISTORY: Laid up Port Chalmers, 31/8/1920. Sold Todd & Borlase, Dunedin, shipbreakers and dismantled 1924. Hull sunk alongside mole, Otago Heads 27/5/1926.

OONAH — 1758 GRT — IN FLEET 1891–1922

BUILT: 1888 by A. & J. Inglis, Glasgow.

PREVIOUS OWNERS: Tasmanian Steam Navigation Co. Ltd., Hobart, 1888–91.

SUBSEQUENT HISTORY: Transferred to Tasmanian Steamers Pty. Ltd., Melbourne, 1922–35. Sold Miyachi K.K.K., Kobe and broken up Osaka 1936.

The one-year-old **Talune** *was the most modern ship of the Tasmanian Steam Navigation Company fleet and she fitted well into Union Company services. She achieved publicity in 1899 when she came across the* **Perthshire**, *which had been adrift in the Tasman Sea for eight weeks with a broken tail shaft, and towed her into Sydney*   WM. LIVERMORE

Upolu *was built for the Pacific Island trade but she was replaced after only 12 years. Under Australian and Chinese owners she lasted until 1930 when she was sunk in Chinese waters*

Another small coaster which had been built in sections in England in 1864 and re-assembled in New Zealand, the **Moa** *was already 30 years old when acquired by the Union Company. It retained her for only three years. The photograph shows her ashore on one of her many strandings at Wanganui*   ALEXANDER TURNBULL LIBRARY

TALUNE　　　1991 GRT　　　IN FLEET 1891–1925

BUILT: 1890 by Ramage & Ferguson, Leith.

PREVIOUS OWNERS: Tasmanian Steam Navigation Co. Ltd., Hobart, 1890–91.

SUBSEQUENT HISTORY: Laid up Auckland, 16/2/1921. Sold Todd & Borlase, Dunedin, shipbreakers 5/1925 for dismantling at Auckland. Hulk sold to N.Z. Government Public Works Dept. for use as breakwater at Waikokopu. Towed to Waikokopu by *Hinemoa* 21/11–25/11/1925 and sunk 22/1/1926.

UPOLU　　　1141 GRT　　　IN FLEET 1891–1903

BUILT: 1891 by Fleming and Ferguson, Paisley.

SUBSEQUENT HISTORY: Sold Lever's Pacific Plantations Ltd., Sydney, 1903–11. Sold The Brisbane Milling Co. Ltd., Brisbane, 1911–15. Sold A.B. Iffland van Ess, Shanghai, 1915–21. Sold Shaw Hsing S.S.Co. Ltd,. Newchang, 1921–30 and renamed *Tongan* (China). Sunk in collision off Shantung Promontory 12/8/1930 with *Lienhsing* (1562/1892) on passage Tsingtao to Newchang.

MOA　　　188 GRT　　　IN FLEET 1894–1897

BUILT: 1864 by Temple & Co., London, in sections and assembled at Lyttelton by Henry Phillips.

PREVIOUS OWNERS: E. Reece, Lyttelton, 1864–66. H.P. Murray-Aynsley, Lyttelton, 1866–74. J.S. Cameron & G Hutchinson, Lyttelton, 1874–76. D. McIntyre, Wellington, 1876–82. Black Diamond Line, Wellington, (W.R. Williams) 1882–90. J.H. Williams, Wellington 1890–94.

SUBSEQUENT HISTORY: Sold Wellington Steam Packet Co., (C. Seagar & J. Joseph), Wellington, 1897–1901. Sold Wellington and Wanganui Steam Packet Co. Ltd., Wellington, 1901–14. Destroyed by fire following explosion off Wanganui Heads 3/2/1914 on passage Wellington to Wanganui.

Rakanoa *was another vessel purchased on the stocks by the Union Company. She was mainly employed as a collier and in September 1904 she established a coaling record by delivering 1000 tons of coal to* HMS **Euryalus** *in 9 hours 40 minutes*
ALEXANDER TURNBULL LIBRARY

Bellinger *was acquired when the Union Company purchased T.A. Reynolds and Company of Hobart in 1896. She was too small for the burgeoning Strahan trade and was sold to the Northern Steam Ship Company of Auckland*

The Union Company also acquired the little steamer **Glenelg** *from the takeover of T.A. Reynolds and Company and sold her within two years*

RAKANOA 2246 GRT IN FLEET 1896–1925

BUILT: 1896 by W. Dobson & Co., Low Walker-on-Tyne. Launched as *Bells* for Bell Bros. (Geo. & Chas. R. Bell), Newcastle, but renamed *Rakanoa* prior to completion.

SUBSEQUENT HISTORY: Used as coal storage hulk at Wellington 1925–28 and hull scuttled in Cook Strait 23/4/1928.

BELLINGER 225 GRT IN FLEET 1896–1897

BUILT: 1884 by J. McArthur & Co., Paisley.

PREVIOUS OWNERS: G.W. Nicoll, Sydney 1884. Belfast & Koroit Steam Navigation Co. Ltd., Port Fairy, Victoria, 1884–87. B.B. Nicoll, Sydney, 1887–90. T.A. Reynolds & Co., (E.T. Miles) Hobart, 1890–96.

SUBSEQUENT HISTORY: Sold Northern Steam Ship Co. Ltd., Auckland, 1897 and renamed *Muritai* 1897–08. Wrecked West Chicken Island, near Whangarei 27/5/1908 on passage Russell to Auckland.

GLENELG 210 GRT IN FLEET 1896–1898

BUILT: 1875 by Aitken & Mansel, Glasgow.

PREVIOUS OWNERS: Elder, Smith & Co., Adelaide, 1875–1881. Wm. Wells, Port Adelaide, 1881–82. Port Jackson S.S.Co. Ltd., Sydney, (T. Hesselton, Mgr) 1882–91. T.A. Reynolds & Co., (E.T. Miles), Hobart, 1891–96.

SUBSEQUENT HISTORY: Sold A.J. Ellerker, Melbourne, 1898–1900. Foundered in Bass Strait, about 40 miles west of Lakes Entrance 25/3/1900 on passage Melbourne to Gippsland Lakes.

PIONEER 34 GRT IN FLEET 1896–1901

BUILT: 1892 by Paul & Co., Dumbarton, in sections and assembled at Dunedin by R.S. Sparrow.

PREVIOUS OWNERS: Anderson's Bay Ferry & Baths Co. Ltd., Dunedin, 1892–96.

SUBSEQUENT HISTORY: Sold Henry Marks & Co. Ltd., Fiji, 1901, later transferred to Fiji Shipping Co., Suva, (Brown & Joske Ltd., Mgrs). Laid up 1915, dismantled and remains subsequently buried in reclamation, Walu Bay, Suva.

54 *Union Fleet*

In 1896 the Union Company purchased the goodwill of the Donald & Edenborough services from Auckland to Rarotonga and Tahiti and acquired the 748-ton steamer **Richmond** *which the company subsequently renamed* **Haupiri**
ALDERSLEY

Built in 1897, the collier **Hawea**, *shown here at Dunedin, had a short life of only 11 years before she was lost on the North Tip Head, Greymouth, in October 1908. Earlier that same year her tail shaft broke on 30 July and four company vessels were searching for her in the vicinity of Lord Howe Island. She was lost for 30 days*
HARRAWAY COLLECTION, HOCKEN LIBRARY

For many years the mainstay of the New Zealand east coast general cargo service, the **Wanaka** *of 1897 served in the fleet for 30 years before her partly dismantled hull was scuttled off Great Barrier Island* DE MAUS

HAUPIRI — 748 GRT — IN FLEET 1896–1915

BUILT: 1885 by Gourlay Bros. & Co., Dundee as *Richmond* 1885–1897.

PREVIOUS OWNERS: B.B. Nicoll, Sydney 1885–87. Donald & Edenborough, Auckland, 1887–1896.

SUBSEQUENT HISTORY: Laid up Wellington 2/7/1913. Sold Sun Shipping Co. Ltd., London, (Mitchell, Cotts & Co. Ltd. Mgrs) 1915–19. Sold M.C. Stamatopoulos Fils, Piraeus, 1919 and renamed *Margarita* (Greece) 1919–21. Foundered off Milos, on passage Piraeus to Crete 6/2/1921.

HAWEA — 1758 GRT — IN FLEET 1897–1908

BUILT: 1897 by A. McMillan & Son Ltd., Dumbarton.

SUBSEQUENT HISTORY: Wrecked North Tip Head, Greymouth 30/10/1908 on sailing Greymouth for Launceston and Adelaide.

WANAKA — 2425 GRT — IN FLEET 1897–1927

BUILT: 1887 by Chas. Connell & Co., Scotstoun, Glasgow, as *Liddlesdale*.

PREVIOUS OWNERS: Robert Mackill & Co. Ltd., Glasgow, 1887–1897.

SUBSEQUENT HISTORY: Laid up Auckland, 11/1/1926. Sold to Borlase & McKay, Dunedin, shipbreakers, 19/2/1927 and broken up Auckland. Hull sunk off Great Barrier Island 25/6/1927.

The 3915-ton **Moana** *was designed for the Trans Pacific service as a replacement for the* **Monowai** *and entered service in 1897. When the San Francisco service terminated in 1900,* **Moana** *was able to take up running to Vancouver in the following year. A successful vessel, she ran the fastest passage between Wellington and Lyttelton in 1900 in 10 hours 15 minutes, heads to heads*

The 3071-ton **Waikare** *is shown here at Vavau on the 1899 Pacific Island cruise. Cruising was to be her downfall, as on the West Coast Sounds cruise in January 1910 she struck a rock and sank in Dusky Sound. The annual Sounds cruise was then discontinued* BURTON BROS.

Kini *was purchased second-hand in 1898 to supplement the cargo requirements around the New Zealand coast. She had an uneventful career and was disposed of in 1924* DE MAUS

| **MOANA** | **3915 GRT** | **IN FLEET 1897–1927** |

BUILT: 1897 by Wm. Denny & Bros., Dumbarton.

SUBSEQUENT HISTORY: Laid up Port Chalmers from 13/3/1921. Dismantled at Port Chalmers, 1927. Hull sold Otago Harbour Board and sunk alongside mole, Otago Harbour entrance 31/10/1927.

| **WAIKARE** | **3071 GRT** | **IN FLEET 1897–1910** |

BUILT: 1897 by Wm. Denny & Bros., Dumbarton.

SUBSEQUENT HISTORY: On cruise around West Coast Sounds from Dunedin, struck uncharted rock Dusky Sound, West Coast, New Zealand 4/1/1910 and beached Stop Island. Subsequently sank 5/1/1910.

| **KINI** | **1122 GRT** | **IN FLEET 1898–1924** |

BUILT: 1894 by Short Bros., Sunderland, as *Ella* 1894–1898.
PREVIOUS OWNERS: J.S. Barwick, Sunderland, 1894–98.
SUBSEQUENT HISTORY: Sold to Todd & Borlase, Dunedin, shipbreakers, 11/1924. Dismantled Wellington and hull sunk Cook Strait 11/2/1925 in position 41.31 S, 174.56 E.

Rotoiti was built in 1898 for the coastal passenger traffic around New Zealand and she spent 14 years on Union Company service before being sold to the Northern Steam Ship Company of Auckland in 1912. On 30 July 1906 she was the first vessel to officially open the new channel through the Boulder Bank, Nelson
S. RAWSON

The little 300-ton **Kia Ora** had a variety of roles within the Union Company during the five years she was in its service. In 1900 she was chartered by a telegraph company to lay cable in Bass Strait and a year later she was sent to Fiji   DE MAUS

A sister ship to the **Rotoiti**, the **Mapourika** is shown bustling out of Greymouth in December 1911 with many of the passengers on the fore deck as the ship moves to cross the bar
S. RAWSON

| ROTOITI | 1159 GRT | IN FLEET 1898–1912 |

BUILT: 1898 by Wm. Denny & Bros., Dumbarton.

SUBSEQUENT HISTORY: Sold Northern Steam Ship Co. Ltd., Auckland, 1912–26 and renamed *Manaia*. Wrecked Slipper Island, Bay of Plenty, 10/6/1926 on passage Tauranga to Auckland.

| KIA ORA | 300 GRT | IN FLEET 1898–1903 |

BUILT: 1896 by Robert Duncan & Co. Ltd., Port Glasgow.

PREVIOUS OWNERS: McGregor Steam Ship Co., Auckland, (W.A. McGregor) 1896–98.

SUBSEQUENT HISTORY: Sold Northern Steam Ship Co. Ltd., Auckland, 1903–07. Wrecked Piritoki Reef off Turua Point 13/6/1907 on passage Waitara to Kawhia.

| MAPOURIKA | 1203 GRT | IN FLEET 1898–1921 |

BUILT: 1898 by Wm. Denny & Bros., Dumbarton.

SUBSEQUENT HISTORY: Sold Anchor Shipping & Foundry Co. Ltd., Nelson, 1921–35 and renamed *Ngaio*. Broken up at Nelson by Jackson & Co., 1935–36.

Mapourika *went ashore on the seaward side of the North Tiphead at Greymouth on 1 October 1898 and in order to salvage the vessel it was necessary to virtually slide her over the breakwater and re-launch her into the river. Nearly 100 men spent 4 months in preparation and she was successfully re-launched 10 March 1899. The illustration shows the vessel in preparation for being raised over the breakwater on the left* J. RING

A larger version of the **Waikare**, *the 3502-ton* **Mokoia** *entered service in 1898 and was placed on the "Horseshoe run" from Wellington, Lyttelton, Dunedin, Bluff, Hobart, Melbourne and then back again. Apart from a voyage to San Francisco in 1918 she spent her 22 active years with the Union Company on the Tasman services*   WM. LIVERMORE

The 80-ton **Yolla** *had a very brief life with the Union Company, being wrecked on the west coast of Tasmania 16 days after being purchased. She had been intended for use in Macquarie Harbour, Strahan*

Koonya *was purchased in 1899 for the Tasmanian trade but rail competition saw her transferred to the New Zealand coast by 1901, although she returned to Tasmania in 1913. On 1 January 1908 she sailed from Lyttelton with the Shackleton expedition vessel* **Nimrod** *in tow and became the first steel vessel to cross the Antarctic Circle*

ALLAN C. GREEN

| **MOKOIA** | **3502 GRT** | **IN FLEET 1898–1928** |

BUILT: 1898 by Wm. Denny & Bros., Dumbarton.

SUBSEQUENT HISTORY: Laid up Port Chalmers, 18/12/1920. Dismantled at Port Chalmers, 1929. Hull sunk in Carey's Bay, Port Chalmers, 4/3/1931 but in 1941 was taken over by Dept. of Industries and Commerce, raised 16/7/1941 and scrapped to the waterline. Remains sunk alongside mole, Otago Harbour entrance 28/11/1945.

| **YOLLA** | **80 GRT** | **IN FLEET 1898–1898** |

BUILT: 1890 by Robert Inches, Hobart.

PREVIOUS OWNERS: Risby Bros., Hobart, 1890–98.

SUBSEQUENT HISTORY: Wrecked Sandy Cape, West Coast of Tasmania, 23/12/1898 on passage King Island to Strahan.

| **KOONYA** | **1091 GRT** | **IN FLEET 1899–1919** |

BUILT: 1898 by Grangemouth Dockyard Co., Grangemouth, as *Yukon*,

PREVIOUS OWNERS: S.S. Yukon Co. Ltd., Swansea, (F. Le Boulanger, Swansea, Mgr) 1898–99.

SUBSEQUENT HISTORY: Wrecked Sandy Cape, West Coast of Tasmania, 3/6/1919 on passage Strahan to Burnie.

Moura *was a "white elephant" which the Union Company decided to buy in 1898 to protect the cargoes of the mining companies being shipped out of Strahan, Tasmania. Despite being a misfit in its fleet,* **Moura** *spent another 40 years in service after being sold in 1915*   WM. LIVERMORE

The distinctive three-masted **Kittawa** *was purchased second-hand in 1899 and served in the coastal and coal trades for 29 years.*

The 573-ton **Herald** *had been on charter to the Union Company for 12 years from 1888 to 1900. The company then purchased her but she was sold five years later and then spent a further 30 years under Japanese owners*   DE MAUS

| MOURA | 2027 GRT | IN FLEET 1899–1915 |

BUILT: 1899 by Sir W.G. Armstrong, Whitworth & Co. Ltd., Newcastle-upon-Tyne as *North Lyell*.
PREVIOUS OWNERS: North Mount Lyell Copper Co. Ltd., Melbourne, 1899.
SUBSEQUENT HISTORY: Laid up Auckland, 28/1/1914. Sold Douglas Steamship Co. Ltd., Hong Kong, 1915, renamed *Hai Hong* (Britain) 1916–28. Sold Fernandez Hermanos Inc., Manila, (later Compania Maritima – same managers) 1928 and renamed *Mactan* (Philippines) 1928–56. Requisitioned in Manila by US Army 12/1941–45 but within this period was employed as ammunition storage vessel in Sydney for Royal Australian Navy and later as canteen and recreation ship in South Pacific. Returned to owners 22/6/1945. Sold Chiap Hua Shipbreaking Co. Ltd., Hong Kong, 1955 and towed Manila to Hong Kong mid 1955 for demolition between 1/1956–3/1956.

| KITTAWA | 1247 GRT | IN FLEET 1899–1928 |

BUILT: 1898 by Osbourne, Graham & Co., Sunderland, as *Glosterhill*.
PREVIOUS OWNERS: Broomhill Shipping Co. Ltd., Newcastle. (R. Jack, Mgr) 1898–99.
SUBSEQUENT HISTORY: Laid up Wellington 10/3/1928. Sold Wing Hong Co. Ltd., (S.T. Williamson, Mgr) 9/1928–32. Sunk following collision with *Bhutan* (6104/1929) in Astrea Channel, Whangpoo River (Hwangpu Kiang) 6/7/1932. Wreck removed 9/1932–10/1933.

| HERALD | 573 GRT | IN FLEET 1900 – 1905 |

BUILT: 1884 by Pearce Bros., Dundee.
PREVIOUS OWNERS: James Stone, Auckland, 1884–85. C.B. Stone & Partners, Auckland, 1885–00. (Union Line held part interest in *Herald* 1888–1900 until acquired outright and she was also on charter for most of this period).
SUBSEQUENT HISTORY: Sold S. Yamashita, Hakodate, 1905 and renamed *Rensho Maru* (Japan) 1905–07. Sold Kanamori Gomei Kaisha, Hakodate, 1907–12. Sold C. Nishimura, Nanao, 1912–19. Sold Hamaguchi K.K.K., Amagasaki, 1919–22. Sold Kyukichi Fujita, Amagasaki, 1922–24. Sold Zoga Shigimatsu, Amagasaki, 1924–26. Sold Fujita Tomizo, Fuchu, 1926–30. Sold Matsuura Shizuo, Fuchu, 1930–34 and renamed *Matsu Maru* (Japan) 1932–34. Sold Tai Kong S.S. Co. Chefoo, (Hwei Tung S.S. Co., Mgrs) 1934 and renamed *Tai Kong* (China) 1934–35. Sunk near Chinwangtao 10/1935.

*One of the larger cargo vessels, **Whangape,** carried coal to South Africa for the Imperial Government on her delivery voyage in 1900. She made two round trips to India but spent most of her 27 active years with the company on the Trans Tasman trade*

__Kakapo__ was purchased in 1900 as a light draft steamer for the Tasmanian trade but on her delivery voyage she ran aground just south of Cape Town and became a total loss. The illustration shows her sitting upright well secured in position by wind blown sand   CAPE ARCHIVES

*Apart from a brief time in Tasmania, the **Kotuku** of 1900 spent her life as a collier and had a comparatively short life when she was wrecked in 1912 on the breakwater at Greymouth*   WM. LIVERMORE

WHANGAPE   2931 GRT   IN FLEET 1900 – 1928

BUILT: 1900 by Sir Raylton Dixon & Co. Ltd., Middlesbrough.

PREVIOUS OWNERS: Laid down as *Adriana* for British Maritime Trust Ltd., London. Sold Elder Dempster & Co. Ltd., Liverpool, and became *Asaba* but again resold and completed as *Whangape* for Union Company.

SUBSEQUENT HISTORY: Laid up Auckland, 6/9/1927. Sold Chun Young Zan, Shanghai, 1928 and renamed *Nanking* (China) 1928–35. Broken up in China 1935.

KAKAPO   1093 GRT   IN FLEET 1900 – 1900

BUILT: 1898 by Grangemouth Dockyard Co., Grangemouth, as *Clarence*.

PREVIOUS OWNERS: S.S. Clarence Co. Ltd., Swansea. (F. Le Boulanger, Mgr.) 1898–00.

SUBSEQUENT HISTORY: Wrecked Chapman's Bay, 15 miles south of Cape Town, 25/5/1900 on delivery voyage United Kingdom to New Zealand.

KOTUKU   1054 GRT   IN FLEET 1900 – 1912

BUILT: Laid down by Carmichael, McLean & Co., Greenock, for Fearnley & Eger, Christiania, (Oslo) but completed 1900 by Russell and Co., Greenock.

SUBSEQUENT HISTORY: Wrecked North Tip Head, Grey River entrance, Greymouth while outward bound 16/5/1912.

The 73-ton wooden tug **Natone** *was initially purchased for use at Strahan, Tasmania but from 1904 to 1947 she was employed as a tug and tender at the port of Wellington*

Warrimoo *had been built in 1892 for James Huddart's Trans Tasman service but when Huddart ran into financial trouble, the Union Company purchased the vessel. She was lost during World War 1*   WM. LIVERMORE

NATONE 73 GRT IN FLEET 1900 – 1947

BUILT: 1900 by Walter Ford, Berry's Bay, Sydney, for James Wallace, Sydney and purchased on stocks by Union Company.
SUBSEQUENT HISTORY: Sold A.J. Long, Wellington 1947, resold 1947 to R.L. Clark, Petone. Abandoned derelict near Havelock 1955.

WAIPORI 1919 GRT IN FLEET 1901–1928

BUILT: 1901 by Campbeltown Shipbuilding Co., Campbeltown. (Laid down as Campbeltown standard type and sold on the stocks to Union Company).
SUBSEQUENT HISTORY: Sold Kaitsu Koshi Goshi Kaisha, Dairen (later Kaitsukosi & Co., Shanghai) and renamed *Waipori Maru* (Japan) 1928–34. Sold Zee Yu Kun, Shanghai, 1934 and renamed *Chingsun* (China) 1934. Sold Tientsin Navigation Co. Ltd., Shanghai, and renamed *Tung Lee* (China) 1934–37. Requisitioned by Chinese Government during Sino-Japanese war and sunk as blockship in midstream Yangtze River 1937.

Purchased on the stocks in 1901, **Waipori** *was a standard collier and spent 27 years in the carriage of coal. She was the first steamer to discharge coal at the Napier breakwater in December 1901*   ALLAN C. GREEN

WARRIMOO 3529 GRT IN FLEET 1901–1916

BUILT: 1892 by C.S. Swan & Hunter, Wallsend.
PREVIOUS OWNERS: N.Z. & Australasian S.S.Co., London, (J. Huddart, Mgr) 1892–1893. Canadian Australian Royal Mail Line, London, 1893–1898. New Zealand Shipping Co. Ltd., London, 1898–1901.
SUBSEQUENT HISTORY: Sold 18/10/1916 (but not delivered until 29/1/1917) to Khiam Yik & Co. Ltd., (Tan Kah Kee, Mgr), Singapore, 1916–18. Sunk following collision with escorting French destroyer *Catapulte* north of Galita Island, off the coast of Tunis 18/5/1918 on passage Singapore to Marseilles via Bizerta.

68   Union Fleet

Kamona *was another cargo vessel purchased for the Tasmanian trade but most of her 30-year service was spent around the New Zealand coast. In 1904 she lifted a record 800,000 super feet of timber from Greymouth to Sydney and in December 1913 she became the largest vessel to call at Gisborne*   HARRAWAY COLLECTION, HOCKEN LIBRARY

The 5704-ton **Aparima** *was specially designed for the Union Company's Indian service. Completed in 1902 she made over 30 round voyages to Calcutta before being lost in 1917 on wartime service*

Moeraki, *built in 1902, was the largest twin screw steamer then built for the Union Company and she was employed on the Trans Tasman services. In 1904 she made a record passage of 76 hours between Wellington and Sydney and was one of the more popular passenger ships in the fleet*   WM. LIVERMORE

KAMONA　　1425 GRT　　IN FLEET 1901–1931

BUILT: 1901 by Grangemouth & Greenock Dockyard Co., Grangemouth, as *Rollesby Broad* for Hawthorn Bros. & Co., London.

SUBSEQUENT HISTORY: Laid up Port Chalmers, 29/12/1930. Sold Shun Hong S.S.Co. Ltd., Hong Kong, (S.T.Williamson, Mgr.) 1931–36. Broken up Kowloon Bay, Hong Kong, 9/1936.

APARIMA　　5704 GRT　　IN FLEET 1902–1917

BUILT: 1902 by Wm. Denny & Bros., Dumbarton.

SUBSEQUENT HISTORY: Torpedoed and sunk in English Channel, 6 miles SW from Anvil Point, 19/11/1917 on passage London to New York.

MOERAKI　　4392 GRT　　IN FLEET 1902–1933

BUILT: 1902 by Wm. Denny & Bros., Dumbarton.

SUBSEQUENT HISTORY: Laid up Sydney 30/9/1930. Sold Japanese shipbreakers through H.C. Sleigh Ltd., Melbourne, and sailed Sydney 25/2/1933. Broken up by Amakasu & Co., Osaka, 8/1933.

The name **Kakapo** *was revived in 1903 for a two-year-old shallow draft cargo ship. She spent much of her 25 years with the company in the Australian trade*   WM. LIVERMORE

A second-hand ship purchased in 1903 for the Tasmanian trade, **Karori** *was later employed as a collier on the New Zealand coast until she was sold in 1928*

The 4505-ton passenger ship **Manuka** *was the 34th vessel built by Wm. Denny & Bros. for the Union Company and apart from a period in the trans Pacific service, she proved a very popular Trans Tasman vessel. In January 1904 she made a fast passage of 10 hours 29 minutes between Lyttelton and Wellington. She was wrecked at Long Point, South Otago in 1929 without loss of life*   WM. LIVERMORE

| KAKAPO | 1521 GRT | IN FLEET 1903–1928 |

BUILT: 1901 by Grangemouth & Greenock Dockyard Co., Greenock, as *Scarisbrick* 1901–03.
PREVIOUS OWNERS: Scarisbrick S.S. Co. Ltd., Cardiff, (Elvidge & Morgan, Mgrs) 1901–03.
SUBSEQUENT HISTORY: Converted to coal hulk at Auckland, 1926. Fitted out as oil barge 1927. Sold to F. Appleton, Auckland and dismantled 8/1936. Hull beached Shakespear Bay, Whangaparoa Peninsula 18/12/1937.

| PILOT | 39 GRT | IN FLEET 1903–1907 |

BUILT: 1884 by Denis Sullivan, Berry's Bay, N.S.W.
PREVIOUS OWNERS: John Dalton, Newcastle, 1884–03. W.H. Baker, A. Dalton, Newcastle and E.A. Mitchell, Sydney, 1903. (Under Union Company management 1898–03).
SUBSEQUENT HISTORY: Sold Wellington Harbour Ferries Ltd., Wellington, 1907–13. Sold Fisheries Ltd., (E.G.F. Zohrab) Wellington, 1913–19. Sold M. Beck, Wellington, 1919–20. Sold V. Picone, Napier, 1920–33. Wrecked Port Ahuriri, Napier, 2/4/1933, striking broken wharf piles while attempting to tow trawler *Phantom* into Napier.

| KARORI | 1863 GRT | IN FLEET 1903–1928 |

BUILT: 1902 by Craig, Taylor & Co., Stockton-on-Tees as *Minas* (Spain).
PREVIOUS OWNERS: Sociedad Espanola de Minas (R. de Madariaga), Bilbao, Spain 1902–03.
SUBSEQUENT HISTORY: Laid up Wellington 12/8/1927. Sold Moller & Co., Shanghai, and ownership registered to Chun Yung Zan, Shanghai, and renamed *Shanghai* (China) 1928–30. Ownership transferred Moller & Co., Shanghai, 1930 and renamed *Katie Moller* (China) 1930–32. Sold Tientsin Navigation Co. Ltd., Shanghai, 1932 and renamed *Tung Cheng* (China) 1932–37. Sunk in air attack on Shanghai, 8/1937 during Sino-Japanese war.

| MANUKA | 4505 GRT | IN FLEET 1903–1929 |

BUILT: 1903 by Wm. Denny & Bros., Dumbarton.
SUBSEQUENT HISTORY: Wrecked Long Point, South Otago, 16/12/1929 on passage Melbourne to Dunedin via Bluff.

Navua *was yet another vessel specially designed for the Pacific Island service and made her first trip to Fiji in October 1904. She had a lucky escape in August 1908 when she ran aground on a reef at Mauke, Cook Islands and damaged 60 hull plates* WM. LIVERMORE

The **Loongana** *was the first vessel in the fleet to have steam turbine propulsion and indeed the first turbine vessel to operate in the Southern Hemisphere. She was built for the express passenger service between Melbourne and Launceston. In December 1904 she made a record passage of 9 hours between the two ports. She remained in this service for 32 years* ALLAN C. GREEN

Kaituna *was purchased in 1905 as a standard type cargo carrier and spent the next 25 years in the service of the company. In 1907 she loaded 1,060,000 super feet of timber in Greymouth for Lyttelton – the largest timber cargo to leave the West Coast at that time*

| NAVUA | 2930 GRT | IN FLEET 1904–1926 |

BUILT: 1904 by David J. Dunlop & Co., Port Glasgow.
SUBSEQUENT HISTORY: Laid up Port Chalmers, 31/12/1924. Sold Khedivial Mail Steamship and Graving Dock Co. Ltd., London, 1926 and renamed *Roda* (Br) 1927–32. Sold Pol C. Gallia, Alexandria 9/1932 and broken up Egypt 1933.

| LOONGANA | 2448 GRT | IN FLEET 1904–1922 |

BUILT: 1904 by Wm. Denny & Bros., Dumbarton.
SUBSEQUENT HISTORY: Transferred to Tasmanian Steamers Pty. Ltd., Melbourne, 1922–36. Sold Tanaka K.K.K. Osaka, shipbreakers and left Melbourne for Osaka in tow of *Kanna* 3/11/1936.

| KAITUNA | 1977 GRT | IN FLEET 1905–1931 |

BUILT: 1904 by Osbourne, Graham & Co., Hylton, Sunderland, as *Needwood* 1904–05.
PREVIOUS OWNERS: Wm France, Fenwick & Co. Ltd., London, 1904–05.
SUBSEQUENT HISTORY: Laid up Auckland, 27/12/1930. Sold Wing Hong & Co. Ltd., Hong Kong, (S.T. Williamson, Mgr) 1931–37, later Foo Hong S.S. Co. Ltd., (same mgr). Sold Wallem & Co., Panama, 1937 and renamed *Needwood* (Pan) 1937–41. Captured by Japanese at Tsingtao 12/1941 and renamed *Kaiyo Maru* (Japan) 1941–42. Sunk near Kominase Lighthouse, Inland Sea, Japan following collision with *Nichiun Maru* (2723/1941) 22/12/1942.

When the **Wairuna** *was purchased in 1905 she was the second largest cargo carrier in the company and was mainly employed on the trade to the West Coast of North America, called the Pacific Slope service at the time. She was captured by the German raider* **Wolf** *near the Kermadec Islands in June 1917 and after the raider had transferred coal and stores,* **Wairuna** *was sunk*   S. RAWSON

Arahura *was built in 1905 for the passenger service between Wellington, Nelson, Westport and Greymouth, although in later years she was employed on other short-sea passenger services. She was seriously damaged at Gisborne on 1 March 1917 when the 5610-ton* **Waimate** *crashed into her. She remained with the Union Company for 20 years before being sold to the Anchor Company of Nelson for its overnight service to Wellington. She spent nearly 20 years on this run*   S. RAWSON

The 1376-ton **Karitane** *was a shallow-draft general cargo carrier purchased second-hand for the Tasmanian trade. On two occasions, in January 1907 and December 1915, she struck a rock near Strahan and the damage in each case required extensive repairs in dry dock*   WM. LIVERMORE

| WAIRUNA | 3947 GRT | IN FLEET 1905–1917 |

BUILT: Laid down by Sir W.G. Armstrong Whitworth & Co. Ltd., Newcastle, as *Lady Strathcona* 1904.

PREVIOUS OWNERS: W. Petersen Ltd., Newcastle, 1904 but resold 1904 to Bucknall Steamship Lines Ltd., London, and renamed *Matoppo* 1904–05.

SUBSEQUENT HISTORY: Captured Sunday Island, Kermadec Group, South Pacific 2/6/1917 by German raider *Wolf* and sunk 17/6/1917 nearby. On passage Auckland to San Francisco.

| ARAHURA | 1596 GRT | IN FLEET 1905–1925 |

BUILT: 1905 by Wm. Denny & Bros., Dumbarton.

SUBSEQUENT HISTORY: Sold Anchor Shipping & Foundry Co. Ltd., Nelson, 1925–50. Withdrawn from service and laid up Shelly Bay, Wellington, 6/1949. Sold B.T. Daniel, Wellington, 1950 and partly dismantled there before being sunk by RNZAF Mosquito bombers on practice mission in Cook Strait, 15 miles south of Baring Head, 24/1/1952.

| KARITANE | 1376 GRT | IN FLEET 1905–1921 |

BUILT: 1903 by S.P. Austin & Son Ltd., Sunderland, as *Cavalier* 1903–05.

PREVIOUS OWNERS: Stewart Steamship Co. (Liv) Ltd., (W.J. Stewart, Mgr), Liverpool, 1903–05.

SUBSEQUENT HISTORY: Ran aground Deal Island, Bass Strait 24/12/1921, later beached Squally Bay and totally wrecked while on passage Devonport to Port Kembla.

One of the finest Trans Tasman passenger vessels was the triple screw turbine steamer **Maheno,** *which entered service in 1905 and thereafter broke many of the passage records between Melbourne and Sydney, Wellington and Sydney as well as Bluff to Hobart. She was one of the first turbine steamers to cross the Pacific in 1906 and in 1914 she was converted to a twin screw steamer with geared turbines. She was in service for 30 years and on her way to Japanese shipbreakers in 1935 she ran aground on Fraser Island, north of Brisbane, where her remains form a tourist attraction on that island*

ALLAN C. GREEN

The 112-ton wooden steamer **Tuatea** *was employed as a passenger tender at Gisborne and in the illustration taken 26 December 1912, the wreck of the* **Star of Canada** *can be seen in the background. Sold by the Union Company after 24 years service,* **Tuatea** *was acquired by fishing interests and remained in service for a further 41 years* S. RAWSON

| MAHENO | 5282 GRT | IN FLEET 1905–1935 |

BUILT: 1905 by Wm. Denny & Bros., Dumbarton. (Machinery converted from triple screw direct drive turbines to twin screw geared turbines at Port Chalmers, 4–7/1914).

SUBSEQUENT HISTORY: Sold Miyachi K.K.K., Kobe and Osaka, 1935. Left Sydney 3/7/1935 in tow of *Oonah* but broke adrift 8/7/35 and went ashore 9/7/35 on Ocean Beach, Fraser Island, 168 miles north of Brisbane. Hull used as target for RAAF aircraft 1939–44.

*During World War 1, **Maheno** became a hospital ship and served from May 1915 until June 1919. In this role, she is shown alongside George Street Pier, Port Chalmers on 25 April 1916*   S. RAWSON

*A recent view of the remains of the **Maheno** on Fraser Island, Queensland*

| TUATEA | 112 GRT | IN FLEET 1905–1929 |

BUILT: 1905 by Chas. Bailey Jnr., Auckland.

SUBSEQUENT HISTORY: Sold A.A. Perano, Picton, 1929–1945. Transferred to J.A. Perano & Co. Ltd., Picton, 1945–65. Sold Otakou Fisheries Ltd., Dunedin, 1965–1970. Caught fire 23/4/1970, 20 miles SE of Taieri Mouth, Otago, taken in tow for Port Chalmers but beached sinking (same day) at Little Papanui Inlet, near Wickcliffe Bay, Otago Peninsula.

Atua, like **Navua**, *was specially designed for the Pacific Island service and she made her first voyage to Fiji on 24 July 1906. She remained in this service for 18 years* WM. LIVERMORE

The coaster **Squall** *was purchased by the Union Company in 1906 to operate a feeder service to Auckland from Gisborne and Hawke's Bay in competition with Richardson and Company. She was sold to that company in 1912 when Union and Richardson joined forces in this trade*
ALEXANDER TURNBULL LIBRARY

The 2003-ton **Kaiapoi** *was fitting out for other owners when the Union Company purchased her. She was usefully employed in the coal and general cargo trades for 24 years*

ATUA — 3444 GRT — IN FLEET 1906–1926

BUILT: 1906 by D.J. Dunlop & Co., Port Glasgow.

SUBSEQUENT HISTORY: Laid up Port Chalmers, 6/8/1924. Sold Khedivial Mail Steamship & Graving Dock Co. Ltd., London 1926 and renamed *Rashid* (Br) 1927–1932. Sold Pol. C. Gallia, Alexandria, 9/1932 and resold 8/1933 for demolition at Savona, Italy.

SQUALL — 369 GRT — IN FLEET 1906–1912

BUILT: 1904 by J. Meyer, Zalt Bommel, Holland.

PREVIOUS OWNERS: Shipping Investments Ltd., (C.H. Pile) London, 1904–05. Stewart Bros., Auckland, (Geo. Niccol, James Stewart, R.S. Lamb & Partners) 1905–06.

SUBSEQUENT HISTORY: Sold Richardson & Co. Ltd., Napier, 1912–16. Struck uncharted rock off Horoera Point, 1 mile north of East Cape, New Zealand 1/2/1916 and was totally wrecked on passage Te Araroa to Port Awanui.

KAIAPOI — 2003 GRT — IN FLEET 1906–1930

BUILT: 1906 by Osbourne, Graham & Co., Hylton, Sunderland, as *Holywood* 1906.

PREVIOUS OWNERS: Wm. France, Fenwick & Co. Ltd., London, 1906.

SUBSEQUENT HISTORY: Sold Kin Hong S.S. Co. Ltd., Hong Kong, (S.T. Williamson, Mgr) 1930–39. Sold Wallem & Co. Ltd., Hong Kong, 1939 and registry transferred to Panama. Struck rocks and foundered 25/1/1939 outside Wenchow Bay (28.16N, 121.38E) on passage Shanghai to Wenchow and Ningpo.

80   *Union Fleet*

Komata *was a general purpose freighter built for the company in 1907 and apart from grounding at Pencarrow Heads on 31 January 1916, she had an uneventful 25 active years with the Union Company. In this illustration she is shown with her derricks rigged to transfer coal*   J. DICKIE

At 4638 tons, **Waihora** *was one of the larger coal and general cargo carriers and spent much of her 20 years with the company in the Trans Tasman trade, taking coal out of Newcastle*

In 1907 the Union Company commissioned the powerful salvage tug **Terawhiti.** *She was based at Wellington for 40 years, mainly on harbour work, but undertaking salvage tasks on many mishaps around the country*

| KOMATA | 1994 GRT | IN FLEET 1907–1934 |

BUILT: 1907 by Swan Hunter & Wigham Richardson Ltd., Newcastle.

SUBSEQUENT HISTORY: Laid up Wellington 31/10/1932. Sold to Miyachi K.K.K., Kobe, 1934 and towed by *Kaimanawa* to Japan (sailed Auckland, 12/1/1935). Registered under Chinese flag to Fan Shien Ho, Tsingtao, 1935–37 and renamed *Fu Ho* (China) 1935–38. Under Song Wen Kwei (V.K. Song), Tsingtao, 1937–38 (same name).Transferred Miyachi K.K.K., Kobe, and renamed *Toyama Maru* (Listed as *Huzan Maru/Fusan Maru* in Lloyd's Register) (Japan) 1938–43. Sunk 33kms WSW of Maoka (46.57N, 141.42E) in collision with *Juzan Maru* (3943/1941) 16/7/1943 on passage Rumoe, Hokkaido to Maoka, Sakhalin.

| WAIHORA | 4638 GRT | IN FLEET 1907–1927 |

BUILT: 1907 by Swan Hunter & Wigham Richardson Ltd., Newcastle.

SUBSEQUENT HISTORY: Sold Naigai K.K.K., Kobe and Amagaski, and renamed *Tairyu Maru* (Japan) 1927–38. Sold Kuribashi Shosen K.K., Tokyo, 1938–44 (same name). Sunk by US Army aircraft 19/2/1944 (25.25N, 121.30E).

| TERAWHITI | 260 GRT | IN FLEET 1907–1947 |

BUILT: 1907 by Ramage & Ferguson Ltd., Leith.

SUBSEQUENT HISTORY: Sold Australian Steamships Pty. Ltd., (Howard Smith Ltd., Mgrs), Melbourne, 1947. Sank following collision at Melbourne with *City of Khartoum* (9955/1946) 30/9/1950, declared constructive total loss and broken up Melbourne 5/1951.

82   *Union Fleet*

MARAMA — 6437 GRT — IN FLEET 1907–1937

BUILT: 1907 by Caird & Co. Ltd., Greenock.

SUBSEQUENT HISTORY: Sold Linghua Dock & Engineering Works Ltd., Shanghai and left Wellington 10/8/1937. Resold 1938 to Miyachi Kisen K.K., Kobe, and broken up Osaka 1938/39.

◂ *One of the few passenger ships of that era not built by Denny & Bros.,* **Marama** *of 1907 was one of the more popular Trans Tasman passenger vessels. She was placed in the Vancouver service in 1908 and again in 1909, while during World War 1 she was converted to a hospital ship and saw service in this role from 5 October 1915 to 21 July 1919*   ALLAN C. GREEN

MAORI — 3399 GRT — IN FLEET 1907–1946

BUILT: 1907 by Wm. Denny & Bros., Dumbarton.

SUBSEQUENT HISTORY: Laid up Wellington 6/1/1944. Sold United Corporation of China Ltd., Shanghai and renamed *Hwa Lien* (China) 1946–50. Laid up Keelung 1950, then owned by Chung Lien S.S. Co., Keelung. Sunk in storm 13/1/1951, raised during 5/1951, broken up and portion of hull converted to floating crane barge.

◂ *The growth of the passenger traffic between Wellington and Lyttelton saw the company order the triple screw turbine steamer* **Maori** *in 1907. With a speed of 19 knots and accommodation for 600 passengers, she was a stalwart of the service for 37 years*   W. HILLSDON

KOROMIKO — 2479 GRT — IN FLEET 1907–1928

BUILT: 1907 by Wm. Doxford & Sons Ltd., Sunderland.

SUBSEQUENT HISTORY: Laid up Wellington 1/4/1927. Sold Shun Hong S.S. Co. Ltd., Hong Kong (S.T. Williamson, Mgr) 1928–36. Sold Yu Chung Steamship Co. Ltd., Shanghai, and renamed *Yu Ping* (China) 1936–41. Sunk 12/1941 at Hankow, Yangtse River, and became constructive total loss.

◂ **Koromiko** *was an unusual cargo ship as she had a turret deck. This was meant to keep the net tonnage low while providing a good carrying capacity. It was primarily designed to save Suez Canal dues, which had little relevance to her service in New Zealand. She remained an oddity in the fleet throughout her years with the company*

The **Kaitangata** was yet another general-purpose collier and general cargo carrier. She served in the fleet from 1908 to 1930

Maitai, *purchased in 1908, was a sister ship to the* **Warrimoo** *and the Union Company had been managing the vessel since 1901. She seemed to be accident-prone and had numerous mishaps which culminated in her being wrecked at Rarotonga in 1916* DE MAUS

Tofua *was built in 1908 as a larger edition of* **Atua** *for the Pacific Islands service. She remained on this run until 1932, apart from requisition as a troopship 1915 to 1919 and in the San Francisco run in 1919* WM. LIVERMORE

KAITANGATA — 1983 GRT — IN FLEET 1908–1930

BUILT: 1907 by Osbourne, Graham & Co. Ltd., Sunderland, as *Ladywood*.

PREVIOUS OWNERS: Wm. France, Fenwick & Co. Ltd., London, 1907–08.

SUBSEQUENT HISTORY: Sold Ling Nam S.S. Co. Ltd., Hong Kong (S.T. Williamson, Mgr), 1930–37. Sank following explosion and fire 25/10/1937 in South China Sea (21.40N, 112.00E) on passage Hong Kong to Haiphong.

MAITAI — 3393 GRT — IN FLEET 1908–1916

BUILT: 1892 by C.S. Swan & Hunter, Wallsend, as *Miowera* 1892–1908.

PREVIOUS OWNERS: N.Z. and Australasian S.S. Co., London (J. Huddart, Mgr), 1892–93. Canadian Australian Royal Mail Line, London, 1893–99. New Zealand Shipping Co. Ltd., London, 1899–1908 (Union Company-joint owners and managers from 1901).

SUBSEQUENT HISTORY: Wrecked 25/12/1916 at Avarua, Rarotonga, after dragging anchor and drifting on to reef on passage San Francisco to Wellington.

TOFUA — 4345 GRT — IN FLEET 1908–1934

BUILT: 1908 by Wm. Denny & Bros., Dumbarton.

SUBSEQUENT HISTORY: Laid up Auckland, 12/4/1932. Sold to Miyachi K.K.K., Kobe. Broken up Osaka 1934.

86 Union Fleet

Built to the company's order in 1908, the **Waitemata** *had a cargo capacity for 5000 tons. Shortly after she arrived in New Zealand she was chartered by Shaw Savill & Albion Company for a voyage to London with wool. From there she proceeded to Glasgow to load general cargo for Vancouver. She then sailed to San Francisco to load 1200 mules for Fiji and for that voyage she was painted white. On her return she remained in the general cargo/collier trade until she was requisitioned during World War 1 and was sunk in 1918* DE MAUS

The **Paloona** *had already spent nine years on the Tasman passenger trade as the* **Zealandia** *when the Union Company purchased and renamed her. She remained on the Tasman services apart from voyages across the Pacific to San Francisco in 1917 and 1919 and to Fiji also in 1919* ALLAN C. GREEN

Another large passenger ship built for the Vancouver mail service, the **Makura** *entered service in 1908. She was the first vessel built by Alexander Stephen & Son, Glasgow, for the Union Company since the little* **Bruce** *in 1874. She remained with the company for 28 years* WINKELMAN'

| WAITEMATA | 5432 GRT | IN FLEET 1908–1918 |

BUILT: 1908 by Wm. Hamilton & Co. Ltd., Port Glasgow.

SUBSEQUENT HISTORY: Torpedoed and sunk 100 miles NE from Marsa Susa, Mediterranean Sea 14/7/1918.

| PALOONA | 2771 GRT | IN FLEET 1908–1928 |

BUILT: 1899 by Gourlay Bros. & Co., Dundee, as *Zealandia*.

PREVIOUS OWNERS: Huddart, Parker & Co. Pty. Ltd., Melbourne, 1899–08.

SUBSEQUENT HISTORY: Laid up Port Chalmers, 28/12/1922. Dismantled at Port Chalmers, 1928 and sunk alongside mole stonework, Otago Harbour entrance 20/9/1928.

| MAKURA | 8075 GRT | IN FLEET 1908–1936 |

BUILT: 1908 by A. Stephen & Sons Ltd., Linthouse, Glasgow.

SUBSEQUENT HISTORY: Sold to China Shipbreakers Limited, Shanghai, 11/1936 and left Wellington for Shanghai via Australian ports 30/1/1937.

Completed in 1909, **Kurow** *was an improved collier/general cargo carrier and had an uneventful career during her 24 years with the company*

Aorangi, *acquired in 1910, was the third vessel which had previously been associated with J. Huddart's North American service. Built in 1883 for the New Zealand Shipping Company, she was already 27 years old when she joined the fleet. She was sold to the British Admiralty in 1914 for use as a blockship at Scapa Flow and there her remains still lie. Despite her short life with the company she was the first ship in the fleet to be fitted with wireless equipment*

WM. LIVERMORE

One of the few early Union Company coasters with engines aft, the **Kowhai** *was engaged in the carriage of coal and timber around both the New Zealand and Australian coasts. She had a lucky escape from disaster when she stranded on Farewell Spit on 9 June 1919 and it was not until after strenuous salvage efforts that she was finally refloated on 14 July*   ALLAN C. GREEN

KUROW 2581 GRT IN FLEET 1909–1933

BUILT: 1909 by Wm. Doxford & Sons Ltd., Sunderland (Originally intended to be named *Kamo*).

SUBSEQUENT HISTORY: Laid up Auckland, 18/7/1931. Sold Moller and Co., Shanghai, 1933 and renamed *Mabel Moller* (Br) 1933–35. Went ashore 18/9/1935 on south coast of Sakhalin on passage Petropavlovsk to Otaru. Refloated and sold to Japanese shipbreakers.

AORANGI 4268 GRT IN FLEET 1910 – 1914

BUILT: 1883 by John Elder & Co., Govan, Glasgow.

PREVIOUS OWNERS: New Zealand Shipping Co. Ltd., Christchurch, 1883–1896. (Chartered to Canadian Australian Royal Mail Line, Melbourne, 1894–96). James Huddart, Melbourne, 1896–97. Canadian Australian Royal Mail S.S. Co. Ltd., London (J. Huddart), 1897–99. New Zealand Shipping Co. Ltd., Christchurch, 1899–1910 (Union Company joint owners and managers 1901–10).

SUBSEQUENT HISTORY: Sold to British Admiralty 11/1914 and scuttled 10/8/1915 as blockship in Holm Sound, Scapa Flow, Orkney Islands by Royal Navy. On being raised 8/9/1920, was swept ashore by strong current and subsequently broke up.

KOWHAI 792 GRT IN FLEET 1910 – 1950

BUILT: 1910 by W. Harkess & Son Ltd., Middlesbrough.

PREVIOUS OWNERS: Launched as *Hopeful* for F.H. Powell & Co., Liverpool, but renamed *Devon Coast* – all in 1910.

SUBSEQUENT HISTORY: Laid up Melbourne, 3/1949. Sold to Steels & Metals Ltd., Melbourne, shipbreakers, 1950 but not completely demolished until 1957.

90 *Union Fleet*

| KANNA | 1948 GRT | IN FLEET 1911–1936 |

BUILT: 1911 by Ramage & Ferguson Ltd., Leith.

SUBSEQUENT HISTORY: Laid up Auckland, 9/4/1936. Sold Sakamoto Shoji K.K. Osaka, 9/1936 but registered under Chinese flag to Tsui Tsung Chu, Tsingtao, 1936 and renamed *Chung Tai* (China) 1937–38. Transferred Sakamoto Shoji K.K., Osaka, and renamed *Seian Maru* (Japan) 1938–44. Sunk by USS *Snapper* 1/10/1944 450 miles south of Yokohama (28.11N–139.30E).

◀ *The largest steamer constructed at Leith for many years, the 1948 ton* **Kanna** *was employed in the company's general and bulk cargo trades, including voyages to Walpole Island to load guano and also a period in 1915 coaling British warships under Admiralty control*

| TAHITI | 7585 GRT | IN FLEET 1911–1930 |

BUILT: 1904 by A. Stephen & Sons Ltd., Linthouse, Glasgow as *Port Kingston*.

PREVIOUS OWNERS: Imperial Direct West India Mail Service Co. Ltd., Liverpool, (Elder Dempster & Co., Mgrs) 1904–11.

SUBSEQUENT HISTORY: Broke starboard tail shaft 15/8/1930, which punctured hull, about 460 miles south of Rarotonga on passage Wellington to San Francisco. Sank 17/8/1930 in position 24.40S–166.15W.

◀ *Built in 1904 as the* **Port Kingston** *for service from Avonmouth to Kingston, Jamaica, this vessel was purchased by the Union Company in 1911 for the Pacific service and was renamed* **Tahiti**. *She had two lucky escapes from being sunk by enemy action in 1916 and 1917 but her fate was sealed in 1930 when her propellor shaft fractured and pierced the hull. The slow steady ingress of water saw the ship sink in mid Pacific three days later*   WM. LIVERMORE

| MAUNGANUI | 7527 GRT | IN FLEET 1911–1947 |

BUILT: 1911 by Fairfield Shipbuilding & Engineering Co. Ltd., Govan, Glasgow.

SUBSEQUENT HISTORY: Laid up Wellington 14/8/1946. Sold Cia. Nav. de Atlantico S.A., Panama (Hellenic Mediterranean Lines Co. Ltd., Piraeus, Mgrs) 1947–50 and renamed *Cyrenia* (Panama) 1947–57. Transferred to Hellenic Mediterranean Lines Co. Ltd., Piraeus, 1950–57 (same name but Greek registry). Arrived Savona, Italy, for demolition 6/2/1957.

◀ *Completed in 1911, the* **Maunganui** *proved another very successful passenger ship, whether she was in the Trans Tasman or Pacific services. She was converted to a troopship and served in this role from 1914 to 1919. During a following refit her engines were converted from coal to oil burning. She remained under the Union Company for 36 years and spent a further 10 years as a passenger ship under Greek owners*   ALLAN C. GREEN

The collier **Katoa**, *completed in 1912, was pressed into war service in 1916 mainly carrying stores and equipment between India and the Persian Gulf. In June 1923 she had the distinction of being the largest ship to call at Port Craig, west of Bluff in Southland, to load timber* D. JONES

Karamu, *another engines aft cargo ship slightly larger than* **Kowhai**, *came into service in 1912 and nine years later was transferred to the Dunedin-Wanganui run of the Canterbury Steam Shipping Company, in which the Union Company had a financial interest. She returned to Union Company service in 1922 running between Port Kembla and Strahan until she foundered off the west coast of Tasmania in 1925*

The 2833 ton **Kauri** *of 1912 was little more than a larger collier/general cargo vessel of the general purpose type introduced just after the turn of the century. She had only 16 years service with the company but survived another nine years under Shanghai owners in eastern waters*

| KATOA | 2484 GRT | IN FLEET 1912–1933 |

BUILT: 1912 by Osbourne, Graham & Co. Ltd., Sunderland.

SUBSEQUENT HISTORY: Laid up Wellington 23/6/1931. Sold Moller Line Ltd., (Moller & Co., Mgrs) Shanghai, 1933 and renamed *Winifred Moller* (Br) 1934–48. Sold Zui Kong S.S.Co. Ltd., Shanghai, (C.Y. Tung, Mgr) 1946–48 and renamed *Tsze Yung* (China 1948–49, Taiwan 1949–58). Ownership transferred Chinese Maritime Trust Ltd., Shanghai, 1948–49, Keelung 1949–58. Broken up 1958.

| KARAMU | 934 GRT | IN FLEET 1912–1921 & 1922–1925 |

BUILT: 1912 by Ramage & Ferguson Ltd., Leith.

SUBSEQUENT HISTORY: Sold Canterbury Steam Shipping Co. Ltd., Christchurch, 1921–22 and renamed *Gale*. Resold Union Company and renamed *Karamu* 1922. Struck on bar, Macquarie Harbour entrance 1/9/1925 outward bound from Strahan to Hobart. Subsequently developed a leak in heavy weather and foundered one mile east of South West Cape, Tasmania 4/9/1925.

| KAURI | 2833 GRT | IN FLEET 1912–1928 |

BUILT: 1905 by Furness, Withy & Co. Ltd., West Hartlepool, as *Harmony* 1905–12.

PREVIOUS OWNERS: J & C Harrison Ltd., London, 1905–12.

SUBSEQUENT HISTORY: Laid up Lyttelton 5/8/1927. Sold N.E.A. Moller, Shanghai (Moller & Co., Mgrs), 1928 and renamed *Minnie Moller* (Br) 1928–36. Sold Hwah Sung S.S. Co. Ltd., Shanghai, 1936 and renamed *Hwah Foo* (China) 1936–37. Sunk as blockship in Yangtse River, 8/1937 during Sino-Japanese war.

▲ In 1912 the Union Company purchased four large steamers, originally built for the Houlder Bros. Australasian trade, for employment on a new service to the United Kingdom. The **Rippingham Grange** was renamed **Limerick** but she had little peacetime service before the outbreak of World War 1. She was lost in 1917.
J. DICKIE
ALEXANDER TURNBULL LIBRARY

The **Oswestry Grange** was renamed **Roscommon** and she too was sunk in 1917
R. HILDEBRAND

All the four ships were named after Irish counties and the **Tyrone**, formerly **Drayton Grange**, had an even shorter life as she was wrecked in heavy fog when she ran aground south of the entrance to Otago Harbour in September 1913 and became a total loss
ALEXANDER TURNBULL LIBRARY

| **LIMERICK** | **6827 GRT** | **IN FLEET 1912–1917** |

BUILT: 1898 by Workman, Clark & Co. Ltd., Belfast as *Rippingham Grange* 1898–1912.

PREVIOUS OWNERS: Rippingham Grange Steamship Co. Ltd., London (Houlder Bros & Co. Ltd.), Mgrs) 1898–99. Houlder Line Ltd., London (Houlder Bros & Co. Ltd., Mgrs), 1899–12. New Zealand Shipping Co. Ltd., London, 1912 and renamed *Limerick* (Br) 1912.

SUBSEQUENT HISTORY: Torpedoed and sunk by *U-86*, 140 miles SW of Bishop Rock (48.53N – 09.45W) 28/5/1917 on passage Sydney to London.

| **ROSCOMMON** | **7381 GRT** | **IN FLEET 1912–1917** |

BUILT: 1902 by Workman, Clark & Co. Ltd., Belfast, as *Oswestry Grange* 1902–12.

PREVIOUS OWNERS: Oswestry Grange Steamship Co. Ltd., London (Houlder Bros & Co. Ltd., Mgrs), 1902–12. New Zealand Shipping Co. Ltd., London, 1912 and renamed *Roscommon* (Br).

SUBSEQUENT HISTORY: Torpedoed and sunk by *U-53*, 20 miles NE of Tory Island, (55.27N–08.00W) 21/8/1917 on passage Manchester to Australia.

| **TYRONE** | **6664 GRT** | **IN FLEET 1912–1913** |

BUILT: 1901 by Workman, Clark & Co. Ltd., Belfast, as *Drayton Grange* 1901–12.

PREVIOUS OWNERS: Houlder Line Ltd., London (Houlder Bros & Co. Ltd., Mgrs), 1901–12. New Zealand Shipping Co. Ltd., London, 1912 and renamed *Tyrone* (Br) 1912.

SUBSEQUENT HISTORY: Ran aground Rerewahine Point, 1 mile south of Taiaroa Head, Otago 27/9/1913 and became total loss, on passage Manchester to Dunedin.

The **Westmeath**, *previously* **Everton Grange**, *was the only one of the quartet to survive World War 1 and she was disposed off in 1925*

The passenger liner **Niagara**, *completed in 1913 for the Pacific service, had accommodation for 278 passengers in first class, 224 in second and 200 in third class. She was propelled by two sets of quadruple expansion reciprocating engines, and the exhaust steam from these passed to a low-pressure turbine which powered a third propellor.* **Niagara** *had a very successful career until she was mined and sunk off Whangarei in 1940*

The 4436 ton **Waitomo** *was chiefly engaged in the coal trade out of Newcastle as well as the occasional voyage to Nauru or Ocean Island for phosphate rock. She had a lucky escape in 1928 when her tail shaft broke on passage from Newcastle to Bluff with a full cargo of coal. She drifted for 60 hours before being taken in tow by the* **Kaitoke** *and eleven and a half days later she was towed into Auckland*   DE MAUS

| WESTMEATH | 8096 GRT | IN FLEET 1912–1925 |

BUILT: 1903 by Furness, Withy & Co. Ltd., West Hartlepool, as *Everton Grange* 1903–12.

PREVIOUS OWNERS: Empire Transport Co. Ltd., London (Houlder Bros & Co. Ltd., Mgrs), 1903–11. New Zealand Shipping Co. Ltd., London, 1911 and renamed *Westmeath* (Br) 1912.

SUBSEQUENT HISTORY: Sold Soc. Ligure Nav. a Vap., Genoa 1925 and renamed *Nordico* (Italian) 1925–27. Sold Ditta D.E. Fratelli Bozzo, Genoa 1927–32 (same name). Laid up Genoa 29/3/1930. Sold Giacomo Pittaluga, Genoa and arrived Savona for demolition 2/5/1932.

| NIAGARA | 13415 GRT | IN FLEET 1913–1931 |

BUILT: 1913 by John Brown & Co. Ltd., Clydebank.

SUBSEQUENT HISTORY: Transferred to Canadian-Australasian Line Ltd., London (Union Company, Wellington, Mgrs), 1931–40. Sunk by mine off Bream Head, Whangarei, 19/6/1940 (35.53S – 174.54E) on passage Auckland to Vancouver.

| WAITOMO | 4214 GRT | IN FLEET 1913–1933 |

BUILT: 1911 by Northumberland Shipbuilding Co. Ltd., Howdon-on-Tyne, Newcastle, as *Gifford* 1911–13.

PREVIOUS OWNERS: The Gifford Trading Co. Ltd., Glasgow, (Andrew Weir & Co. Ltd., Mgrs) 1911–13.

SUBSEQUENT HISTORY: Laid up Auckland, 9/1928. Sold China Pacific Nav. Co. Ltd., Shanghai, 1933 and renamed *Meishun* (China) 1933. Broken up at Osaka, Japan 1933.

The second fast passenger ferry specially built for the service between Wellington and Lyttelton was the **Wahine**, *completed in 1913. She was a 20.5-knot vessel with three propellers and a bow rudder, which enabled her to go astern in a very manoeuvrable state. During World War 1 she was requisitioned for service in European waters 1915-1920*

The 1236 ton **Kamo** *was built in Scotland in 1913 for coastal service and in her 17 years' service with the Union Company she ran from main ports to Napier and Gisborne, to Westport and Greymouth and also between Brisbane and Sydney to Hobart*

Waimarino *was 15 years old when chartered by the Union Company which employed her in the trade from the West Coast of North America and for bulk liftings of grain or coal from Australia to New Zealand. She was not a favourite ship and on one occasion in 1924 the crew refused to sail, claiming the vessel was unseaworthy and rolled dangerously. Although the men lost their case and were fined one day's pay, the company sold the ship two years later*

J. DICKIE   ALEXANDER TURNBULL LIBRARY.

| **WAHINE** | **4436 GRT** | **IN FLEET 1913–1951** |

BUILT: 1913 by Wm. Denny & Bros., Dumbarton.

SUBSEQUENT HISTORY: Wrecked on reef, SE end of Masela Island, Arafura Sea 15/8/1951 on passage Wellington to Kure with New Zealand troops for Korean War.

In November 1943, **Wahine** *made a voyage from Wellington to Sydney as a safe conduct "protected ship" carrying non-combatant Japanese nationals who were being repatriated to their own country and the illustration shows her painted for that voyage. The vessel was lit up at night and the Japanese Government had guaranteed safe passage*

| **KAMO** | **1236 GRT** | **IN FLEET 1913–1930** |

BUILT: 1913 by Campbeltown Shipbuilding Co. Ltd., Campbeltown.

SUBSEQUENT HISTORY: Sold Foo Hong S.S. Co. Ltd., Hong Kong, 1930–35 (same name, British registry). Sold Akai Shoten, Osaka, 1935 but registered under Chinese flag to Fan Shien Ho, Tsingtao, renamed *Lung Ho* (China) 1935–37. Sold Nippon Kaiun Kogyo K.K., Tokyo, 1937, renamed *Ryuan Maru* (Japan) 1937–38. Renamed *Ryuwa Maru* (Japan) 1938–45 (same owner). Sunk by US, carrier-based aircraft off Chongjin, Korea, 9/8/1945 (42.30N – 129.45E)

| **WAIMARINO** | **4204 GRT** | **IN FLEET 1915–1926** |

BUILT: 1900 by A. McMillan & Son. Ltd., Dumbarton, as *Lord Roberts* 1900.

PREVIOUS OWNERS: The Irish Shipowners Co. Ltd., Belfast, (Thos. Dixon & Sons, Mgrs) 1900. Sold British Maritime Trust Ltd., London, 1900–09 and renamed *Wyandotte* (Br) 1900–15. Furness, Withy & Co. Ltd., West Hartlepool, 1909–12. British & Argentine Steam Navigation Co. Ltd., London, 1912–15 (All three companies under management of Furness, Withy & Co. Ltd., London). (On charter to Union Company 1914–15)

SUBSEQUENT HISTORY: Laid up Sydney, 31/8/1925. Sold Moller & Co., Shanghai and ownership registered to Chun Young Zan, Shanghai, 1926 and renamed *King Sing* (China) 1926–29. Ownership transferred N.E.A. Moller, Shanghai (Moller & Co., Mgrs), 1929–34 and renamed *Daisy Moller* (Br) 1929–34. Broken up in Japan 1934.

Taken on charter in 1913 for the service from Pacific coast ports of North America, the **Canada Cape** was purchased by the company in 1914 and renamed **Waihemo**. Less than four years later she was torpedoed and sunk on Imperial Government service

In 1915 the Union Company purchased the Maoriland Steamship Company and took over its three ships, one of which, the collier **Lauderdale**, became the **Kokiri**. The 1214-ton vessel served until sold 12 years later

WAIHEMO   4283 GRT   IN FLEET 1914–1918

BUILT: 1904 by Northumberland Shipbuilding Co. Ltd., Howdon-on-Tyne, Newcastle.

PREVIOUS OWNERS: Laid down as *Gloriana* for the British Maritime Trust Ltd. (Furness Withy & Co., London) and sold on stocks to Elder Dempster Shipping Ltd., Liverpool and completed as *Canada Cape* 1904–14. Elder Dempster Shipping Ltd., Liverpool, 1904–1911. Transferred Elder Line Ltd., Liverpool (Elder Dempster & Co. Mgrs) 1911–12. H. & C. Grayson Ltd., Liverpool, 1912–14. (On charter to Union Company 1913–14).

SUBSEQUENT HISTORY: Torpedoed and sunk in Gulf of Athens, Mediterranean Sea 17/3/1918.

KOKIRI   1214 GRT   IN FLEET 1915–1927

BUILT: 1911 by Campbeltown Shipbuilding Co. Ltd., Campbeltown, as *Lauderdale* 1911–15.

PREVIOUS OWNERS: Maoriland Steamship Co. Ltd., Wellington, (Ferdinand Holm, Mgr) 1911–15.

SUBSEQUENT HISTORY: Sold Madrigal & Co., Manila, 1927 and renamed *Josefina* (Phil) 1927–31, *Visayas II* (Phil) 1931 (same owners), *Taurus* (Phil) 1931–41 (same owners). Scuttled off Luzon 12/1941 under US Navy orders to prevent capture by Japanese. Refloated by Japanese and on liberation of Manila, was sunk off Manila Bay 2/1945.

KAHIKA   1148 GRT   IN FLEET 1915–1933

BUILT: 1902 by Ailsa Shipbuilding Co. Ltd., Troon, as *Ennerdale* 1902–15.

PREVIOUS OWNERS: Robert Simpson, Whitehaven, 1902–07. Ferdinand Holm, Wellington, 1907–08. Maoriland Steamship Co. Ltd., Wellington (Ferdinand Holm, Mgr) 1908–15.

SUBSEQUENT HISTORY: Laid up Port Chalmers, 3/8/1931, dismantled 10/1933 and remains sunk alongside mole, Otago Harbour entrance 4/12/1933.

◀ *A sister ship to the* **Lauderdale**, *the* **Ennerdale** *was renamed* **Kahika**. *Employed on New Zealand coastal services, she had a lucky escape from disaster when she drove ashore on Waikanae Beach, at Gisborne on 24 October 1929. She was successfully refloated five days later with assistance from the company's tug* **Terawhiti**   D. JONES

The third vessel taken over from the Maoriland Steamship Company was formerly an auxiliary sailing ship that had been converted to a steamer. The little 267-ton vessel **Karu** *was a "misfit" within the Union Company fleet and crew often referred to her as "the tub" or some other uncomplimentary name. She was chartered out for three years of her nine-year company ownership*
(DE MAUS) HARRAWAY COLLECTION, HOCKEN LIBRARY

Waikawa *was a former captured German vessel. Built as the* **Schlesien** *in 1907, she had a short life with the Union Company, being purchased in 1915 and sunk in the English Channel on Imperial Government service two years later*

Under the name of **Aotearoa**, *this 15,000 ton passenger liner was intended as a "running mate" for the* **Niagara**. *However, due to war time requirements she was requisitioned by the British Admiralty prior to launching and was completed as the armed merchant cruiser HMS* **Avenger**. *She was lost after little more than one year's service and the illustration shows her in naval garb*

| KARU | 267 GRT | IN FLEET 1915–1925 |

BUILT: 1901 by Moss Iron Foundry & Mechanical Works, Moss, Norway as *Torgauten* (auxiliary steamer) 1901–08.

PREVIOUS OWNERS: Aas & Cappelen, Fredikstad, 1901–04. West Coast Steamship Co. Ltd., Greymouth, 1904–07. Maoriland Steamship Co. Ltd., Wellington (Ferdinand Holm, Mgr) 1907–15 and renamed *Holmdale* 1908–15.

SUBSEQUENT HISTORY: (On charter to Reece Bros., Lyttelton, 11/1917–9/1918 and to Canterbury Steam Shipping Co. Ltd, Christchurch, 4/1919–8/1921). Laid up Port Chalmers, 10/8/1921. Sold 1924 to Melbourne syndicate and towed Port Chalmers, to Sydney by *Waikouaiti* 11–19/4/1924. Sale fell through and vessel laid up Sydney for 18 months. Sold A.F. Watchlin, Auckland, 1925. Foundered 28/2/1926 in Twilight Bay, off Cape Maria van Diemen, after vessel sprang leak, having apparently struck submerged rock or log when leaving Whangape for Sydney 27/2/1926.

| WAIKAWA | 5642 GRT | IN FLEET 1915–1917 |

BUILT: 1907 by Flensburger Schiffsbau-Gesellschaft, Flensburg, as *Schlesien* 1907–14.

PREVIOUS OWNERS: Norddeutscher Lloyd, Bremen, 1907–14. Captured by HMS *Vindictive* 7/8/1914 in English Channel. Condemned by Prize Court and sold by auction 1/1915 to Wm. Thomas Sons & Co. Ltd., London. Under its management, renamed *Maritime* (Br) registered to Maritime Steamship Co. Ltd., London, 21/1/1915.

SUBSEQUENT HISTORY: Torpedoed and sunk 19/10/1917, 4 miles east from Start Point, English Channel.

| AOTEAROA | 14744 GRT | IN FLEET — – — |

BUILT: Laid down 1913 by Fairfield Shipbuilding & Engineering Co. Ltd., Glasgow, but taken over by Admiralty 21/6/1915.

PREVIOUS OWNERS: Launched 30/6/1915 and completed as AMC *Avenger* for Royal Navy 1916.

SUBSEQUENT HISTORY: Torpedoed and sunk by *U-69* in North Sea 14/6/1917 (60.20N – 3.58W) on passage from North Sea patrol to Scapa Flow.

Leitrim *was built as a replacement ship for the United Kingdom trade following the loss of the* **Tyrone** *in 1913. Built in 1915,* **Leitrim** *was transferred to a subsidiary company in 1929 and renamed* **Narbada**. *In this role, with an Asian crew, she was the mainstay of the Union Company's Indian Service for 19 years*   WM. LIVERMORE

The nine year old **Waitotara** *was acquired for the Pacific coast North American service in 1916. Less than a year later she caught fire south of Noumea and was abandoned at sea. The master of the ship that picked up the crew said they spotted the flaming vessel from 45 miles away and at night some of the plates were blazing red with the heat and every so often great gusts of flames burst out from the ship. No lives were lost*   J. DICKIE

| LEITRIM | 9540 GRT | IN FLEET 1916–1929 |

BUILT: 1915 by Sir Raylton Dixon & Co. Ltd., Middlesbrough. (Delivered 22/1/1916).

SUBSEQUENT HISTORY: Transferred to Indo-Pacific Shipping Co. Ltd., London, 1929 (Union Company, Wellington, Mgrs) and renamed *Narbada* (Br) 1929–48. Sold Scheepswerf en Machinehandel N.V., Holland for demolition at Hendrik Ido Ambacht (arrived 27/9/1948).

| WAITOTARA | 4717 GRT | IN FLEET 1916–1917 |

BUILT: 1907 by Scott's Shipbuilding & Engineering Co. Ltd., Greenock, as *Dalmore* 1907–16.

PREVIOUS OWNERS: Steamship "Dalblair" Co. Ltd, Glasgow (John M. Campbell & Son, Mgr) 1907–12. Alliance Shipping Co. Ltd., Glasgow, (John M. Campbell & Son, Mgr) 1912–16.

SUBSEQUENT HISTORY: Caught fire 17/6/1917, 240 miles south of Noumea; abandoned and vessel sank 18/6/1917 on passage Suva to Sydney.

| ARMAGH | 12269 GRT | IN FLEET 1917–1923 |

BUILT: 1917 by Swan, Hunter & Wigham Richardson Ltd., Newcastle.

SUBSEQUENT HISTORY: Wrecked Taylor's Bank Revetment, entrance Mersey River, 15/12/1923 on passage Liverpool to Brisbane.

◀ **Armagh** *was the largest cargo ship then built for the Union Company when she entered service in 1917. Of 12,269 tons, she was designed for the United Kingdom service, the masts and the funnel being telescopic to enable the ship to navigate the Manchester Ship Canal. She was wrecked in 1923 as she left Liverpool outward bound for Australia*

WM. LIVERMORE

106   *Union Fleet*

| KAIWARRA | 3051 GRT | IN FLEET 1919–1942 |

BUILT: 1919 by J. Blumer & Co., Sunderland. Laid down as *War Star* for British Government.

SUBSEQUENT HISTORY: Stranded 4/12/1942 1.5 miles north of Motunau Island, North Canterbury and became total loss on passage Sydney to Lyttelton.

◀ *The 3051-ton cargo ship* **Kaiwarra** *was one of a World War 1 standard type, which the Union Company purchased in 1919 while under construction. Her 23 years with the company were somewhat mundane, although she did strike the headlines in 1936 when she came across the Tasman directly from Sydney to Picton with overseas air mail. The mail was then distributed by Union Airways from Blenheim to the main centres*

| WAIRUNA | 5832 GRT | IN FLEET 1919–1945 |

BUILT: 1914 by Flensburger Schiffsbau Gesellschaft, Flensburg, as *Schneefels* (Ger) 1914.

PREVIOUS OWNERS: Deutsche Dampfschiffahrts Ges. Hansa, Bremen, 1914. Captured by Royal Navy 5/8/1914 and renamed *Gibraltar* 1914–16 (Houlder, Middleton & Co. Ltd., London, Mgrs). Renamed *Polescar* 1916–17 (same mgrs 1916–17, G.Heyn & Sons Ltd., Belfast, Mgrs 1917–19). British India Steam Navigation Co. Ltd., London, Owners and Mgrs 1919.

SUBSEQUENT HISTORY: Sold British Ministry of War Transport 20/3/1945 (J. & J. Denholm Ltd., Glasgow, Mgrs) and used as storeship on the Clyde. Badly damaged by fire at Greenock 12/8/1945. Hull loaded with 8432 tons condemned ammunition and scuttled in Atlantic, 120 miles north west of Ireland 30/10/1945 (55.30N – 11.00W).

◀ *A former German ship captured in 1914, the* **Wairuna** *was taken over by the Union Company in 1919 and employed on the overseas services to North America and occasionally India. She was sold in 1945 and subsequently became one of 60 ships which were scuttled between 1945 and 1964 with cargoes of poison gas shells, unwanted or obsolete ammunition*

| WAITEMATA | 5666 GRT | IN FLEET 1919–1932 |

BUILT: 1919 by Northumberland Shipbuilding Co. Ltd., Newcastle. Laid down as *War Bastion* for British Government.

SUBSEQUENT HISTORY: Laid up Auckland, 5/8/1930. Sold Wm. Crosby & Co., Melbourne, 1932 and intended to be renamed *Willandra* but resold 1933 to Dairen Kisen K. K., Dairen and renamed *Yuki Maru* (Japan) 1933–44. Sunk by submarine USS *Bream* 16/6/1944 (2.19N – 128.40E).

◀ **Waitemata** *was another standard war-built ship purchased to replace war losses. She was mainly employed in the North American service but on at least one occasion she carried bagged wheat from Wallaroo to Yokohama. In 1922 her cargo in Vancouver was loaded twice. Originally stevedored by non-union labour, a dispute arose and a condition of the settlement was that the cargo had to be loaded by union labour so the cargo already loaded, was discharged and then re-loaded!*

The 5637 ton steamer **Waikawa**, *another standard war-built freighter, was purchased on the stocks. Mainly employed in the Trans Pacific cargo service, she had one around-the-world voyage in 1927. Chartered to load coal at Port Kembla for Buenos Aires, she then loaded maize in the River Plate for Barcelona. From there she proceeded to Oran to load bunker coal for a ballast voyage to Bunbury in West Australia where she loaded jarrah for New Zealand – the journey covering over 30,000 miles*   D. JONES

A war-built sister ship to the **Waikawa**, *the* **Waihemo** *was completed to Union Company requirements. She had an unobtrusive 15 years under the company's flag until sold in 1934. One of her later owners employed her for two seasons as a floating cannery, packing King crab meat in the Tartarski Strait. She was not finally broken up until 1958*

Another standard war-built C class vessel, **Kaitoke** *was employed mainly as a collier during her 12 years with the Union Company*

WAIKAWA   5627 GRT   IN FLEET 1919–1934

BUILT: 1919 by Northumberland Shipbuilding Co. Ltd., Newcastle. Laid down as *War Donjon* for British Government.

SUBSEQUENT HISTORY: Sold Tower Steamship Co. Ltd., London, (Rethymnis & Kulukundis Ltd., London, Mgrs) 25/10/1934, but not delivered until 27/3/1935 and renamed *Tower Ensign* (Br) 1935–36. Sold Hunter Shipping Co. Ltd., London, (A.G. Hunter, Mgr) 1936 and renamed *Huntress* (Br) 1937–39. Sold African & Continental S.S. Co. Ltd., London, (D.P. Barnett, Mgr) 1938–39 (Same name). Sold M.V. Vassiliades, Panama, 1939 and renamed *Ronin* (Pan) 1939, (Greek) 1939–41. Sold Ronin S.S. Co., Panama, (Wallem & Co., Mgrs) 1941 and renamed *Iran* (Pan) 1941–42. Transferred to Iran S.S. Co., Panama (M. Nemazee, Mgr) 1941 but still Wallem subsidiary 1941–44. Badly damaged by fire as a result of explosion on *Fort Stikine* at Bombay 14/4/1944 and subsequently sold for breaking up Bombay.

WAIHEMO   5627 GRT   IN FLEET 1919–1934

BUILT: 1919 by Northumberland Shipbuilding Co. Ltd., Newcastle. (Constructed as standard warbuilt "B" class vessel – probable allocated name *War Keep*, but contract negotiated between Union Company and builders – not the Shipping Controller).

SUBSEQUENT HISTORY: Sold Theofano Maritime Co. Ltd., Chios, 1934–37 (Livanos Bros, Piraeus, Mgrs 1934–36, N.G. Livanos, Piraeus, 1936–50) and renamed *Evinos* (Gr) 1934–50. Transferred Livanos Maritime Co. Ltd., Chios, 1937–50 (same name). Sold Cia Maritima Internacional, Panama, 1950, renamed *Rio* (Panama registry, later Honduran) 1950–51. Sold Matsuoka K.K.K., Ashiya and renamed *Shokyu Maru* (Japan) 1951–56. Sold Nippon Suisan K.K., Tokyo, 1956–58 (same name). Sold Taiyo Kaijo K.K. Osaka, shipbreakers 1958 and arrived Osaka for demolition 6/6/1958.

KAITOKE   3167 GRT   IN FLEET 1920 – 1935

BUILT: 1918 by Sir Raylton Dixon & Co. Ltd., Middlesbrough, as *War Palace* for British Government (Japp, Hatch & Co. Ltd., London, Mgrs) 1918–19.

PREVIOUS OWNERS: British Africa Shipping & Coaling Co. Ltd., Cape Town, (Mitchell, Cotts & Co., Mgrs) 1919–20 and renamed *Cape Colony* (Br) 1919–21. (Not renamed *Kaitoke* until 1921).

SUBSEQUENT HISTORY: Laid up Auckland, 11/8/1932. Sold Sakamoto Shoji K.K., Osaka, 1935 but registered under Chinese flag to Fan Shien Ho, Tsingtao and renamed *Kong Ho* (China) 1935–37. Transferred Chou Jen Chen, Tsingtao, 1937 and renamed *Tai Yang* (China) 1937–38. Reverted to Sakamoto Shoji K.K., Osaka 1938 and renamed *Seitai Maru* (Japan) 1938–43. Sunk by submarine USS *Plunger* off Hokkaido 20/8/1943 (42.15N – 139.58E).

Kawatiri *was another C class war built steamer and although owned by the Union Company for 16 years, she was laid up for almost 5 years. She was sold to Japanese owners in 1936 and was torpedoed and sunk in 1942* E. FLUCK

Although a sister ship to both **Kaitoke** *and* **Kawatiri**, **Kaikorai** *had a much longer life with the Union Company, serving 28 years before being sold to mainland Chinese buyers in 1948* E. FLUCK

The last of the standard war-built C class steamers acquired by the Union Company was the **Kekerangu**. *She was a successful vessel, initially employed in the Trans Tasman trades, but in later life operating out of Tasmanian ports to the Australian mainland mainly with cargoes of zinc concentrates from Port Pirie to Risdon. After 33 years with the company she was sold and broken up in Japan* E. FLUCK

| **KAWATIRI** | **3127 GRT** | **IN FLEET 1920 – 1936** |

BUILT: 1919 by John Priestman & Co., Sunderland.

PREVIOUS OWNERS: Laid down as *War Beacon* for British Government but completed as *Shahristan* for F.C. Strick & Co. Ltd., London, 1919–20. (Not renamed *Kawatiri* until 1921).

SUBSEQUENT HISTORY: Laid up Port Chalmers, 31/8/1930. Sold Sakamoto Shoji K.K., Osaka, 1936 but registered under Chinese flag to Sung Wen Kwei, Tsingtao, (Kawasaki K.K.K., Tokyo, Mgrs) and renamed *Wen Yuan* (China) 1936–38. Transferred Sakamoto Shoji K.K. and renamed *Seikai Maru* (Japan) 1938–40. Sold Kita Nippon K.K.K., Tokyo, 1940–42 (same name). Torpedoed and sunk by submarine USS *Guardfish* east of Northern Honshu 24/8/1942 (38.12N – 141.30E).

| **KAIKORAI** | **3151 GRT** | **IN FLEET 1920 – 1948** |

BUILT: 1918 by Wm. Gray & Co. Ltd., West Hartlepool, as *War Foam* for British Government (G.B. Harland & Co, West Hartlepool, Mgrs) 1918–19.

PREVIOUS OWNERS: British Africa Shipping & Coaling Co. Ltd., Cape Town, (Mitchell, Cotts & Co., Mgrs) 1919–20 and renamed *Cape Natal* (Br) 1919–21. (Not renamed *Kaikorai* until 1921).

SUBSEQUENT HISTORY: Laid up Port Chalmers, 31/10/1947. Sold Hwah Lee Steam Ship Co., Shanghai, 1948–49 (same name). Sold Purple Star S.S. Co., Shanghai, 1949–51 but transferred Grande Shipping Corp. Soc. Anon, Panama (same name) 1951; reverted to Purple Star S.S. Co., Shanghai, 1952 when Panamanian registry cancelled. Deleted from Lloyd's Register 1968–69 and not reported for 10 years, so likely out of service from early 1950s.

| **KEKERANGU** | **3146 GRT** | **IN FLEET 1920 – 1953** |

BUILT: 1919 by Tyne Iron Shipbuilding Co. Ltd., Newcastle as *War Coast* for British Government (C. Doresa, London, Mgr) 1918–19.

PREVIOUS OWNERS: J.S. Ambrose, Cardiff, 1919 and renamed *Cosmos* (Br) 1919–21. Severn Shipping Co. Ltd., Cardiff (N.G.Hallett, Mgr) 1920 (same name) but sold Union Company 1920 through F.C. Strick & Co. Ltd., London. (Not renamed *Kekerangu* until 1921 and originally intended to be renamed *Karaka*).

SUBSEQUENT HISTORY: Sold Gilbert's (A'sian) Agency(Vic) Pty. Ltd., Melbourne, 1953 and broken up in Japan 1953.

Another former German vessel, the **Waikouaiti** *was a very well-built cargo ship. She was only six years old when the Union Company acquired her and she was employed in the Tasman services. In 1939 she was wrecked on Dog Island in Foveaux Strait with 5400 tons of cargo on board. A quantity of cargo was salvaged from the wreck and for the first time in New Zealand electro magnets were used to lift steel plates*   D. JONES

| WAIOTAPU | 5886 GRT | IN FLEET 1920 – 1945 |

BUILT: 1913 by Flensburger Schiffsbau-Ges., Flensburg as *Stolberg* (Ger) 1913–20.

PREVIOUS OWNERS: Deutsche Australische D.G., Hamburg, 1913–19. Surrendered 24/8/1919. British Government (British India Steam Navigation Co. Ltd., Mgrs) 1919–20.

SUBSEQUENT HISTORY: Sold David Williamson Ltd., London, 1945–46 (same name). Sold Peak Shipping Co. Ltd., London, (Wallem & Co., Hong Kong subsidiary and Lambert Bros Ltd, London, Mgrs) 1946 and renamed *Victoria Peak* (Br) 1946–47. Sold Shahin S.S. Co., Hong Kong, (Wallem & Co. Ltd., Mgrs) 1946 and renamed *Shahrokh* (Pan) 1947. Sold Dah Loh Nav. Co. Ltd., Shanghai and renamed *Dah Hung* (China) 1947–48. Broken up Shanghai, 1948.

◀ *The 5886 ton* **Waiotapu** *was the largest of five vessels acquired by the Union Company under war reparations. Surrendered in 1919, the vessel was formerly the* **Stolberg** *and the illustration identifies her as a former German Australian Line vessel with the distinctive small well deck forward. She was mainly employed on the trans Pacific service*   E. FLUCK

| WAIKOUAITI | 3926 GRT | IN FLEET 1920 – 1939 |

BUILT: 1914 by Neptunwerft Rostock Schiffswerft und Maschinenfabrik G.m.b.H, Rostock, as *Imgard* (Ger) 1914–20.

PREVIOUS OWNERS: Hamburg-Bremer Afrika Linie A.G., Bremen, 1914–19. British Government (T. Dunlop & Sons, Glasgow, Mgrs) 1919–20.

SUBSEQUENT HISTORY: Wrecked Dog Island, Foveaux Strait, New Zealand, 28/11/1939 on passage Sydney to Lyttelton.

| KORANUI | 1266 GRT | IN FLEET 1920 – 1952 |

BUILT: 1914 by Schiffswerft von Henry Koch, Lubeck as *Cleopatra* (Ger).

PREVIOUS OWNERS: Adolph Kirsten, Hamburg, 1914–19. British Government 1919–20.

SUBSEQUENT HISTORY: Sold S.P. Bell, Sydney, 17/12/1952 but not delivered until 16/1/1953. Resold 4/1953 to Jean Hagen, Noumea and renamed *Neo Hebridais 11* (Fr) 1953–56. Sold to Hong Kong Rolling Mills for demolition and arrived Hong Kong, 5/9/1956.

◀ *Built in 1914 as the* **Cleopatra**, *the 1266-ton German freighter was purchased by the Union Company as part of the war reparations. She was renamed* **Koranui** *and although she spent some time on the New Zealand coast, most of her 32 years with the Union Company were spent in Australia, particularly because of her suitability for carrying heavy cargoes*   ALLAN C. GREEN

Another ex-German ship, the **Kaimanawa**, *originally named* **John Heidmann**, *was specially built as a collier in 1909 and she proved equally suitable in this role on the New Zealand coast. She was fitted with special friction winches at the side of each hatch and with this equipment she could discharge a full cargo of coal in 13 hours. She was in the company's service from 1920 to 1934*

Built as the **Antwerpen** *in 1914, the* **Wingatui** *was the fifth former German ship purchased by the Union Company after the World War 1. A high-sided, low-powered vessel, she had many incidents of colliding with other vessels, wharves and sandbanks. On one voyage she sailed from Wellington on 25 May 1945 in ballast for Westport but she met heavy winds and kept being blown northwards. She eventually circumnavigated the North Island, arriving back in Wellington 38 days later on a voyage that should have taken five days. She was the slowest ship in the fleet and on one voyage from Wellington to Lyttelton she was passed three times by the inter-island express steamer* **Wahine**

The increasing demand for oil fuel for its liners in the Pacific service prompted the company to purchase its own tanker, **Orowaiti**, *in 1921. It acquired its own tank farm at Miramar, Wellington, in 1923.* **Orowaiti** *had a short life, being wrecked on the Californian coast in 1924*

KAIMANAWA   2416 GRT   IN FLEET 1920 – 1934

BUILT: 1909 by Flensburger Schiffsbau-Ges, Flensburg as *John Heidmann* (Ger) 1909–1919, British 1919–20.

PREVIOUS OWNERS: H.W. Heidmann, Hamburg, 1909–18. Hugo Stinnes, Mulheim 1918–19. British Government (J. Cormack & Co. Ltd., Leith, Mgrs 1919–20.

SUBSEQUENT HISTORY: Laid up Auckland, 1/7/1931. Sold Miyachi Kisen K.K. Kobe, 1934 and towed to Japan by *Komata* (sailed Auckland, 12/1/1935). Registered under Chinese flag to An Kwea Hung, Chefoo, 1935 and renamed *Lee An* (China) 1935–41. Transferred to An Kwea Feng, Chefoo, 1937–41. Reverted to Japanese owners, Nitto Kogyo K.K.,Tokyo, 1941 and renamed *Nitto Maru* (Japan) 1941–43. Sunk in collision with Japanese destroyer *Namikaze* near Omaezaki (Cape Omae), Japan, in position 34.33N – 138.44E, 7/2/1943.

WINGATUI   2378 GRT   IN FLEET 1920 – 1951

BUILT: 1914 by Schiffswerft von Henry Koch, Lubeck as *Antwerpen* (Ger) 1914–19.

PREVIOUS OWNERS: Oldenburg-Portugiesische Dampfschiffs-Rhederei, Hamburg, 1914–19. Shipping Controller, (W.A. Young & Co. Ltd., London, Mgrs) 1919–20. (Vessel initially named *Kairanga* 1920–21 by Union Company).

SUBSEQUENT HISTORY: Laid up Wellington 4/11/1949. Sold Mrs E.J. Chandris, Piraeus, 1951 and renamed *Thoula Chandris* (Gr) 1951–52. Ran aground on Arnemuiden Shoal, near Jakarta 12/6/1952. Refloated and sold Mollers Ltd., Hong Kong and arrived Hong Kong for demolition 3/12/1952.

OROWAITI   6684 GRT   IN FLEET 1921–1924

BUILT: 1921 by Greenock Dockyard Co. Ltd., Greenock. Laid down as *Oakpark* and purchased on stocks from J.& J Denholm Ltd, Glasgow.

SUBSEQUENT HISTORY: (Under charter to Wm. Cory & Sons Ltd., London, during Union Company ownership). Wrecked Point Sal, 18 miles south of San Luis Obispo, California, 12/8/1924 on passage Wellington to San Luis Obispo.

The 7113 ton **Hauraki** *was the first motor ship in the Union Company fleet. Built in 1922, she burned an average of 14 tons of oil fuel per day in service. All her winches and auxiliary equipment were powered by electricity. She was the 41st ship built by Wm. Denny & Bros. for the company. She was in the fleet for 20 years before being captured by Japanese surface craft in the Pacific in 1942* D. JONES

Sussex *was purchased from the Federal Steam Navigation Company (a P & O subsidiary company) in 1923 for the service to India and throughout the six year ownership the vessel remained under London registry and was painted in Federal Line colours. It was always publicly stated that the ship was under charter, thus allowing an Indian crew to be employed* WM. LIVERMORE.

A former iron sailing vessel and Union Company coal hulk, the **Opihi** *dated from 1886. In 1918 she was fitted with engines from the* **Opouri**, *which had been wrecked at Greymouth in 1917. She was purchased from Reece Bros of Christchurch in 1923 and spent 13 years with the Union Company on New Zealand coastal services before the 50-year old vessel was scuttled in Cook Strait*

HAURAKI   7113 GRT   IN FLEET 1922–1942

BUILT: 1922 by Wm. Denny & Bros. Ltd., Dumbarton.

SUBSEQUENT HISTORY: Captured by Japanese naval units in Indian Ocean 12/7/1942 and converted to Japanese transport *Hoki Maru* 1943 under Japanese Navy control. Bombed and sunk by U.S. carrier-based planes at Truk, Caroline Islands 17/2/1944.

SUSSEX   6957 GRT   IN FLEET 1923–1929

BUILT: 1900 by Hawthorn, Leslie & Co. Ltd., Newcastle.

PREVIOUS OWNERS: Federal Steam Navigation Co. Ltd., London, 1900–23.

SUBSEQUENT HISTORY: (While under Union Company, Federal Steam Navigation Co. Ltd., remained as registered nominal owners). Sold shipbreakers 1929 through John Summers & Co. Ltd., Kobe. Arrived Osaka 15/7/1929 and demolition undertaken by Osaka Marine Co. Ltd., 8/1929.

OPIHI   1117 GRT   IN FLEET 1923–1936

BUILT: 1886 by Rostocker Schiffsund Maschinenbau-Actien Gesellschaft, Rostock as sailing vessel *Lilla* (Ger) Jean Hintze, Hamburg, 1886–98.

PREVIOUS OWNERS: F. Th. Eckhusen, Hamburg, 1898–06. Acties Lilla (Pettersen & Ullenaes, Porsgrund, Mgrs) 1906–08. (H. Jeremiassen, Porsgrund, Mgr 1908–14). (Under Norwegian flag 1906–14). Union Steam Ship Co. of N.Z. Ltd., Dunedin, 1914–17 and converted to coal hulk at Wellington 1914. Daniel Reese, Christchurch (Reese Bros., Mgrs) 1917–23 and towed Lyttelton for conversion to steamer. Renamed *Opihi* (N.Z.) 1918. Opihi Shipping Co. Ltd., Christchurch (same managers) 1923.

SUBSEQUENT HISTORY: Laid up Wellington 28/1/1935. Dismantled Wellington 7/1936 and remains scuttled off Turakirae Heads, Cook Strait 28/8/1936.

118 *Union Fleet*

| KAIRANGA | 2830 GRT | IN FLEET 1924–1956 |

BUILT: 1921 by Livingstone & Cooper Ltd., Hessle-on-Humber. Launched as *Saint Dominique* but name changed to *Saint Rominique*.

PREVIOUS OWNERS: Built for Societe Navale de L'Ouest, Paris but registered to Forth Shipbuilding & Engineering Co (1921) Ltd, Alloa 1921–24.

SUBSEQUENT HISTORY: Sold Teh Hu S.S. Co. Ltd., Hong Kong, 1956 and renamed *Amelia* (Pan). 1956–67 registered to Cia. de Nav Victoria Neptuno S.A., Panama. Sold Fuji Marden & Co. for demolition at Hong Kong, 1967.

◀ *The distinctive "goal post" masts identified the* **Kairanga**, *which was built for French owners, but purchased directly from the shipbuilders, by the Union Company in 1924. Built for the French wine trade, she was mainly employed in the Trans Tasman services and was one of the first company vessels to be fitted for oil fuel. She had a narrow escape from disaster on 7 March 1940 when the 11095 ton* **Sydney Star** *collided with her in Sydney harbour. The larger ship chopped off the bow of* **Kairanga** *and she had to be beached to prevent her sinking*   E. FLUCK

| KONINI | 1435 GRT | IN FLEET 1924–1924 |

BUILT: 1924 by Grangemouth Dockyard Co. Ltd., Grangemouth. (Laid down as speculation or for other owners and purchased by Union Company after launching).

SUBSEQUENT HISTORY: Wrecked on Whale Head, Ocean Beach, Bluff 22/12/1924 on passage Adelaide to Dunedin.

◀ *The 1435 ton* **Konini** *had a short life with the Union Company, being wrecked at Bluff at the end of her delivery voyage from Grangemouth in 1924. The master had lost sight of landmarks due to poor visibility and he was censured for not reducing speed. The illustration shows* **Konini** *at Adelaide prior to her ill-fated Tasman crossing*

| KAIMAI | 1435 GRT | IN FLEET 1924–1952 |

BUILT: 1924 by H. Veldhuis, Papendrecht as *Charlois* (Du) 1924 for J. Van Santen and C. Schmid, Rotterdam 1924. Fitted out for Union Company by Livingstone & Cooper Ltd., Hessle-on-Humber.

SUBSEQUENT HISTORY: Laid up Wellington 22/12/1948. Sold Mrs E.J. Chandris, Piraeus and renamed *Mina Chandris* (Gr) 1952–55. Sold Saints Anaryroi Cia Ltda., Puerto Limon and renamed *Pothoula* (Costa Rica) 1955–58. Sprung leak and sank 40 miles north of Hercules Lighthouse, Bay of Biscay 8/6/1958 on passage Rouen to Vigo.

◀ **Kaimai** *was specially built for the Baltic timber trade as the* **Charlois** *for Dutch owners but she was purchased by the Union Company prior to completion. She was a successful New Zealand coastal vessel and was in the fleet from 1924 until 1952*   D. JONES

Although the 3219 ton steamer **Karetu** *was completed to Union Company requirements in 1924, she had been originally laid down for French owners. A stalwart of the Tasman and coastal trades for 25 years, she was sold in 1952 and was in service for another 25 years in the Mediterranean and Black Seas – lasting a record 53 years. The illustration shows her off the coast of Gisborne in 1939* RNZAF

As a result of continuing losses, the Tasmanian Government sold its steamers **Poolta** *and* **Melbourne** *to the Union Company in 1925. The latter was quickly sold but the* **Poolta** *served until 1950. The illustration shows the vessel in the colours of the Tasmanian Government*

| **KARETU** | **3210 GRT** | **IN FLEET 1924–1951** |

BUILT: 1924 by Wm. Gray & Co. Ltd., West Hartlepool. Originally laid down for Societe Navale de L'Ouest, Paris but taken over by Union Company prior to launching.

SUBSEQUENT HISTORY: Laid up Wellington 14/12/1949. Sold Mrs E.J. Chandris, Piraeus and renamed *Keti Chandris* (Gr) 1951–54. Sold Cia. de Vap. Marine Ltda, Panama, 1954 and renamed *Marina* (Pan) 1954. Sold to Riza ve Asian Sadikoglu, Istanbul and renamed *Umran* (Turkey) 1954–57. Sold to Cemal Pehlivan Varisleri, Istanbul and renamed *Muzzaffer Pehlivan* (Turkey) 1957–60. Sold Ufuk Vapuru Donatma Istiraki, Istanbul, 1960 and renamed *Ufuk* (Turkey) 1960–77. Broken up at Aliaga Demolition site, Izmir, Turkey from 5/3/1977.

| **AORANGI** | **17491 GRT** | **IN FLEET 1924–1931** |

BUILT: 1924 by Fairfield Shipbuilding & Engineering Co. Ltd., Glasgow.

SUBSEQUENT HISTORY: Transferred to Canadian-Australasian Line Ltd., Vancouver, (Union Company, Mgrs) 1931–53. Sold British Iron and Steel Corporation and allocated to W.H. Arnott Young, Dalmuir for demolition and arrived Dalmuir 25/7/1953.

◀ *When built, the 17,491 ton* **Aorangi** *was the largest and fastest (18.5 knots in trials) motor liner in the world. She had accommodation for 386 passengers in first class, 56 interchangeable first or second, 284 in second and 227 in third class. She was built for the trans Pacific service and her ownership was transferred to a subsidiary company in 1931 but under Union Company management. In 1941 she was requisitioned by the British Ministry of War Transport and served as a troopship and depot ship until 1946. She resumed in the Vancouver mail service from 1948 to 1953, being initially painted with a white hull and copper green boot-topping until 1949, when she was repainted with the regular Union Company colours*

| **POOLTA** | **1675 GRT** | **IN FLEET 1925–1952** |

BUILT: 1921 by Burgerhout's Mach. & Scheeps. Naamlooze Vennootschap, Rotterdam. Laid down as *Graaf Jan* for N.V. Scheepvaart Maatschappij 'Orange Nassau' Rotterdam but sold on the stocks to Tasmanian Government, Hobart, and renamed *Poolta* (Aust) 1921–25.

SUBSEQUENT HISTORY: Laid up Wellington 7/7/1950. Sold to Mrs E.J. Chandris, Piraeus and renamed *Despo Chandris* (Gr) 1952–53. Sold Emin Sadikoglu, Istanbul 1953 and renamed *Arif* (Turkey) 1953–61. Broken up at Istanbul by Emin Sadikoglu, 5–6/1961.

*The **Limerick** was similar in design to the New Zealand Shipping Company's **Tongariro**, also built in 1925 but the latter vessel was a steamer while **Limerick**, when completed had the largest diesel machinery then installed in a British vessel, apart from **Aorangi**. Because of her large cargo capacity she was employed on the Indian or Pacific coast trades until torpedoed in 1943* E. FLUCK

*Following the loss of the tanker **Orowaiti** in 1924, the Union Company purchased a replacement vessel the following year. Named **Otokia**, she had a capacity for 9300 tons of oil fuel. As with the earlier vessel, she was under charter to Wm. Cory & Sons during her eight active years with the Union Company* ALEXANDER TURNBULL LIBRARY

*The 2347 ton **Kartigi** was the first of a series of specialist colliers built for the Union Company. Completed in 1925, she was fitted with all the latest equipment for coal handling including patented corrugated steel hatch covers, which replaced the traditional wooden hatch boards. She also had additional ballast tanks to keep the vessel in stable trim during ballast voyages* E. FLUCK

| **LIMERICK** | **8734 GRT** | **IN FLEET 1925–1936** |

BUILT: 1925 by Wm. Hamilton & Co. Ltd., Port Glasgow.

SUBSEQUENT HISTORY: Transferred to Indo-Pacific Shipping Co. Ltd., London (Union Company, Mgrs), 1936–38. Transferred Irish Counties Steamers, London (Union Company, Mgrs), 1938–43. Torpedoed and sunk by Japanese submarine *I-26* about 20 miles SE off Cape Byron, New South Wales, 26/4/1943 (28.54S–153.54E) on passage Sydney to Brisbane in convoy.

| **OTOKIA (OIL TANKER)** | **7277 GRT** | **IN FLEET 1925–1935** |

BUILT: 1925 by Livingstone & Cooper Ltd., Hessle-on-Humber. Laid down as speculation by builders and purchased on stocks by Union Company.

SUBSEQUENT HISTORY: (Under charter to Wm. Cory & Sons Ltd., London during Union Company ownership). Laid up Port Chalmers, 20/2/1933. Sold Summers & Co. Ltd., Kobe, with Nippon Tanker K.K., Tokyo controlling owners 1935–37 (same name but Panamanian registry). Sold Cia Maritima Istmenia Ltda, Panama 1937 and renamed *Panam* (Panama) 1937–43. Sold Panamanian Government, Panama 1943 (same name). Torpedoed and sunk by *U-129* on the night of 4–5/5/1943, 31 miles south of Cape Lookout, North Carolina (34.11N – 76.12W).

| **KARTIGI** | **2347 GRT** | **IN FLEET 1925–1955** |

BUILT: 1925 by Wm. Gray & Co. Ltd., West Hartlepool.

SUBSEQUENT HISTORY: Laid up Wellington 20/3/1952. Sold Grosvenor Shipping Co. Ltd., Hong Kong (Moller's Ltd, Hong Kong, Mgrs). Towed to Hong Kong by tug *Golden Cape* (sailed Wellington in tow 15/3/1955). Sold shipbreakers 2/1956 and broken up Hong Kong.

124 *Union Fleet*

| KIWITEA | 2350 GRT | IN FLEET 1925–1955 |

BUILT: 1925 by Wm.Gray & Co. Ltd., West Hartlepool.

SUBSEQUENT HISTORY: Laid up Wellington 27/8/1952. Sold Grosvenor Shipping Co. Ltd., Hong Kong (Moller's Ltd, Hong Kong, Mgrs). Towed to Hong Kong by tug *Golden Cape* (sailed Wellington in tow 15/3/1955). Sold shipbreakers 2/1956 and broken up Hong Kong.

◀ A sister ship to **Kartigi**, *the* **Kiwitea** *had almost an identical career which saw both vessels in service for 27 years. They were also disposed of together, being towed in tandem to Hong Kong in 1955 for demolition*

| KAPONGA | 2346 GRT | IN FLEET 1925–1932 |

BUILT: 1925 by Wm. Gray & Co. Ltd., West Hartlepool.

SUBSEQUENT HISTORY: Wrecked on bar, Grey River mouth 27/5/1932 outward bound from Greymouth to Auckland.

◀ *The third specialist collier was the* **Kaponga,** *but she had a short life, being stranded on the Greymouth river bar on 27 May 1932 when outward bound with a full cargo of coal. The Court of Inquiry found that the Harbour Master at Greymouth had given the master of the ship inaccurate information on the depth of water on the bar. Within a few months the vessel had completely broken up*   E. FLUCK

| TAMAHINE | 1989 GRT | IN FLEET 1925–1962 |

BUILT: 1925 by Swan, Hunter & Wigham Richardson Ltd., Wallsend-on Tyne.

SUBSEQUENT HISTORY: Sold Hong Kong Shipping Co. (Panama) Ltd., Hong Kong, 1962 and renamed *Kowloon Star* (Pan) 1963–69. Left Wellington for Hong Hong 5/1/1963. Ownership later transferred to Cia. de Nav. Sunlite S.A., Panama (same owners). Sold Leung Yau Shipbreaking Co. Hong Kong and broken up Hong Kong, 1969.

◀ *The twin-funnelled* **Tamahine** *was the first passenger vessel built for the Picton-Wellington service. Completed in 1925, she could carry 637 passengers but there was only limited cabin accommodation because of the short passage. When she was retired in 1962 it was estimated she had made over 15,000 crossings, carrying over 2 million passengers. She had a slight permanent list as well as a corkscrew motion in heavy seas, so there were few trips across Cook Strait that some passengers were not seasick*

Built as a general purpose coastal vessel, **Waipahi** *was subsequently adapted for the Pacific Island fruit trade. She made her first voyage in this service in 1927 and was painted white with a green band around the hull. She also was fitted with air shoots to give better air circulation in the holds. From 1936 she reverted to the New Zealand coastal trade* D. JONES

The 887 ton steamer **Kakariki** *was built in 1926 for the ore trade between Tasmania and the mainland of Australia. Her short life was ended when she was in collision with the steamer* **Caradale** *in the main shipping channel into Melbourne in January 1937. The wreck had to be cleared and several attempts were made over a period of seven years until the full channel depth was restored* ALLAN C. GREEN

Built for the Dunedin – Auckland coastal service via the East Coast, **Waipiata** *entered service in 1926. She had a stable, uneventful career until the night of the 5th May 1950 when she collided with the larger* **Taranaki** *inside Wellington Heads. The damage took 15 months to repair. The wartime illustration shows the* **Waipiata** *in 1943 with guns on the bow and stern* RNZAF

WAIPAHI   1783 GRT   IN FLEET 1925–1955

BUILT: 1925 by Northumberland Shipbuilding Co. Ltd., Howdon-on-Tyne.

SUBSEQUENT HISTORY: Laid up Wellington 11/12/1952. Sold Agean Navigation Typaldos Bros. Steamship Co., Piraeus, 1955 and renamed *Kefallinia* (Gr) 1955–62. Broken up in Piraeus area, Greece between 12/1959 and 9/1960.

KAKARIKI   887 GRT   IN FLEET 1926–1937

BUILT: 1926 by Cochrane & Sons Ltd., Selby.

SUBSEQUENT HISTORY: Collided with *Caradale* (1881/1921) near Gellibrand Light, Hobson's Bay, Melbourne and sank 29/1/1937 on passage Strahan to Melbourne. Wreck removed following three attempts between 1938–45.

WAIPIATA   2826 GRT   IN FLEET 1926–1956

BUILT: 1926 by Napier & Miller Ltd., Glasgow.

SUBSEQUENT HISTORY: Sold San Roberto S.S. Co. S.A., Panama, (John Manners & Co. Ltd., Hong Kong, Mgrs) 1956 and renamed *San Roberto* (Pan) 1956–63. Sold Coastal Shipping Corp., Hong Kong, 1963–66 (same name). Sold Intertrader Shipping Co. S.A., Panama 1966 and renamed *Intertrader* (Pan) 1966–68. Sold Leung Yau Shipbreaking Co., Hong Kong and arrived Hong Kong, 26/1/1968 for demolition.

Waimea *was in the Union Company fleet from 1928 to 1935. She was an Anchor Company ship from 1909 to 1928 and again from 1935 to 1939 and her transfer to the Union Company was at the Union Company behest as it had effective control of the Anchor Company at the time and sought to use the vessel in the Auckland-Gisborne trade*

Kaimiro *was the first of a pair of self-trimming colliers built in 1929. With a carrying capacity of 3400 tons, the vessel was used for coal, timber and bulk cargoes. Cargo was carried in three holds and accessed through six hatches served by 12 winches. She played a significant role in the salvage of the steamer* **Kotor** *when she was pulled off a beach near North Cape on 27 June 1944*   E. FLUCK

An identical sister to **Kaimiro**, *the 2563 ton* **Karepo** *spent 25 years in service before both she and her sister were sold in 1954 to Sydney owners to be employed as colliers on the 60 mile run from Newcastle to Sydney. The 1943 illustration shows her under wartime conditions with life rafts fitted and a gun on the stern*   RNZAF

WAIMEA — 454 GRT — IN FLEET 1928–1935

BUILT: 1909 by Mackie & Thomson Ltd., Glasgow.

PREVIOUS OWNERS: Anchor Shipping & Foundry Co. Ltd., Nelson 1909–28.

SUBSEQUENT HISTORY: Resold Anchor Shipping & Foundry Co. Ltd., Nelson 1935–39. Resold to Union Company 1939, which required vessel's boiler for its *Wingatui*. Left Nelson 31/5/1939 in tow of *Kaitoa* for Wellington. Hull later scuttled off Turakirae Heads, Cook Strait 8/8/1939.

KAIMIRO — 2562 GRT — IN FLEET 1929–1954

BUILT: 1929 by Cammell Laird & Co. Ltd., Birkenhead.

SUBSEQUENT HISTORY: Laid up Wellington 9/10/1952. Sold R.W. Miller & Co. Pty. Ltd., Sydney, 1954 and renamed *Branxton* (Aust) 1954–69. Sold Goldfields Metal Traders, Fremantle and delivered Sydney 4/6/1969. Intended to be demolished at Sydney but subsequently towed to Hong Kong by tug *Nullagine* (sailed Sydney 12/5/1970 and arrived Hong Kong, 21/6/1970). Broken up by Ming Hing & Co.

KAREPO — 2563 GRT — IN FLEET 1929–1954

BUILT: 1929 by Cammell Laird & Co. Ltd., Birkenhead.

SUBSEQUENT HISTORY: Laid up Auckland, 14/3/1952. Sold R.W. Miller & Co. Pty. Ltd., Sydney, 1954 and renamed *Teralba* (Aust) 1954–70. Transferred SS William McArthur Pty. Ltd., (R.W. Miller & Co. Pty. Ltd. Mgrs) 1962–70. Sold Goldfields Metal Traders, Fremantle and delivered Sydney 24/4/1970. Sailed Sydney 11/5/1971 in tow for Taiwan for demolition.

Early in 1930 the Union Company acquired three steamers from R.S. Lamb of Sydney. **Gabriella** had been laid down in 1914 but as a result of the war, German army engineers removed some plates and prevented the ship from being completed. It was not until 1920 that she was delivered to Belgian owners. She served the Union Company for 20 years

Kalingo was only three years old when purchased from R.S. Lamb of Sydney and she proved a useful general purpose ship in the Trans Tasman trade for 13 years until she was torpedoed and sunk east of Sydney in 1943

The third ship purchased from R.S. Lamb of Sydney was the 15 year old **Omana**. In June 1935 she had a narrow escape when she stranded on a gravel bank in the Grey River and some 300 tons of timber had to be discharged before she swung free four days later. In May 1936 she became the first steamer to load milling timber direct from Bruce Bay in Westland for Melbourne   E. FLUCK

| **GABRIELLA** | **1587 GRT** | **IN FLEET 1930 – 1951** |

BUILT: Laid down 1914 by Antwerp Engineering Co. Ltd., Hoboken but dismantled during World War 1. Keel re-laid 6/5/1919 and completed 3/5/1920.

PREVIOUS OWNERS: Handel en Scheepvaart S.A. Ostend (M. Vandesompel, Ostend, Mgr) 1920–22. Gabriella Steamship Ltd, Sydney (R.S. Lamb & Co. Ltd., Mgrs) 1922–30.

SUBSEQUENT HISTORY: Laid up Wellington 1/11/1950. Sold 12/12/1951 but not delivered until 4/2/1952 to Mrs E.J. Chandris, Piraeus, and renamed *Dora Chandris* (Gr) 1951–55. Sold Santa Kyriaki Nav. Ltda, Puerto Limon, (D.N. Mitropoulos, Piraeus, Mgr) 1955 and renamed *Capetan Costas* (Costa Rica) 1955–59. Sold Sidiremboriki Ltd, Piraeus, for demolition 1959 and broken up St George's Bay 10–11/1959.

| **KALINGO** | **2047 GRT** | **IN FLEET 1930 – 1943** |

BUILT: 1927 by The Clyde Shipbuilding & Engineering Co. Ltd., Port Glasgow.

PREVIOUS OWNERS: Kalingo Steamship Ltd., Sydney (R.S. Lamb & Co. Ltd., Mgrs) 1927–30.

SUBSEQUENT HISTORY: Torpedoed and sunk by Japanese submarine *I-21*, 18/1/1943 about 110 miles east of Sydney (34.07S – 153.15E) on passage Sydney to New Plymouth.

| **OMANA** | **2550 GRT** | **IN FLEET 1930 – 1951** |

BUILT: 1915 by Osbourne, Graham & Co., Hylton, Sunderland.

PREVIOUS OWNERS: Omana Steamship Pty. Co. Ltd., Sydney (R.S. Lamb & Co. Ltd, Mgrs) 1915–30.

SUBSEQUENT HISTORY: Sold Mrs E.J. Chandris, Piraeus and renamed *Youla Chandris* (Gr) 1951–53. Sold San Anastasias Cia. Ltda, Puerto Limon, 1953 and renamed *Tassos* (Costa Rica) 1953–59. Laid up Piraeus 9/1958. Sold Greek shipbreakers at St. George's Bay 7/1959.

Wainui *was built for the Dunedin-Gisborne service via intermediate East Coast ports, but shortly after she went on the Trans Tasman (described as the intercolonial trade at that time) service from Melbourne to Bluff and Dunedin. She was in the fleet for 28 years* ALLAN C. GREEN

The three-masted **Talune** *was built in 1930 and ran under the Union Company flag for 29 years, 27 of them in the trade between New South Wales ports and Tasmania. During World War 2 she spent two years as a naval supply ship based at Colombo* E. HUMPHERY

An improved larger version of the **Waipiata**, *the 3066 ton* **Waimarino** *was a familiar sight on the Bluff to Auckland service for 27 years. She was also known for her fast passages between ports* D. JONES

WAINUI   1633 GRT   IN FLEET 1930 – 1958

BUILT: 1930 by R. & W. Hawthorn, Leslie & Co. Ltd., Hebburn-on-Tyne.

SUBSEQUENT HISTORY: Sold Teh-Hu Steamship Co. Ltd., Hong Kong, 1958 (under subsidiary Cia de Nav. Victoria Neptuno S.A., Panama) and renamed *Amonea* (Pan) 1958–60. Went aground south of Palawan Island (117.13E – 8.10N) 14/12/1960 and subsequently abandoned as total loss on passage Sandakan to Jesselton.

TALUNE   2742 GRT   IN FLEET 1930 – 1959

BUILT: 1930 by Blythswood Shipbuilding Co. Ltd., Glasgow.

SUBSEQUENT HISTORY: Sold Transporte de Minerales S.A., Panama, 1959 and renamed *Amos* (Pan) 1959–60. Sold Taiwan shipbreakers and arrived Kaohsiung for demolition 13/6/1960.

WAIMARINO   3067 GRT   IN FLEET 1930 – 1957

BUILT: 1930 by Ardrossan Dockyard Ltd., Ardrossan.

SUBSEQUENT HISTORY: Sold San Roberto S.S. Co. S.A., Panama (John Manners & Co. Ltd., Hong Kong, Mgrs) 1957 and renamed *San Eduardo* (Pan) 1957–64. Sold Mercantile Shipping Development Corp., Hong Kong (Ta Hing Co. Ltd., Hong Kong, Mgrs), 1964 and renamed *Flores* (Pan) 1964–66. Subsequently repossessed by John Manners & Co. Ltd., 1965 and resold Oriental Trader Navigation Co. S.A., Panama (China Pacific Navigation Co. Ltd., Hong Kong, Mgrs), 1966 and renamed *Continental Trader* (Pan) 1966–68. Sold Leung Yau Shipbreaking Co., Hong Kong and arrived Hong Kong for demolition 3/12/1968.

Following the loss of the Trans Pacific liner **Tahiti**, *the Union Company acquired the five year old* **Razmak** *from P & O and renamed her* **Monowai**. *She proved a popular ship during her 30 years with the company and during World War 2 she saw extensive service firstly as an armed merchant cruiser and then as a troopship. She is shown at Auckland prior to World War 2*

When the Union Company purchased the three steamers of R.S. Lamb of Sydney, that company had just ordered a new specialist timber carrier from an Aberdeen shipyard. Intended to be named **Ihumata** *(pronounced ishumata) she was taken over by the Union Company and renamed* **Kini**. *She had two large open hatches, ideally suited to the carriage of long poles, with long heavy derricks to handle them. She was employed on a number of services but in the years up to her retirement in 1956 she was engaged in the Tasmanian trades*

E. FLUCK

The turbo-electric express steamer **Rangatira** *was one of the most graceful and popular vessels ever owned by the Union Company. She was built for the Wellington-Lyttelton express service. The 6152 ton, 22 knot vessel in April 1939 made the fastest passage ever from Lyttelton to Wellington – 8 hours 8 minutes at an average speed of 21.4 knots*

MONOWAI — 10852 GRT — IN FLEET 1930 – 1960

BUILT: 1925 by Harland & Wolff Ltd., Greenock as *Razmak*.

PREVIOUS OWNERS: Peninsular & Oriental Steam Navigation Co., London, 1925–30.

SUBSEQUENT HISTORY: Sold Far East Metal Industry and Shipping Co. Ltd., Hong Kong, and arrived Hong Kong for demolition 6/9/1960.

KINI — 1388 GRT — IN FLEET 1930 – 1956

BUILT: 1930 by J. Lewis & Sons Ltd., Aberdeen. (Laid down as *Ihumata* for R.S. Lamb & Co. Ltd., Sydney).

SUBSEQUENT HISTORY: Sold Isabel Navigation Co. S.A. Panama (John Manners & Co. Ltd., Hong Kong, Mgrs) 1956 and renamed *Brenda* (Pan) 1956–61. Sold San Raimundo Cia. Nav S.A. Panama, (Lanena Shipping Co. Ltd., Hong Kong, Mgrs) 1961 and renamed *Jade* (Pan) 1961–62. Broken up at Hong Kong, 1/1962.

RANGATIRA — 6152 GRT — IN FLEET 1931–1967

BUILT: 1931 by Vickers-Armstrongs Ltd., Barrow-in-Furness.

SUBSEQUENT HISTORY: Laid up Wellington 16/12/1965. Sold John Manners & Co. Ltd., Hong Kong, 26/5/1967 but resold 2/8/67 to Fortune & Co. Ltd., Hong Kong. Sailed Wellington 25/10/1967 in tow of tug *Fuji Maru* and delivered Hong Kong, 27/11/1967 for demolition there 1968.

Rangatira *had a number of incidents in her career including running aground in heavy weather off Sinclair Head, Cook Strait, on 2 February 1936, and in dense fog she ran aground in Pigeon Bay, Banks Peninsula on 29 December 1940. On Christmas Day 1959 she ran aground just inside the entrance to Tory Channel but was safely refloated 26 hours later. The illustration shows her aground in Pigeon Bay* RNZAF

136   *Union Fleet*

| **WAITAKI** | **2212 GRT** | **IN FLEET 1934–1958** |

BUILT: 1934 by A. Stephen & Sons Ltd., Linthouse, Glasgow.

SUBSEQUENT HISTORY: Laid up Wellington 21/12/1957. Sold Ta Hsing Steamship Co. Ltd., Keelung and renamed *Tai Yuin* (Taiwan) 1958–60. Sold Taiwan Maritime Transportation Co. Ltd., Keelung 1960–66 (same name). Broken up Kaohsiung 1966.

◀ *A slightly larger version of the* **Wainui**, *the 2212 ton* **Waitaki** *spent almost all her 24 years with the Union Company on the run from Melbourne to Wellington via South Island east coast ports*

| **KARU** | **1044 GRT** | **IN FLEET 1935–1964** |

BUILT: 1935 by A. Stephen & Sons Ltd., Linthouse, Glasgow.

SUBSEQUENT HISTORY: Sold Australia Pacific Shipping (H.K.) Ltd., Hong Kong, (Jas. Lee, Mgr) and intended to be renamed *Dorothie* (Hong Kong), 1964. Wrecked as *Karu* on reef in Jomard Passage, Louisade Archipelago, south east of Papua 11/7/1964 on passage Sydney to Guam.

◀ *The* **Karu**, *built in 1935 to replace the* **Opihi** *in the South Island – New Plymouth trade was unlike the other vessels of that era. She had a cruiser stern, a quarter deck aft, a full bridge and was the company's first coastal motorship. The lines of the vessel both above and below the water line were designed to give the best economy in propulsion and fuel consumption.* **Karu** *was on the New Zealand coast for 29 years*   BAIN-WRIGHT COLLECTION

| **MATUA** | **4166 GRT** | **IN FLEET 1936–1968** |

BUILT: 1936 by R. & W. Hawthorn, Leslie & Co. Ltd., Hebburn, Newcastle-on-Tyne.

SUBSEQUENT HISTORY: Sold "K" Shipping Corporation, Manila (Litonjua Shipping Co. Inc., Mgrs) 1968 and renamed *Sultan K.L* (Phil) 1968–69. Ran aground during typhoon, Manila Bay 1969, later salvaged by Taiwan shipbreakers and broken up Kaohsiung 1970.

◀ *The yacht-like appearance of the* **Matua** *made her a popular ship on the run to the Pacific Islands. She had accommodation for 40 passengers and a round trip from Auckland to Rarotonga, Nukualofa, Apia and Suva and return was the equivalent of $156 in 1936. She also had 94,000 cubic feet of insulated space and her main southbound cargo was bananas. Apart from several instances of striking reefs and the effects of cyclones,* **Matua** *was a very successful vessel and served the Union Company for 32 years*

Kauri *was the first of a new series of motorships built by the Union Company for the Trans Tasman trade. She had three holds, with exceptionally large hatchways, double sets of derricks at each hatch, powered by 12 electric winches. She spent 26 years with the Union Company and a further 16 years in eastern waters under various flags before being broken up at Bangkok in 1978* E. FLUCK

| AWATEA | 13482 GRT | IN FLEET 1936–1942 |

BUILT: 1936 by Vickers, Armstrongs Ltd., Barrow-in-Furness.

SUBSEQUENT HISTORY: Requisitioned by British Ministry of War Transport 1941. In service as troopship, bombed and sunk 1 mile north of Bougie Breakwater, Algeria 11/11/1942 outward bound from Bougie to Algiers.

◀ Long recognised as the finest ship ever built for the Union Company, the 13,482 ton liner **Awatea** was completed in 1936 for the Trans Tasman service from Auckland and Wellington to Sydney. Her record-breaking passages – 55 hours 28 mins Auckland to Sydney and 55 hours 47 minutes Sydney to Wellington – attracted world wide attention. She had accommodation for 377 passengers in first class and 151 in second. The twin screw liner was powered by Parsons turbines developing up to 22,500 shaft horse power for a maximum speed of 23 knots, making her one on the fastest liners in the world

◀ Another view of the magnificent **Awatea**. From December 1939 she was employed transporting Commonwealth troops but in the latter part of 1941 she was requisitioned by the Ministry of War Transport and converted to a troopship. It was during one of these voyages that she cut the American destroyer **Buck** in two when it suddenly swung across her bows. She was then fitted out as a Landing Ship, Infantry (L.S.I.) and took part in the North African landings. When sailing out of Bougie, Algeria, she was attacked by waves of German bombers and eventually sank. The naval officer in command of the landing, known as Operation Torch, said the **Awatea** 'fought like a battleship'

| KAURI | 2361 GRT | IN FLEET 1936–1962 |

BUILT: 1936 by A. Stephen & Sons Ltd., Linthouse, Glasgow.

SUBSEQUENT HISTORY: Sold Cronulla Shipping Co. Ltd., Hong Kong, (John Manners & Co. Ltd., Hong Kong, Mgrs) 1962 and renamed *Carolina* (H.K.) 1962–63. Transferred San Jeronimo S.S. Co. S.A., Panama (same name, Panamania registry) 1963–67. Sank in Hong Kong harbour during typhoon 'Ruby' 5/9/64, raised and repaired. Sold Primal Nav. Co. Ltd., Hong Kong, 1967 and renamed *Miranda* (Pan) 1967–68. Transferred Luen Seng Nav. Co. S.A., Panama 1968 and renamed *Primal Prosperity* (Pan) 1968. Renamed *Golden Dragon* (Pan) 1968 (same owners). Sold The Africa Shipping Co. S.A. (Asia Selatan Enterprises Ltd., Hong Kong, Mgrs subsidiary of Kie Hock Shipping (1971) Ltd., Singapore) 1969 and renamed *Gambali* (Pan) 1969–77. Renamed *Gautari* (Pan) 1977–78 (same owners). The Africa Shipping Co. S.A. declared bankrupt 26/5/1978 and *Gautari* transferred to Talihai Shipping Co. Ltd., Hong Kong (subsidiary of Kie Hock Shipping (1971) Ltd.) 1978 and renamed *Talihai* (Honduras) 1978. Broken up near Bangkok, Thailand, 12/1978.

To replace the **Wingatui** *in the New Zealand east coast service, the company built the 3363 ton* **Waiana** *in 1937. Her 29 years with the company was marred by only one major incident when she ran aground at French Pass on 5 June 1958. Considerable bottom damage resulted and repairs included the renewal of 27 hull plates*

In the pre-war years the Union Company always came under considerable pressure from the seafaring trade unions to employ New Zealand seafarers on all its ships. The company contended that it could not afford New Zealand crews on competitive international services and always managed to 'flag out' the ships employed on the service to India. In 1937 it purchased the 5348 ton motorship **Tolten** *from Scottish shipbuilder Lithgows and ran her with a foreign crew, but placed the ship under the nominal ownership and management of Trinder Anderson and Company of London to avoid union problems! She was sold five years later*   E. FLUCK

| **WAIANA** | **3363 GRT** | **IN FLEET 1937–1966** |

BUILT: 1937 by A. Stephen & Sons Ltd., Linthouse, Glasgow.

SUBSEQUENT HISTORY: Sold Intertrader Shipping Co. S.A., Panama 1966 and renamed *Express Trader* (Panama) 1966–69. Sold Welfare Navigation Inc., Taipeh, 1969 and renamed *Welfare* (Panama) 1969. Mined by Viet Cong guerilla forces 6/7/1969 while anchored in Nha Be river, 8 miles south east of Saigon. Sunk same day about 1.5 miles down river.

| **TOLTEN** | **5348 GRT** | **IN FLEET 1937–1942** |

BUILT: 1930 by Lithgows Ltd., Port Glasgow, for Compania Sud Americana de Vapores, Valparaiso, but repossessed by Lithgows Ltd., 1932–33.

PREVIOUS OWNERS: Transferred to Glen Line Ltd., Liverpool, (Lowden, Connell & Co. Ltd., London, Mgrs) 1933 and renamed *Glenearn* (Br) 1933–35. Reverted to *Tolten* (Br) 1935 under ownership Lithgows Ltd., Port Glasgow, (Lowden, Connell & Co. Ltd., London, Mgrs) 1935–37.

SUBSEQUENT HISTORY: (While under Union Company, Trinder, Anderson & Co. Ltd., London was registered nominal owner and vessel ran under charter to Indo-Pacific Shipping Co. Ltd., London.) Sold South American Saint Line Ltd., Cardiff, 1942–50 and renamed *St. Merriel* (Br) 1945–50. Sold A/B Oceanfart (B. Krogius, Mgr) Helsingfors and renamed *Helios* (Finland) 1950–59. Sold Santa Irini Shipping Co. Ltd., Beirut, and renamed *Tassos* (Lebanon) 1959–67. Sold Leung Yau Shipbreaking Co., Hong Kong, and arrived Hong Kong for demolition 14/4/1967.

| **KAKAPO** | **2498 GRT** | **IN FLEET 1937–1960** |

BUILT: 1937 by A. Stephen & Sons Ltd., Linthouse, Glasgow.

SUBSEQUENT HISTORY: Sold Cia de Nav Victoria Neptuno S.A., Panama (Teh Hu Steamship Co. Ltd., Hong Kong, Mgrs) 1960–64 (same name). Transferred Teh Hu Steamship Co. Ltd., Hong Kong, 1964 and renamed *Teh Ping* (Taiwan) 1964–70. Sailed Hong Kong, 21/10/1970 for Keelung and subsequently broken up in Taiwan 1970.

◀ *Built as a replacement ship for the* **Kanna** *for operation on the New Zealand coast, the 2498 ton* **Kakapo** *was launched at Govan, Glasgow, in 1937 by Mrs W.J. Jordan, wife of the New Zealand High Commissioner in London. Her comments attracted considerable attention in the British press when she concluded the traditional launching phrase with the comment in Maori, "Haere ra te moana pai waka" (Go in peace over the ocean, good ship).* **Kakapo** *did prove to be a successful vessel and was finally sold out of the fleet in 1960*   J.Y. FREEMAN

Following the loss of the **Kakariki** *in 1937, the company quickly ordered a replacement vessel. This was the twin screw motor ship* **Kahika** *which entered the Tasmanian ore trade in June 1938. Less than two years later, she struck an uncharted rock off West Point, Tasmania and sank within five minutes*

Wanaka *was built in 1938 for the New South Wales – Tasmanian trade. In 1942 she was fitted out as an aircraft tender for the Royal Australian Air Force carrying armed forces personnel and supplies to forward areas of combat in the Pacific. On 15 December 1943 during cyclonic conditions the ship ploughed into Eden Reef off the Queensland coast with the loss of 10 lives. The salvaging of the ship was one of the most difficult then attempted in Australia but she was successfully refloated and following her return to peace time service in 1946 she remained with the Union Company for a further 19 years* E.M. HUMPHERY

Not all the new tonnage built in the late 1930s was powered by diesel engines and the 2525 ton **Korowai** *was equipped with triple expansion steam engines powered by coal. She entered service in August 1938 and apart from a fire in Auckland in August 1944, she had a nondescript 27 years with the Union Company. It was the* **Korowai** *that became the first vessel to berth at Mount Maunganui wharf on 5 December 1954 – the start of a port that has subsequently become one of the largest in the country* BAIN-WRIGHT COLLECTION

KAHIKA   1537 GRT   IN FLEET 1938–1940

BUILT: 1938 by Henry Robb Ltd., Leith.

SUBSEQUENT HISTORY: Struck an uncharted rock and foundered off West Point, near Marrawah, Tasmania, 16/3/1940 on passage Strahan to Melbourne.

WANAKA   2259 GRT   IN FLEET 1938–1965

BUILT: 1938 by A. Stephen & Sons Ltd., Linthouse, Glasgow.

SUBSEQUENT HISTORY: Sold Letsena Navigation Inc., Monrovia, 1965 and renamed *Pater Elias* (Liberia) 1965–67. Sold Nansei Kensetsu G.K., Naha, Okinawa, 1967 and renamed *Tainan Maru* (Japan) 1967–68. Broken up at Kaohsiung 1968.

KOROWAI   2525 GRT   IN FLEET 1938–1965

BUILT: 1938 by A. Stephen & Sons Ltd., Linthouse, Glasgow.

SUBSEQUENT HISTORY: Sold Timor Navigation Corp. S.A., Panama, 1965 and renamed *Ermera* (Pan) 1965–69. Laid up Hong Kong from 22/11/1969. Sold Mollers Ltd., Hong Kong, for demolition with work commencing Hong Kong, 3/1970.

The Union Company never ceased to experiment with new developments in ship design and machinery. The 4282 ton steamer **Waipori** *built in 1938 had an Isherwood Arcform hull. This hull form had a bulge outwards along the hull which was designed to increase the carrying capacity without requiring more powerful engines. With a deadweight capacity of 6000 tons,* **Waipori** *was for many years the largest cargo carrier on the Trans Tasman service. The rounded hull caused excessive rolling and in later years, rolling chocks were fitted. She was a familiar sight around the main New Zealand ports for 27 years* BAIN-WRIGHT COLLECTION

Komata *was slightly smaller than the* **Waipori** *but also had an Arcform hull. She ran aground just after leaving Glasgow and was delayed five weeks while new hull plates were fitted. Her life with the Union Company was short. While waiting to load phosphate rock at Nauru Island on 8 December 1940 she was attacked and sunk by the German commerce raider* **Komet** *(Ship 45)* HARRAWAY COLLECTION, HOCKEN LIBRARY

The third vessel with an Arcform hull was the 3900 ton **Kurow**, *an identical sister ship to the* **Komata**. *They were both coal-burning single screw steamers with a deadweight capacity of 4500 tons. She had an uneventful 26 years with the Union Company*

WAIPORI   4282 GRT   IN FLEET 1938–1965

BUILT: 1938 by R. & W. Hawthorn, Leslie & Co. Ltd., Hebburn, Newcastle-on-Tyne.

SUBSEQUENT HISTORY: Sold Australia Pacific Shipping Co. (H.K.) Ltd., Hong Kong, (Jas. Lee, Mgr) 1965 and renamed *Pacific Mariner* (Hong Kong) 1965–67. Transferred Kimberley Shipping Corp. S.A., Panama 1967–69 (same name/mgrs but Panamanian registry). Sold Ming Kee & Co., Hong Kong shipbreakers, and broken up Hong Kong, 1969.

KOMATA   3900 GRT   IN FLEET 1938–1940

BUILT: 1938 by A. Stephen & Sons Ltd., Linthouse, Glasgow.

SUBSEQUENT HISTORY: Sunk off Nauru Island, by gunfire from German raider *Komet* (Ship 45) 8/12/1940. Arrived in ballast, from Auckland, 2 days previously, to load phosphate.

KUROW   3900 GRT   IN FLEET 1939–1965

BUILT: 1939 by A.Stephen & Sons Ltd., Linthouse, Glasgow.

SUBSEQUENT HISTORY: Sold Norse Shipping Co. S.A. Panama (Chinido Shipping & Trading Co. Ltd., Hong Kong, Mgrs) 1965 and renamed *Norse Transporter* (Pan) 1965–68. Sold Borneo Korea Lines S.A., Panama, 1968 and renamed *Bintang Borneo* (Pan) 1968–69. Sold Leung Yau Shipbreaking Co., Hong Kong, and arrived Hong Kong for demolition 14/12/1969.

146   *Union Fleet*

KARITANE　　2534 GRT　　IN FLEET 1939–1965

BUILT: 1939 by Henry Robb Ltd., Leith.

SUBSEQUENT HISTORY: Sold Kinabatangan Shipping Co. Ltd., Hong Kong, 1965 and renamed *Good Philippine Anchorage* (Hong Kong), 1965–66. Sold Century Shipping Lines S.A., Panama, 1966 (same name but Panamanian registry). Renamed *Amaria* (Pan) 1968–70 (same owners) Renamed *Unistar One* (Pan) 1970 (same owners). Sold Haisen Nav. Co. S.A., Panama, 1970 (same name). Sold Lee Sing & Co., shipbreakers, and broken up Hong Kong, 1970.

◀ *Karitane was the last in a series of cargo ships built for the Union Company prior to the outbreak of World War 2. The 2534-ton twin screw vessel was the only motorship in the fleet with steam winches. It was believed they would be more reliable when using grabs to discharge bulk cargoes. Between 1941 and 1943 she was requisitioned for war service in the Pacific and in 1952 she was specially fitted out for the carriage of bulk grain. She was 26 years with the Union Company and proved a very useful cargo handler*　BAIN-WRIGHT COLLECTION

UNDERWOOD　　1990 GRT　　IN FLEET 1941–1944

BUILT: 1941 by Henry Robb Ltd., Leith. (Originally ordered by Captain A.F. Watchlin and intended to be named *Port Underwood*).

SUBSEQUENT HISTORY: Requisitioned by British Ministry of War Transport on completion. (J.T. Duncan & Co. Ltd., Cardiff, Mgrs) 1941–44. Torpedoed and sunk by E boat in western approaches to English Channel 6/1/1944 (49.57N – 05.28W) on passage from the Clyde to a south coast port.

◀ *The 1990 ton* **Underwood** *was built during World War 2. Although ordered for Captain A.F. Watchlin, the Union Company was supervising and funding the vessel. She had two long open holds, designed for carrying long poles across the Tasman. They were also useful for the shipment of heavy war equipment and she was immediately requisitioned on completion for coastal service around the United Kingdom. She was lost in 1944 and of her crew of 22, only eight survived*　NATIONAL MARITIME MUSEUM

NGAKUTA　　1775 GRT　　IN FLEET 1942–1952

BUILT: 1913 by Smith's Dock Co. Ltd., Middlesbrough.

PREVIOUS OWNERS: Blackball Coal Co. Ltd., London, 1913–23. Mann, George & Co. Ltd., London, 1923–27 on behalf of Union Company. Blackball Coal Mines Pty. Ltd., Wellington, 1927–42. (Union Company subsidiary); (under charter to Union Company 1922–42).

SUBSEQUENT HISTORY: Sold Captain J.S. Costello, Sydney, on behalf of Japanese shipbreakers. Sailed Sydney 23/7/1952 in tow of *Wan Yiu* and arrived Tokyo for demolition 30/11/1952.

◀ *From 1922 the Union Company had chartered the Blackball Coal Company colliers and in 1942 the two remaining vessels were purchased outright by the company.* **Ngakuta** *dated from 1913 and was on the New Zealand coast for 39 years. Although designed and equipped as a collier,* **Ngakuta** *was integrated into Union Company requirements and on occasions carried other cargoes, including fruit from Pacific Island ports*　E. FLUCK

The other Blackball Coal Company collier was the smaller **Ngatoro,** which had arrived in New Zealand on her completion in 1910. Both ships were equipped with flying derricks suitable for transferring coal bunkers to larger vessels. Following the charter of **Ngatoro** in 1922, she was sent to Australia on a number of occasions and spent most of her working life operating between Tasmanian ports and the Australian mainland. She was finally disposed of in 1949

Kaimanawa *was similar in design to* **Karitane** *but was a single screw steamer. She was completed in 1944 but was requisitioned for war service maintaining supplies to the armies in Europe and she did not arrive in New Zealand until 1946. She was one of the first ships on the New Zealand coast with steel hatch covers*

Launched by Lady Freyberg on 10 October 1945 at the Leith shipyard of Henry Robb Ltd, the 925 ton motorship **Kanna** *had been originally laid down as a supply ship for service in South East Asia. Instead, she came to New Zealand and spent 21 years on the coastal service between the North and South Islands*

BAIN-WRIGHT COLLECTION

NGATORO — 1140 GRT — IN FLEET 1942–1949

BUILT: 1910 by A. Rodger & Co., Port Glasgow.

PREVIOUS OWNERS: Blackball Coal Co. Ltd., London, 1910–23. Mann, George & Co. Ltd., London, 1923–27 on behalf of Union Company. Blackball Coal Mines Pty. Ltd., Wellington, 1927–42. (Union Company subsidiary); (under charter to Union Company 1922–42).

SUBSEQUENT HISTORY: Sold Madrigal Shipping Co. Inc., Manila, 1949 and renamed *Aeolus* (Phil) 1949–68. Converted to lumber barge 1968 (same owners). Sold Leung Yau Shipbreaking Co., Hong Kong and demolition commenced Hong Kong, 7/1973.

KAIMANAWA — 2577 GRT — IN FLEET 1944–1966

BUILT: 1944 by Henry Robb Ltd., Leith for Union Company.

SUBSEQUENT HISTORY: Requisitioned by British Ministry of War Transport (General Steam Navigation Co. Ltd., London, Mgrs) 1944–46. Sold Madrigal Shipping Co. Inc., Manila, 1966 and renamed *Rosa Anna* (Phil) 1966–67. Grounded on Sibuyan Island, Philippine Islands, 15/1/1967 and subsequently declared constructive total loss. Wreck sold Wo Hing & Co., Hong Kong, shipbreakers and broken up Hong Kong, 1967.

KANNA — 925 GRT — IN FLEET 1946–1967

BUILT: 1946 by Henry Robb Ltd., Leith.(Originally ordered by British Admiralty as supply ship for South East Asia).

SUBSEQUENT HISTORY: Sold Compania Naviera La Luna S.A., Panama (Heap Seng Trading Co, Singapore, Mgrs) 1967 and renamed *Luna Marina* (Pan) 1967–81. Sold Apollo Shipping & Trading Sdn. Bhd., Kuching, 1979–81 (same name but Malaysian registry). Renamed *Seng Giap* (Malaysia) 1981–83 and owners Apollo Agencies (1980) Sdn. Bhd., Kuching. Ran aground Tanjong Batu 30/12/1983 (2.01N – 109.39E) on passage Sibu to Singapore and became total loss.

150   Union Fleet

An identical sister ship to the **Kanna**, *the* **Katui** *arrived in New Zealand shortly after* **Kanna** *in 1946. She spent most of her 21 years on the coast in the service between Auckland and Dunedin until replaced by a roll-on, roll-off vessel in 1967. In 1950 the company was complaining about the cargo handling practices which saw a small ship like* **Katui** *taking seven weeks for a round voyage. At the time of the 1951 Waterfront Strike she spent 10 weeks idle in Dunedin and the local cartoonist described her as 'Dunedin's newest suburb'*   I.J. FARQUHAR

| KATUI | 925 GRT | IN FLEET 1946–1967 |

BUILT: 1946 by Henry Robb Ltd., Leith.(Originally ordered by British Admiralty as supply ship for South East Asia).

SUBSEQUENT HISTORY: Sold Islander Navigation Corp. S.A., Panama (Unique Shipping & Trading Co. Ltd., Singapore, Mgrs) 1967 and renamed *Cindee* (Pan) 1967–74. Delivered 8/1968 on long term hire purchase to P.T. Perusahaan Pelayaran Nusantara 'Bahari Bahtera', Djakarta. Paid off 5/1974 and renamed *Banang* (Indonesia) 1974–78. Sold Yoga Tigris, Medan, 1978 (same name). Ownership transferred to P.T. Perusahaan Pelayaran Nusantara 'Nagah Berlian', Indonesia, 1980–84 (same name). Broken up 4/1984 at Kosambi I Clilincing, Tanjong Priok, Jakarta.

| WAITEMATA | 7364 GRT | IN FLEET 1946–1967 |

BUILT: 1946 by Burrard Dry Dock Co. Ltd., Vancouver. Launched as *Selsey Bill* 11/7/1945 and intended as naval maintenance ship for Royal Navy. Purchased by Union Line 4/1946 and completed to their design.

SUBSEQUENT HISTORY: Sold Cia. Nav. Pearl S.A., Panama, (Teh Hu Steamship Co. Ltd., Hong Kong, Mgrs) 1967 and renamed *Amelia* (Pan) 1967–73. Sold Taiwan shipbreakers and arrived Kaohsiung for demolition 2/3/1973.

◀ *In order to provide new tonnage for the Trans Pacific cargo service, the Union Company purchased a standard Canadian built 'Victory' type vessel which had been launched as the Royal Navy maintenance ship* **Selsey Bill**. *She was subsequently fitted out to company requirements (which included the provision of accommodation for 16 passengers) and renamed* **Waitemata**. *She was sold in 1967 after only 21 years service as the Union Company had decided to abandon its Pacific Coast cargo service to Australia and New Zealand. She had a lucky escape in October 1961, when hove to in fog off San Francisco, she was rammed by a Norwegian freighter, the* **Hoegh Cape**, *and her bow was very badly damaged.* BAIN-WRIGHT COLLECTION

| HINEMOA | 6911 GRT | IN FLEET 1946–1967 |

BUILT: 1946 by Vickers-Armstrongs Ltd., Barrow-in-Furness.

SUBSEQUENT HISTORY: Laid up Wellington 23/8/1966. Sold The Hydro-Electric Commission of Tasmania for use as floating power station and accommodation ship at Bell Bay, Tasmania. Renamed *George H Evans* and sailed Wellington 25/10/1967. Permanently moored Bell Bay 30/10/1967. Sold Hamersley Iron Ore Co. Ltd. 1969 for use as floating power station at Dampier, West Australia. Towed Bell Bay to Dampier by tug *Tusker* 7/4/1969–8/5/1969. Sold Fuji Marden & Co. Ltd., Hong Kong, for demolition and towed to Hong Kong by tug *Salvonia* 12/2/1971–19/3/1971.

◀ *Built as a replacement for the ageing* **Wahine** *and the standby vessel* **Maori**, *the interisland express steamer* **Hinemoa**, *which arrived in New Zealand in February 1947 had a more utilitarian look about her than the graceful lines of her predecessors. The 6911-ton vessel made 22 knots on trials, so she had no difficulty maintaining the steamer express schedules. She had one class accommodation for 740 passengers as well as space for 62 cars. She remained in service for 21 years until new roll-on, roll-off methods made her obsolete and she subsequently saw service as a floating power station at both Bell Bay, Tasmania and Dampier, Western Australia before being scrapped in Hong Kong in 1971. Her turbo-electric generators provided 10,000 kilowatts of power*

152   *Union Fleet*

WAIKAWA 7185 GRT IN FLEET 1946–1959

BUILT: 1944 by The West Coast Shipbuilders Ltd., Vancouver as *Parkdale Park* 1944–46.

PREVIOUS OWNERS: Canadian Government, (Park Steam Ship Co. Ltd., Montreal, Mgrs)1944–46.

SUBSEQUENT HISTORY: Registered to Canadian – Australasian Line Ltd., Montreal, (Union Company, Mgrs) 1946–47, Canadian-Union Line Ltd., Vancouver (Union Company, Mgrs) 1947–50, Wellington 1950–59. Laid up Vancouver 8/12/1958. Sold Marine Development & Supply Co. S.A., Panama and registered to Fulda Marine Corporation, Panama (Marine Industry Corp. Ltd., Mgrs) 1959 and renamed *Fulda* (Pan) 1960–68. Sold World Marine Transportation Corp., Panama 1968–69 (same name). Sold Korean shipbreakers and arrived Pusan for demolition 10/5/1969.

◀ In 1946 the Union Company purchased four 7200-ton Canadian-built standard 'Victory' cargo ships known as the North Sands type. All were originally in the ownership of the Canadian-Australasian Line and later the Canadian Union Line but were managed throughout by the Union Company. The **Parkdale Park** was renamed **Waikawa** and she commenced a monthly service between Vancouver, San Francisco (and some intermediate West Coast timber ports) to the main New Zealand ports, Sydney and Melbourne in 1946. She was sold in 1959 after being laid up in Vancouver for 10 months   BAIN-WRIGHT COLLECTION

WAITOMO 7209 GRT IN FLEET 1946–1963

BUILT: 1944 by The West Coast Shipbuilders Ltd., Vancouver as *Sunnyside Park* 1944–46.

PREVIOUS OWNERS: Canadian Government (Park Steam Ship Co. Ltd., Montreal, Mgrs) 1944–46.

SUBSEQUENT HISTORY: Registered to Canadian-Australasian Line Ltd., Montreal, (Union Company, Mgrs) 1946–47, Canadian-Union Line Ltd., Vancouver (Union Company, Mgrs) 1947–50, Wellington 1950–61. Union Steam Ship Co. of N.Z. Ltd., Wellington 1961–63. Laid up Vancouver 29/12/1962. Sold Blue Shark Steamship Co. S.A., Panama 1963 and renamed *Blue Shark* (Pan) 1963–67. Sold Taiwan shipbreakers and arrived Kaohsiung for demolition 4/2/1967.

◀ Another of the Canadian-built ships was the **Sunnyside Park**, renamed **Waitomo**. She was in the Pacific Coast service for 17 years. She caused some excitement on 16 October 1960 when she ran aground on Seaward Reef, in the approaches to Apia, Samoa and was not refloated until 20 October. The Union Company's **Tofua** succeeded in towing her clear off the reef and she was able to continue her voyage until permanent repairs were effected some months later
BAIN-WRIGHT COLLECTION

WAIRUNA 7212 GRT IN FLEET 1946–1960

BUILT: 1944 by The Victoria Machinery Depot Co. Ltd., Victoria, B.C. as *Salt Lake Park* 1944–46.

PREVIOUS OWNERS: Canadian Government (Park Steam Ship Co. Ltd., Montreal, Mgrs) 1944–46.

SUBSEQUENT HISTORY: Registered to Canadian-Australasian Line Ltd., Montreal (Union Company, Mgrs) 1946–47, Canadian-Union Line Ltd., (Union Company, Mgrs) Vancouver 1947–50, Wellington, 1950–60. Laid up Auckland, 22/10/1958. Sold Marine Development & Supply Co. S.A., Panama and renamed *Bonna* (Pan) 1960–66. Sold Hongfahlee Navigation Co. Inc., Panama, 1966–69 (same name). Sold Taiwan shipbreakers and sailed Yawata 15/12/1968 for Kaohsiung and broken up 1969.

◀ The class of Canadian-built ships was hardly suitable for the types of lumber cargoes which formed the main southbound cargo from Pacific coast ports and the stevedoring was very labour-intensive. Competition from smaller, more modern ships cut into their cargo volumes. The **Wairuna**, formerly **Salt Lake Park**, was finally laid up at Auckland through lack of cargo in 1958. She was later shifted in 1959 to Shoal Bay, off Chelsea and was the largest vessel to go under the Auckland Harbour bridge. She was sold in 1960. The illustration shows **Wairuna** arriving at Auckland with a full deck load of lumber

154   Union Fleet

The fourth Canadian built ship was the **Dominion Park** *which became the* **Waihemo**. *She lasted for 20 years and then saw service for another 12 years under Philippine owners before being sold for demolition in 1972*
BAIN-WRIGHT COLLECTION

| **WAIHEMO** | **7189 GRT** | **IN FLEET 1946–1966** |

BUILT: 1944 by The West Coast Shipbuilders Ltd., Vancouver. Laid down as *Fort Mackinac* but completed as *Dominion Park* 1944–46.

PREVIOUS OWNERS: Canadian Government (Park Steam Ship Co. Ltd., Montreal, Mgrs) 1944–46.

SUBSEQUENT HISTORY: Registered to Canadian-Australasian Line Ltd., Montreal (Union Line, Mgrs) 1946–47, Canadian-Union Line (Union Line, Mgrs) Vancouver 1947–50, Wellington 1950–61. Union Steam Ship Company of N.Z. Ltd., Wellington 1961–66. Sold Pacific Trading & Navigation Ltd., Manila, (Madrigal & Co.Inc, Manila, Mgrs) 1966 and renamed *Maria Susana* (Pan) 1966–72. Transferred Pac-Trade Nav. Co. S.A., Panama, 1968–72 (same name/same mgrs). Sold Taiwan shipbreakers and arrived Kaohsiung for demolition 27/5/1972.

| **KAMO** | **1450 GRT** | **IN FLEET 1947–1958** |

BUILT: 1944 by Rickmers Werft, Wesermunde as minelayer *Gaarden* for German Navy 1944–45.

PREVIOUS OWNERS: Taken by British Government as war reparation 1945–46. New Zealand Government 1946–47.

SUBSEQUENT HISTORY: Laid up Sydney 23/4/1957. Sold Sunning Trading Corp, Panama 1958 and renamed *Sunning* (Pan) 1958–61. Sold Chip Hong Nav. Co. Ltd., (K.L. Chung, Hong Kong, Mgr) 1961 (same name). Sprang leak and foundered 31/12/1961 (8.10N – 116.26E) on passage Kaohsiung to Singapore.

◀ *Under the Allied Reparations Agency at the end of World War 2, there was 800,000 tons of merchant shipping available for distribution to allied countries. New Zealand qualified for 0.14% of this and the vessel secured was the former German minelayer* **Gaarden** *built in 1943–44. She was renamed* **Kamo** *and arrived in New Zealand in August 1947 and in her ten years service with the Union Company she was mainly employed in Australian waters. A noteworthy feature of the ship was her twin rudders, which with her twin screw propulsion, enabled her to make a full turn in a 600 foot circle* M.A.BARTLETT

| **WAIRATA** | **5255 GRT** | **IN FLEET 1947–1967** |

BUILT: 1943 by Pennsylvania Shipyards Inc., Beaumont, Texas as *Cape Igvak* 1943–47.

PREVIOUS OWNERS: United States War Shipping Administration. (Marine Transport Lines, Beaumont, Mgrs 1943–46, Grace Line Inc, New York, Mgrs 1946–47, Parry Navigation Co. Inc., Seattle, Mgrs 1947).

SUBSEQUENT HISTORY: Sold Ta Teh Steamship Co. S.A., Panama, (Tung Lee Navigation Co. Ltd., Hong Kong, Mgrs) 1967 and renamed *Successful Day* (Pan) 1967–72. Sold Taiwan shipbreakers and arrived Kaohsiung for demolition 6/8/1972.

◀ *In 1947 the Union Company purchased the 5255-ton freigher* **Cape Igvak** *from the United States Maritime Commission as a suitable vessel for the service to Indian and other eastern ports. She was one of a standard class of 65 war-built vessels known as the C1-A type. She was an all welded vessel, with diesel engines connected by electro magnetic couplings, which improved manoeuvrability within confined spaces. She had a service speed of 14 knots. Renamed* **Wairata,** *she spent 20 years on the Eastern service* BAIN-WRIGHT COLLECTION

The first of a series of 5300-ton deadweight freighters for the Trans Tasman service, **Komata** *entered service in July 1947. A modern upgrade of the larger pre-war class, her features included glassed in winch houses. She had an uneventful 30 years with the Union Company with the exception of a collision with the freighter* **Broompark** *in Auckland on 10 June 1949 and again in March 1965 when she briefly ran onto rocks at Owhiro Bay at the entrance to Wellington Harbour. The resourcefulness of crew members was also tested in April 1964 when three officers and a stockman were needed to deliver a foal from a mare which had been shipped on board for the passage to Australia gave birth on the deck of the vessel*

I.J. FARQUHAR

The other tug, **Empire Shirley,** *was renamed* **Tapuhi** *(meaning 'to nurse') and she was active in Wellington Harbour for 25 years before being sold to Fiji owners. She was later employed in salvaging fuel and equipment from the wreck of the* **President Coolidge** *at Espiritu Santo and after lying idle for 12 years at Santo, she was scuttled there in 1990*

BAIN-WRIGHT COLLECTION

| KOMATA | 3543 GRT | IN FLEET 1947–1967 |

BUILT: 1947 by A. Stephen & Sons Ltd., Linthouse, Glasgow.

SUBSEQUENT HISTORY: Sold San Miguel Navigation Co. S.A., Panama, (John Manners & Co. Ltd., Hong Kong, Mgrs) 1967 and renamed *Antonia Regidor* (Pan) 1967. Sold Cheh An Navigation Co. S.A. Panama (New Taiwan Marine Transportation Co. Ltd., Keelung, Mgrs) 1967 and renamed *Glory No 2* (Pan) 1967–72. Sold An Lee Navigation Co. Pte. Ltd., Singapore, (Chip Seng & Co. Pte. Ltd., Singapore, Mgrs) 1972 and renamed *An Fu* (Singapore) 1972–77. Sold Kai Fa Navigation Co S.A., Panama 1977 and renamed *Ford* (Pan) 1977. Sold Taiwan shipbreakers and arrived Kaohsiung for demolition 29/12/1977.

| TAIOMA | 232 GRT | IN FLEET 1947–1975 |

BUILT: 1944 by A. Hall & Co., Aberdeen as *Empire Jane*, 1944–48.

PREVIOUS OWNERS: British Ministry of War Transport, 1944–46. Ministry of Transport, 1946–47 (France, Fenwick, Tyne & Wear Co. Ltd., Newcastle, Mgrs) 1944– 47. (Not renamed *Taioma* until 1948).

SUBSEQUENT HISTORY: Sold B.P. New Zealand Ltd., Wellington, 1975 and subsequently registered to B.P. subsidiary, Development Services Ltd., Wellington, 1975–78 (same name)(Union Company, Mgrs 1975–78). Sold Robert A. Owens, Tauranga, 1978. Towed Wellington to Tauranga and placed in permanent position as maritime museum, Tauranga, 8/7/1978. Officially opened as museum 23/7/1979. Due to deteriorating condition, vessel removed from museum status on shore, refloated and scuttled as wreck dive off Motiti Island, near Mount Maunganui 19/3/2000 in position 37.39S, 176.25.4E.

◄ *In 1947 the Union Company purchased two former naval tugs as replacements for the elderly Wellington harbour tugs* **Natone** *and* **Terawhiti.** *They travelled in tandem to New Zealand in October 1947.* **Empire Jane** *was renamed* **Taioma** *meaning 'sweet waters'. She was sold in 1975 but three years later, Tauranga businessman Robert Owens purchased* **Taioma** *and donated her as an exhibit to the Tauranga Historic Village/Museum*   BAIN-WRIGHT COLLECTION

| TAPUHI | 232 GRT | IN FLEET 1947–1973 |

BUILT: 1945 by A. Hall & Co., Aberdeen, as *Empire Shirley*, 1945–47.

PREVIOUS OWNERS: British Ministry of War Transport, 1944–46. Ministry of Transport, 1946–47. (Townsend Bros. (Ferries) Ltd., London, Mgrs) 1945–47. (Not renamed *Tapuhi* until 1948).

SUBSEQUENT HISTORY: Sold Narain Shipping Limited, Suva 1973 and renamed *Tui Tawate* (Fiji) 1973–74, *Tui Tuate* (Fiji) 1974–90. Sold Salvage Pacific Ltd., Fiji, 1976–77 (same name). Sold Reece Discombe, Port Vila 1977 and vessel subsequently beached at Santo, Vanuatu 1978. Raised 1990 and sunk in Segond Channel between Santo and Aore (15.32 N, 167.08E) 16/5/1990.

158 *Union Fleet*

| KOROMIKO | 3552 GRT | IN FLEET 1947–1967 |

BUILT: 1947 by A. Stephen & Sons Ltd., Glasgow.

SUBSEQUENT HISTORY: Sold San Jeronimo Steamship Co. S.A., Panama (John Manners & Co. Ltd., Hong Kong, Mgrs) 1967 and renamed *Jose Regidor* (Pan) 1967–69. Sold on hire purchase to Jaguar Shipping Corp. Ltd., Hong Kong & Singapore 1969 and renamed *New Cronulla* (Pan) 1969–72 (Singapore) 1972–75. Went aground about 100 miles from Khulna, Bangladesh 31/12/1974 (21.34N – 89.45E) on passage Philippines to Chalna. Abandoned 9/1/1975 lying as visible wreck 21.35N – 89.35E.

◀ The second of the 5300-ton deadweight cargo vessels, often described as the 'slow greens', was the **Koromiko**, which entered the Trans Tasman service in March 1948. In 1952 she and others in her class were converted for carrying bulk grain, particularly wheat. She was in the fleet for 20 years and had a nondescript career apart a collision with the vehicle ferry **Ewen W. Alison** in Auckland harbour on 1 December 1951. Repairs to her hull took over a month to complete

BAIN-WRIGHT COLLECTION

| KOPUA | 1525 GRT | IN FLEET 1947–1959 |

BUILT: 1937 by Henry Robb Ltd., Leith, as *Port Tauranga*.

PREVIOUS OWNERS: Captain A.F. Watchlin, Auckland, 1937–47. (Union Company intended to rename ship *Kawa* but renamed *Kopua* 1948).

SUBSEQUENT HISTORY: Sold Hethking Steamships Pty. Ltd., Sydney (Hetherington, Kingsbury Pty. Ltd., Sydney, Mgrs) 1959 and renamed *Cobargo* (Aust) 1960–73. Sold United Steamships Ltd., Apia 1973 and renamed *Samoan Bay* (Br) 1973–74. Sold Universal Dallas Corp. Inc., Panama, (Log & Timber Products Ltd., Singapore, Mgrs) 1974 and renamed *Universal Dallas* (Pan) 1974–77. Arrived Pontianak 25/1/1976 and subsequently sold for demolition 1977.

◀ In December 1947 the Union Company acquired the remaining interest in the ships registered to the ownership of Captain A.F. Watchlin. One of these was the specialist timber carrier **Port Tauranga**, built in 1937. At that time her 96-foot hatchway was the longest recorded in Lloyd's Register and she was ideal for carrying long poles across the Tasman. The Union Company renamed her **Kopua**. The hull structure had been built on the cantilever principle with arched brackets every 12 feet to give a hold clear of any obstructions. She remained in the company for 22 years

I.J. FARQUHAR

| PORT WAIKATO | 676 GRT | IN FLEET 1947–1959 |

BUILT: 1929 by Henry Robb Ltd., Leith.

PREVIOUS OWNERS: Captain A.F. Watchlin, Auckland, 1929–47.

SUBSEQUENT HISTORY: (The vessel which had been on bareboat charter to Holm & Co. Ltd., Wellington from December 1940 for the Chatham Islands trade remained in this service, under charter to 1958). Sold Lanena Shipping Co. Ltd., Hong Kong, 1959 and sailed Wellington 12/2/1959 in tow of tug *Inglis*. Broken up Hong Kong, 1961.

◀ The other Watchlin vessel was the **Port Waikato** but she was not renamed, as from 1940, she had been on bareboat charter to Holm Shipping Company of Wellington. It employed her on the Chatham Islands service until 1958. Her service to the Chathams was not without incident. In November 1944 and again in February 1946, the Wellington tug **Toia** was sent to tow the vessel back, owing to broken intermediate shafts and in May 1948 she got a wire rope around her propeller and had to be towed back to Wellington by the **Kamo**. Ten years later she broke down on the passage and was towed to Lyttelton by HMNZS **Kaniere**. On 6 August 1954 she grounded near Ohau Point causing damage to her bottom plates. The illustration shows her in Holm Shipping colours BAIN-WRIGHT COLLECTION

The 6796-ton **Wairimu** *was the second ship purchased from the United States Maritime Commission. She was one of a class of 95 C1 – B standard ships and was built in 1941 as* **Cape Alava**. *Eighty-five of the class were steam powered with the remaining 10 diesel driven and* **Wairimu** *was one of the motor ships. She remained with the Union Company for 18 years and ran on the Indian and Singapore service with* **Wairata** BAIN-WRIGHT COLLECTION

Kaitoke *was the third of the 5300-ton deadweight ships built by Alexander Stephen & Sons on the Clyde. She entered service in November 1948 and for the next 24 years she remained on the Tasman services apart from a voyage to India and Singapore in 1951. She had an aversion to entering the port of Timaru as in January 1955 she grounded at the end of the harbour and in May 1958 she stuck in the sand in the middle of Caroline Bay* BAIN-WRIGHT COLLECTION

The 2485-ton **Kaitangata** *was the first of six specialist motor ships built for the New Zealand coastal trades. They were very strongly built to cope with the bar conditions at the West Coast ports of Westport and Greymouth.* **Kaitangata** *commenced service in March 1949 and although sold by the company 20 years later, she subsequently operated under various owners in eastern waters for a further 13 years* BAIN-WRIGHT COLLECTION

| WAIRIMU | 6796 GRT | IN FLEET 1948–1966 |

BUILT: 1941 by Seattle-Tacoma Shipbuilding Corp., Tacoma as *Cape Alava* 1941–48.

PREVIOUS OWNERS: Built for American Mail Line but on entry of U.S.A. into World War 2, was taken over by U.S. War Shipping Administration (American Mail Line, Mgrs 1941–1/47, Overlakes S.S. Co. Detroit 1/47–4/47, Sword Line Inc, New York 4/47–6/47, United States Lines Co., New York 6/47–10/47). Laid up James River, Norfolk 10/1947.

SUBSEQUENT HISTORY: Laid up Wellington 20/11/1965. Sold Tung Lee Navigation Co. Ltd., Hong Kong, 1966 and renamed *Ta Tung* (Pan) 1966–69. Transferred Ta Peng Steamship Co. Ltd., Kaohsiung (Ta Lai Steam Ship Co. Ltd., Kaohsiung, Mgrs) 1969 and renamed *Ta Tzong* (1969). Sold Shei Seng Fa Steel & Iron Works Ltd., Kaohsiung, shipbreakers and demolished from 3/1970.

| KAITOKE | 3551 GRT | IN FLEET 1948–1972 |

BUILT: 1948 by A. Stephen & Sons Ltd., Linthouse, Glasgow.

SUBSEQUENT HISTORY: Sold Cronulla Cia. Nav. S.A., Panama 1972 and renamed *Singapore* (Pan) 1972–74. Sold Cia. Nav. Kaohsiung S.A., Panama (Sam U Shipping Co. Ltd., Hong Kong, Mgrs) 1974–75 (same name). Sold Ioansun S.A. Panama (Zea Shipping Ltd., Piraeus, Mgrs) 1975 and renamed *Venus* (Gr) 1975–77, *Mars* (Gr) (same owners) 1977–80. Went aground at Tarifa Point, Spain 20/9/1978 on passage Casablanca to Ravenna and as a result of damage laid up Chalkis, Greece, from 11/11/1978. Sold Greek shipbreakers and arrived Piraeus for demolition 9/11/1980.

| KAITANGATA | 2485 GRT | IN FLEET 1948–1968 |

BUILT: 1948 by Henry Robb Ltd., Leith.

SUBSEQUENT HISTORY: Sold Maritime (Liberia) Inc., Monrovia, (Asafridel (Hong Kong) Ltd., Hong Kong, Mgrs) 1968 and renamed *Paladin* (Liberia) 1968–69, *Karana III* (Liberia) 1969–74. Sold Oportuno Navegacion S.A., Panama (Asia Africa Shipping Co. Ltd., Hong Kong, Mgrs) 1974 and renamed *Tung Pao* (Pan) 1974–78. Sold Syarikat Perkapalan Bersinar Sdn. Bhd., Kuala Lumpur, (Kie Hock Shipping (1971) Pte.Ltd., Singapore, Mgrs) 1978 and renamed *Gembira* (Malaysia) 1978–81. Declared constructive total loss following engine room fire 6/3/1981 while lying off Telukbayur, Padang and sold to Krakatau Steel Company for demolition, arriving Cigading 10/8/1981.

162 *Union Fleet*

KONUI 2485 GRT IN FLEET 1949–1969

BUILT: 1949 by Henry Robb Ltd., Leith.

SUBSEQUENT HISTORY: Sold Express Navigation (Pte.) Ltd.,Singapore, (Unique Shipping & Trading Co. Pte. Ltd., Singapore, Mgrs) 1969 and renamed *Bonatrade* (Singapore) 1969–74. Under Southern Glow Shipping (Pte.) Ltd., Singapore, 1974 (same name/registry). Sold Tung Wo Shipping Co. S.A., Panama, 1974 and renamed *Tung Lee* (Pan) 1974–77. Sold Syarikat Perkapalan Bersinar Sdn. Bhd., Kuala Lumpur, (Kie Hock Shipping (1971) Pte. Ltd., Singapore, Mgrs) 1977–81 (wound up 1978–81), Kie Gwan Shipping (M) Sdn. Bhd., Port Kelang, Mgrs 1981–83, Uni-Ocean Lines Pte. Ltd., Singapore, Mgrs 1983) and renamed *Berjaya* (Malaysia) 1977–83. Sold P.T. Perusahaan Pelayaran Nusantara Nagah Berlian, Indonesia, 1983 (same name). Sold Golden Sea International Co. Ltd., Bangkok, 27/7/1983 and broken up Bangkok 1983.

◀ *The second vessel of the collier series was the* **Konui**, *launched in Scotland by Mary Wootton, Miss New Zealand of 1948. She was commissioned in February 1949 and for the next 20 years became well known around the New Zealand coast. In June 1960 she broke a loading record in Greymouth when 2926 tons of coal was poured into her holds in seven and a half hours. After being sold by the Union Company in 1969 she spent another 14 years in service operating out of Singapore and Malaysia* BAIN-WRIGHT COLLECTION

KAITAWA 2485 GRT IN FLEET 1949–1966

BUILT: 1949 by Henry Robb Ltd., Leith.

SUBSEQUENT HISTORY: Foundered in heavy weather off Pandora Bank about 2.7 miles from Cape Maria van Diemen and 4.9 miles from Cape Reinga, Northland, New Zealand 23/5/1966 on passage Westport to Portland.

◀ **Konui** *was closely followed by* **Kaitawa**. *She was launched in October 1948 and arrived in New Zealand in August 1949. The 2485 ton collier had completed countless voyages from the West Coast with coal when in 1966 she disappeared without trace in heavy weather. It was believed that the ship was swamped in heavy seas off the coast between Cape Maria van Diemen and Cape Reinga on 23 May 1966 with the loss of all 29 officers and crew* BAIN-WRIGHT COLLECTION

KAIAPOI 2485 GRT IN FLEET 1949–1968

BUILT: 1949 by Henry Robb Ltd., Leith.

SUBSEQUENT HISTORY: Sold E-K Litonjua Steamship Co. Inc., Manila, (Litonjua Shipping Co. Inc., Mgrs) 1968 and renamed *Eddie K.L.* (Philippines) 1968–73. Sold Continental Shipbreaking Co. Ltd., Hong Kong, and broken up Junk Bay with demolition commencing 3/1973.

◀ *The fourth of the series of 2485-ton colliers was the* **Kaiapoi,** *which had an unobtrusive 19 years service from 1949 to 1968. She was then sold to Philippine owners and lasted a further five years before being demolished in a Hong Kong scrapyard* BAIN-WRIGHT COLLECTION

Kamona was a 'one-off' type built for the trade between Tasmania and the Australian mainland, mainly carrying pyritic ores from Strahan to Yarraville in Port Phillip Bay, as well as general cargoes out of Tasmanian ports. She entered the fleet in 1949 and was sold for further trading 16 years later

Steamers and Motorships   165

| **KAMONA** | **1785 GRT** | **IN FLEET 1949–1965** |

BUILT: 1949 by Henry Robb Ltd., Leith.

SUBSEQUENT HISTORY: Sold John Manners & Co. (Aust) Pty. Ltd., Sydney, 12/11/1965. Resold 12/11/1965 to Ocean Transport Pty. Ltd., Sydney, (Hetherington, Kingsbury Pty. Ltd., Sydney, Mgrs) and renamed *Harwood* (Aust) 1965–76. Sold Maldives Shipping Ltd., Male, 1976 and renamed *Maldive Express* (Maldive Is) 1976–83. Sold Pakistani shipbreakers and arrived Gadani Beach about 31/10/1983 for demolition.

| **KAWAROA** | **3532 GRT** | **IN FLEET 1950 – 1972** |

BUILT: 1950 by A. Stephen & Sons Ltd., Linthouse, Glasgow.

SUBSEQUENT HISTORY: Sold Karingo Shipping Co. S.A., Panama, (Kie Hock Shipping (1971) Pte. Ltd., Singapore, Mgrs) 1972 and renamed *Tong Soon* (Pan) 1972–78. Owners declared bankrupt 26/5/1978 and vessel sold San Diego Maritime Co. S.A., Panama, 1978 and renamed *Lydia* (Honduras) 1978. Sold Singapore shipbreakers and delivered Jurong for demolition 17/11/1978.

◄ *The fourth in the series of 5300-ton 'slow greens' for the Tasman service was the* **Kawaroa**, *launched in January 1950 and in service by November. Like her earlier sisters, she had three large hatchways with McGregor steel covers and double sets of union purchase gear powered by electric winches at each hatch. There was a 25-ton derrick at No 2. In 1960* **Kawaroa** *became the first ship to discharge cargo at Deep Cove, Doubtful Sound, for the Manapouri hydroelectric power scheme. She brought a complete shipment of earth moving machinery from Melbourne. She was sold to Singapore buyers for further trading in 1972*   BAIN-WRIGHT COLLECTION

| **KAWATIRI** | **2484 GRT** | **IN FLEET 1950 – 1971** |

BUILT: 1950 by Henry Robb Ltd., Leith.

SUBSEQUENT HISTORY: Sold Lineng Enterprises S.A., Panama, (Kie Hock Shipping (1971) Pte. Ltd., Singapore, Mgrs) 1971 and renamed *Kawati* (Panama 1971–76, Malaysia 1976–78). Sold Syarikat Perkapalan Meladju Sdn. Bhd., Kota Kinabalu, (same mgrs) 1976–78. Sold Independent Airlines (Malaysia) Sdn. Bhd., Port Kelang, (Kie Gwan Shipping M Sdn. Bhd., Port Kelang, Mgrs) 1978 and renamed *Hati Senang* (Malaysia) 1978–87. Broken up by Habib Steel Ltd., Chittagong 1987.

◄ *The last in the series of geared colliers, the* **Kawatiri** *arrived on the New Zealand coast in December 1950. The company's experience with the swift-flowing currents of the West Coast rivers over 75 years saw it build a series of very strongly-built vessels with large square rudders, which enabled maximum efficiency to be gained very quickly. The hulls had heavy steel copes along the sides to prevent damage from the constant movement experienced at a river port. The strength and reliability was appreciated by later owners and the* **Kawatiri** *was no exception. Sold in 1971, she was in service out of Singapore until 1987*   BAIN-WRIGHT COLLECTION

▶ On 27 January 1951 the 2437-ton motor ship **Karoon** was launched at the State Dockyard, in Newcastle, Australia. She was one of two ships ordered by the company from Australian ship-builders. The name **Karoon** is aboriginal for 'No 1' and she was employed on the Australian coastal trade. She remained in service for the Union Company until 1968 and then under various owners she operated out of Singapore until 1993. She had two lucky escapes in her Australian career – the first on 23 November 1958 when she collided with the 4500-ton **Warringa** off Eddystone Point in North West Tasmania and then on 8 September 1963 she ran on Corsair Reef at the entrance to Port Phillip Bay. In both cases the damage was easily repairable   J.Y. FREEMAN

WAIMATE 3506 GRT IN FLEET 1951–1972

BUILT: 1951 by Henry Robb Ltd., Leith. (Laid down as *Kurutai* for Union Line).

SUBSEQUENT HISTORY: Sold Eastern Shipping Lines Inc., Manila, (James L. Chongbian, Manila, Mgr) 1972 and renamed *Eastern Planet* (Philippines) 1972–77. Sold Skyluck Steam Ship Co. S.A., Panama, 1977 and reamed *Sky Luck* (Pan) 1977–80. Arrived Hong Kong, 7/2/1979 laden with Vietnamese refugees. Drifted aground on Lamma Island 29/6/1979, after her anchor chain was cut. Seized by Hong Kong authorities and demolition ordered. Refloated 12/4/1980, towed to Junk Bay 14/5/1980 and demolition completed 24/5/1980.

◄ The **Waimate** *was somewhat similar to the 5300-ton class of Trans Tasman traders but she had tween decks in her three holds and was powered by two diesel engines, with electro-magnetic couplings working through reduction gearing driving a single screw. She was the first British-built ship to be fitted with these couplings. She also had a small amount of insulated space and forced draft ventilation in the tween decks for the carriage of fruit. She was designed to be a more versatile vessel, being able to run on the Pacific or Indian services, rather than just the Tasman. Her shorter, cut back funnel and higher poop distinguished her from the other vessels in the series of 5300-tonners. She remained in the fleet from 1951 to 1972. In 1979 she arrived in Hong Kong as the* **Sky Luck,** *laden with Vietnamese refugees and as the authorities refused their entry she lay at anchor for many months until she ran aground and the government eventually ordered her demolition* BAIN-WRIGHT COLLECTION

KAROON 2437 GRT IN FLEET 1951–1968

BUILT: 1951 by New South Wales Government Engineering & Shipbuilding Undertaking, Newcastle, Australia.

SUBSEQUENT HISTORY: Sold The Miller Steamship Co. Pty. Ltd., Sydney, (R. W. Miller & Co. Pty. Ltd., Sydney, Mgrs) 1968 and renamed *Elisa Miller* (Australia) 1968–69, *Lisa Miller* (Australia) 1969–79. Laid up Sydney 1/1978. Sold Southern Navigation Sdn. Bhd., Kuching, 1979 and renamed *Southern Cross* 1979, *Southern Glory* 1979–93 (both Malaysia). Sold Sing Brun Shipping & Trading Ltd., Brunei, (Hsing Weng Shipping (Pte) Ltd., Singapore, Mgrs) 1980–88. Sold Perkapalan Sinwen Marine Sdn. Bhd., Kuala Lumpur, (Jesselton Shipping (Pte.) Ltd., Singapore, Mgrs) 1988–93 (same name). In heavy weather on passage Muara Port to Singapore, vessel developed 12 degreee list and engines became disabled 9/12/1993. Crew abandoned ship and vessel sank 10/12/1993 close to 05.23N–114.41.7E.

KOKIRI 2470 GRT IN FLEET 1951–1968

BUILT: 1951 by Henry Robb Ltd., Leith.

SUBSEQUENT HISTORY: Sold E – K Litonjua Steamship Co. Inc., Manila (Litonjua & Co. Inc., Manila, Mgrs) 1968 and renamed *Junior K.L.* (Philippines) 1968–71. Disappeared without trace in typhoon 'Elaine' on passage Tanjong Mani to Hong Kong. Last reported 5/10/1971 in position 13.00N – 112.46E.

◄ *The sixth ship of the class of colliers,* **Kokiri** *was different in that she was a gearless ship designed to be loaded solely by grabs, shutes and railway wagons and to be discharged by grab cranes. There were two major incidents in her 17 years with the Union Company. On 12 March 1958 when entering Greymouth she ran onto rocks at the end of the breakwater. Although she came off quickly, the repairs required the replacement of 17 hull plates. In the second incident two men were killed when a mystery explosion rocked the forward hold of the vessel as she was arriving at Wellington on 13 March 1965. It was believed a build-up of coal gas caused the explosion* BAIN-WRIGHT COLLECTION

168 Union Fleet

TOFUA   5299 GRT   IN FLEET 1951–1973

BUILT: 1951 by Wm. Denny & Bros. Ltd., Dumbarton.

SUBSEQUENT HISTORY: Sold Khymer Shipping Co. S.A., Panama, (Cheung Ming & Co., Hong Kong, Mgrs) 1973 and renamed *Tack Tai* (Pan) 1973–75. Sold Chinese shipbreakers 19/7/1975 for demolition at Shanghai.

◀ *The last passenger and cargo ship designed and built for the trade to the Pacific Islands was the 5299-ton* **Tofua** *built by Wm. Denny and Bros, Dumbarton in 1951. She had special ventilated spaces for the carriage of fruit and she had accommodation for 73 passengers with allowance for 200 deck passengers on coasting voyages around the islands. She made her maiden voyage from Auckland to Suva, Nukualofa, Vavau, Pago Pago, Apia and Suva on 21 December 1951. In December the following year she carried a record 32,269 cases of bananas to Auckland. She was sold in 1973 and broken up two years later*   MARINE PHOTOS

KURUTAI   3528 GRT   IN FLEET 1952–1972

BUILT: 1952 by A. Stephen & Sons Ltd., Linthouse, Glasgow.

SUBSEQUENT HISTORY: Sold Cronulla Cia. Nav. S.A., Panama, (Jaguar Shipping Corp. Ltd., Hong Kong, Mgrs) 1972 and renamed *New Keelung* (Pan) 1972–74. Sold Cia. Nav. Keelung S.A., Panama, (Sam U Shipping Co. Ltd., Hong Kong, Mgrs) 1974(same name). Sold Hong Kong shipbreaker, Sam Woo & Co., and demolition commenced 5/1978 following arrival Hong Kong, 21/3/1978.

◀ *The 3528-ton motor ship* **Kurutai** *was the fifth ship of the series commenced with the* **Komata** *in 1947. As with the other vessels, she was strongly built and designed for heavy work, with the hull protected by wooden fenders around the stern and heavy steel copes along the sides. The floors of the holds were laid with Australian tallow wood to protect from the wear and tear of steel grabs. The name* **Kurutai** *was a new name for a Union Company vessel. Entering the Tasman trade in September 1952, she remained with the company for 20 years*   UNION COMPANY

KOOTARA   2427 GRT   IN FLEET 1952–1975

BUILT: 1952 by New South Wales Government Engineering & Shipbuilding Undertaking, Newcastle, Australia.

SUBSEQUENT HISTORY: Sold Amigos Navigation Co., Limassol, 1975 and registered to Martrade Shipping Co. Ltd., Limassol, (S.C. Vazeos, Piraeus, Mgr) 1975 and renamed *Sydney* (Cyprus) 1975–80. Sold Ursa Tradeship Ltd., Cyprus (Al Navigation Co. Ltd., Athens, Mgrs) 1980 and renamed *Padma* (Cyprus) 1980. Stranded on Syros Island, Aegean Sea 27/8/1980 after dragging anchor in heavy weather and became constructive total loss on passage Romania to Syros.

◀ *The second of the Australian built colliers,* **Kootara** *(appropriately, an Australian aboriginal name for 'No 2') followed her sister ship* **Karoon** *into service in October 1952. She worked on the Australian coast for 23 years before being sold. She was lost in the Aegean Sea in 1980*   J.Y. FREEMAN

170   Union Fleet

At the launching of the **Kowhai,** *another of the* **Komata** *class, in April 1952, the wind caught the vessel and she was carried up the River Clyde for some distance before tugs brought her under control. She proved a successful cargo carrier, spending all her working life with the Union Company on the Tasman services until she was sold in 1973*

BAIN-WRIGHT COLLECTION

KOWHAI   3528 GRT   IN FLEET 1952–1973

BUILT: 1952 by A. Stephen & Sons Ltd., Linthouse, Glasgow.

SUBSEQUENT HISTORY: Sold Cronulla Cia. Nav. S.A., Panama, (Jaguar Shipping Corp. Ltd., Hong Kong, Mgrs) 1973 and renamed *New Bangkok* (Pan) 1973–74. Transferred Bangkok Maritime Inc., Panama, (Jaguar Shipping Corp. Ltd., Hong Kong, Mgrs) 1974. Sam U. Shipping Co. Ltd., Hong Kong, 1975 and renamed *Hualien* (Pan) 1975–76. Sold Kamsa Cia. Nav. S.A., Panama, (Ventouris Bros, Piraeus, Mgrs) 1976 and renamed *Kleoniko* (Greek) 1976–77. Renamed *Athinoula* (Greek) 1977 (same owners). Laid up Piraeus under arrest from 17/6/1982. Sold Greek shipbreakers and sailed Piraeus 19/3/1986 for demolition at Laurium.

KARAMU   1988 GRT   IN FLEET 1953–1972

BUILT: 1953 by Henry Robb Ltd., Leith.

SUBSEQUENT HISTORY: Sold Guan Guan Shipping (Pte.) Ltd., Singapore, 1972 and renamed *King Luck* (Singapore) 1972–79. Renamed *Tsin Yuen* (Singapore) 1979–84 (same owners). Sold Taiwan shipbreakers and demolished Kaohsiung 10/1984.

◄ *The 1988-ton motorship* **Karamu** *entered service in May 1953. Intended for the coastal trade, she was seen as a general purpose freighter with a 2000-ton deadweight capacity. She was also the first of the "soft nosed" vessels, having a round stem. In 1960 she was fitted with refrigerated capacity to carry frozen cargoes across the Tasman following the withdrawal of the liner* **Monowai**. *She also carried fruit from the Pacific Islands, coal from the West Coast and in 1956 she made a mercy dash to Campbell Island to bring back an injured man. After 19 years with the Union Company she was sold to Singapore owners and spent a further 12 years operating out of that port* BAIN-WRIGHT COLLECTION

WAIMEA   3657 GRT   IN FLEET 1953–1975

BUILT: 1953 by A. Stephen & Sons. Ltd., Linthouse, Glasgow.

SUBSEQUENT HISTORY: Sold Marama Nav. S.A., Panama, (Handel Maats. Oceanhandel N.V., Rotterdam, Mgrs 1975–76, Sealanes N.V., Antwerp, Mgrs 1976–77) and renamed *Arnhem* (Singapore) 1975–77. Sold Kanaris Shipping Co. S.A., Monrovia, (Zoulias Bros & Co., Piraeus, Mgrs) 1976 and renamed *Milos IV* (Greek) 1977–80. Sold Pakistani shipbreakers and arrived Gadani Beach for demolition 13/12/1980.

◄ **Waimea** *was the seventh of the 5300-ton deadweight series and was launched in December 1953. She was fitted out to be employed in the company's regular service from Melbourne to South Island ports and had 14,000 cubic feet of space for refrigerated cargo. It was on this run that she ran aground 9 miles from the entrance to Port Phillip Bay on 4 September 1959 but came off on the following tide. She was sold in 1975* BAIN-WRIGHT COLLECTION

To upgrade the interisland express service, the Union Company returned to shipbuilder Vickers Armstrongs, builders of **Rangatira** *and* **Hinemoa.** *The new ship, however, was built at the Low Walker yard in the Tyne rather than Barrow. She was named* **Maori** *when launched on 27 November 1952 by Princess Margaret and was the first New Zealand – registered ship to be launched by a member of the Royal Family. With a capacity for 966 passengers and 70 to 80 cars, she was the largest vessel to be employed on the Lyttelton-Wellington service to that time. She was also propelled by turbo electric machinery, with a service speed of 21 knots. In 1965 the company decided to convert her to a roll-on, roll-off vessel and she went to Hong Kong where she was fitted with a stern ramp, her two sets of samson posts were removed and a new bow thruster was installed. She was withdrawn from regular running in 1972 and sold for demolition two years later* N.J.KIRBY

In 1955, in anticipation of an upsurge in timber cargoes, the Union Company purchased a six year old specialist timber carrier which they renamed **Kaponga.** *She had two large hatches but her expectations were never realised and although she was sold six years later, she was laid up for much of this time. She also had triple expansion steam engines and her accommodation had to be modified for New Zealand conditions* MARINE PHOTOS

| **MAORI** | **8303 GRT** | **IN FLEET 1953–1974** |

BUILT: 1953 by Vickers-Armstrongs Ltd., Newcastle.

SUBSEQUENT HISTORY: Converted to roll-on, roll-off ferry 1965 by Taikoo Dockyard & Eng. Co. Ltd., Hong Kong, (New GRT 7498). Sold Wiltopps (Asia) Ltd., Hong Kong, 1974 and left Wellington 20/1/1974 in tow of tug *Mariner* for Hong Kong. Resold en route to Yung Tai Steel & Iron Co. Ltd., Taiwan, and arrived Kaohsiung for demolition 6/3/1974. Work commenced 18/4/1974.

| **KAPONGA** | **2772 GRT** | **IN FLEET 1955–1961** |

BUILT: 1949 by Caledon Shipbuilding & Engineering Co. Ltd., Dundee as *Woodland* 1949–55.

PREVIOUS OWNERS: Currie Line Ltd., Leith 1949–55.

SUBSEQUENT HISTORY: Laid up Auckland, 1/4/1958. Sold Hang Fung Shipping & Trading Co. Ltd., Hong Kong, 1961 and renamed *Nam Feng* (Hong Kong) 1961–63. Sold Leecho Steamship Co. S.A., Panama, (Yong & Lee Timber Shipping Co. Ltd., Hong Kong, Mgrs) 1963 and renamed *Empress of Victoria* (Pan) 1963–67. Went aground off Liu Chiu Hsu Island, south of Pescadores 9/8/1967 (23.15N – 119.37E) on passage Sandakan to Kaohsiung and became total loss.

174 *Union Fleet*

NAVUA   1952 GRT   IN FLEET 1955–1971

BUILT: 1955 by Henry Robb Ltd., Leith.

SUBSEQUENT HISTORY: Sold Guan Guan Shipping (Pte). Ltd., Singapore, 1971 and renamed *King Horse* (Singapore) 1971–85. Sold Nan Wah Enterprise, Singapore, 1985 and renamed *Kin Horse 1* (Honduras) 1985. Sold Chinese shipbreakers, Fujian Province, 1985.

◀ Designed as a supplementary fruit carrier in the Pacific Island service, **Navua** entered service in 1955 and was repainted all white for the island service. In 1960 she reverted to the coastal trade and she was again painted with the traditional bronze green hull. On 29 August 1960 she became the first ship to berth at the artificial island harbour at the port of Bluff. She was sold out of the company after only 16 years service, mainly because of changed cargo handling methods, but she ran under Singapore owners for another 14 years   BAIN-WRIGHT COLLECTION

KAWERAU   3698 GRT   IN FLEET 1955–1975

BUILT: 1955 by A. Stephen & Sons Ltd., Linthouse, Glasgow.

SUBSEQUENT HISTORY: Laid up Auckland, 18/8/1975. Sold Imperial Transport Corp., Male, (Maldives Shipping Ltd., Male, Mgrs) 1/10/1975 and renamed *Coral Sea* (Maldive Is) 1975–76. Transferred Panama flag (same owners) and renamed *Imperial Star* (Panama) 1976–84. Sold owners in United Arab Emirates 1984 and renamed *Nafisah* (U.A.E.) 1984. Sold Indian shipbreakers and sailed Port Sudan 22/1/1984 for Bombay.

◀ **Kawerau** was an improved design and the eighth vessel of the **Komata** class to be built by Alexander Stephen in Scotland and the 19th it had built for the Union Company since 1908. Shortly after her arrival in New Zealand she berthed at the new wharf at Mount Maunganui on 3 December 1955, which marked the commencement of that port's great growth in the export of forestry cargoes. She was in the Tasman trade for 20 years   BAIN-WRIGHT COLLECTION

KAIMIRO   3722 GRT   IN FLEET 1956–1975

BUILT: 1956 by A. Stephen & Sons Ltd., Linthouse, Glasgow.

SUBSEQUENT HISTORY: Laid up Auckland, 16/1/1975. Sold Climax Shipping Corporation, Monrovia, (Maldives Shipping Ltd., Male, Mgrs) 26/8/1975 and renamed *Climax Topaz* (Maldive Is.) 1975–76. Transferred Panama flag (same owners/mgrs) 1976. Transferred Maldives Shipping Ltd., Male, 1981 and renamed *Maldive Topaz* (Pan) 1981 (Maldive Is.) 1981–84. Sold Pakistan shipbreakers and arrived Gadani Beach for demolition 5/5/1984.

◀ **Kawerau**'s *sister ship* **Kaimiro** *entered the Tasman service in June 1956. She was also fitted with permanent partial centre line bulkheads for the carriage of bulk grain as well as portable steel slab bulkheads able to be removed when the vessel transferred to another trade. Like her sisters, she was sold before her economic life was over because of the changing cargo patterns. Disposed of in 1975, she had a further nine years life around the Indian Ocean before being scrapped*   BAIN-WRIGHT COLLECTION

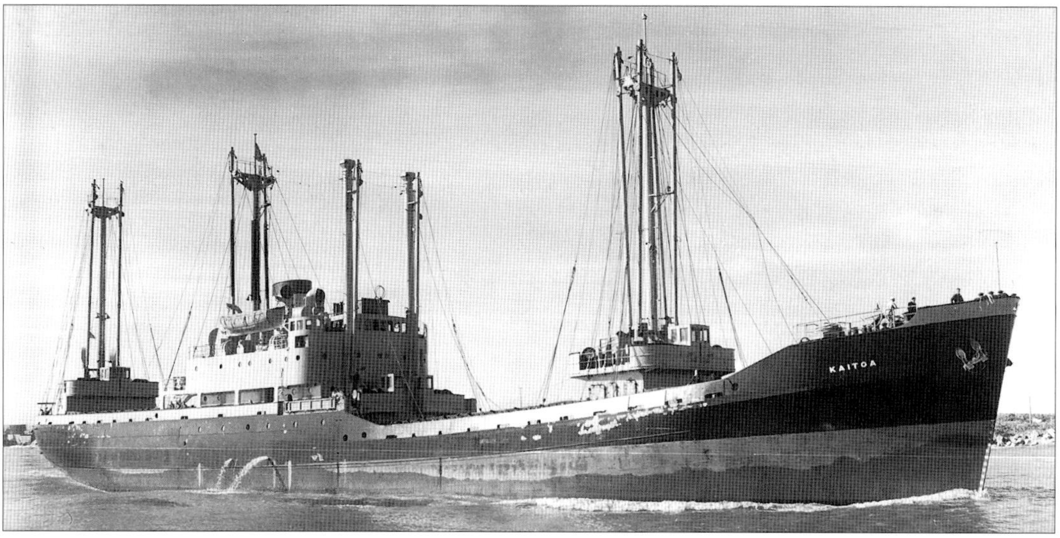
KAITOA

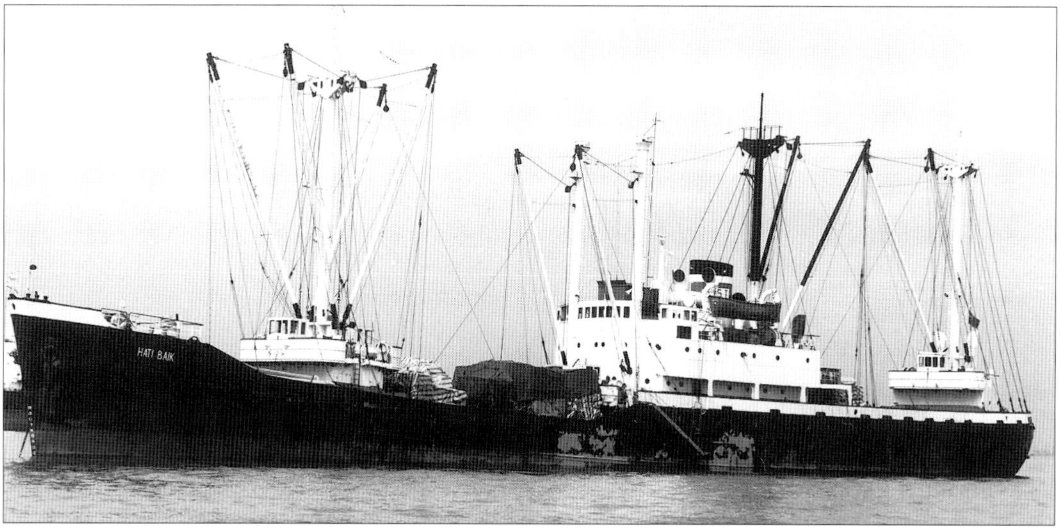
HATI BAIK

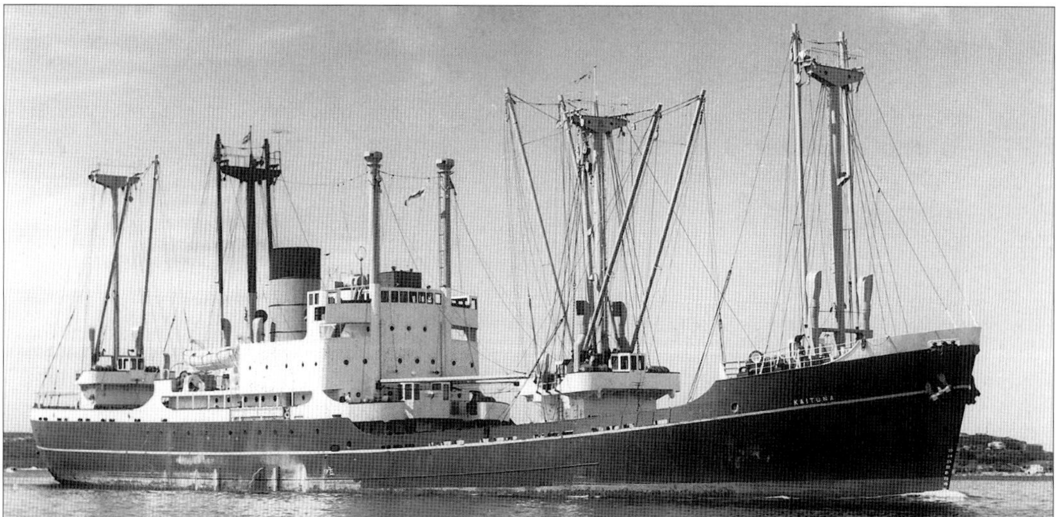
KAITUNA

KAITOA — 2584 GRT — IN FLEET 1956–1971

BUILT: 1956 by Henry Robb Ltd., Leith.

SUBSEQUENT HISTORY: Sold Lineng Enterprises S.A., Panama, (Kie Hock Shipping 1971 (Pte.) Ltd., Singapore, Mgrs) 1971 and renamed *Katoa* (Pan) 1971–76, (Malaysia) 1976–79. Sold Syarikat Perkapalan Meladju Sdn. Bhd., Kota Kinabalu, 1976–78 (same name). Sold Independent Airlines (Malaysia) Sdn. Bhd., Port Kelang, 1978–79. (same name) Sold Kie Gwan Shipping M Sdn. Bhd., Port Kelang, 1979 and renamed *Hati Baik* (Malaysia) 1979–90, (Panama) 1990–92. Transferred Perkapalan Senang Sdn. Bhd., Port Kelang, (Kie Gwan Shipping M Sdn. Bhd., Mgrs) and ownership registered Shing Li Shipping Co. S.A., Panama, 1990. Sold Natsteel Shipbreakers Pte. Ltd., Singapore, and demolished Jurong, from 22/7/1992.

◀ **Kaitoa** *was a 3000-ton deadweight general-purpose freighter built for the New Zealand coastal service. She entered service in July 1956. In 1960 she was one of the first of the cargo vessels to change from the black hulls and orange-buff upperworks to the traditional bronze green hull and white deck and bridgework. After 15 years with the Union company she was sold and operated out of Singapore for a further 21 years*

◀ **Kaitoa** *as the* **Hati Baik** *at Singapore in the 1970s. The distinctive lines of the former Union Company vessel are still very much apparent. Her builders, Henry Robb Ltd. of Leith in Scotland, would have been proud of their skills as the vessel was in active service for 36 years, mainly operating out of Singapore to Malaysian ports* N.J. KIRBY

KAITUNA — 3722 GRT — IN FLEET 1956–1975

BUILT: 1956 by A. Stephen & Sons Ltd., Linthouse, Glasgow.

SUBSEQUENT HISTORY: Laid up Auckland, 5/12/1974. Sold Climax Shipping Corp., Monrovia, (Maldives Shipping Ltd., Male, Mgrs) 23/7/1975 and renamed *Climax Jade* (Maldive Is.) 1975–76 (Panama) 1976–81. Transferred Maldives Shipping Ltd., Male, 1981 and renamed *Maldive Jade* (Maldive Is.) 1981–85. Sold Fortune Shipping Co. Ltd., Male, (Maldives National Shipmanagement Ltd., Male, Mgrs) 1981 and renamed *Fortune Seagull* (Maldive Is.) 1985–85. Laid up Colombo 29/7/1984–13/1/1985. Sold Pakistan shipbreakers and arrived Gadani Beach for demolition 23/1/1985.

◀ *Shipbuilders Alexander Stephen and Sons of Linthouse, Scotland, having built nine similar 5300-ton cargo ships for the Union Company, got quite bold with the construction of the tenth ship, the* **Kaituna***, by undertaking to build the ship at a fixed price – something very rare in 1956 when United Kingdom shipbuilders were often strikebound.* **Kaituna** *was launched by Barbara Twhigg, a daughter of Sir John Roberts, a director of the Union Company from 1903 to 1931. As one of the 'slow greens',* **Kaituna** *had an uneventful career and was disposed off in 1975* J.Y. FREEMAN

178 *Union Fleet*

| **KAIMAI** | **2007 GRT** | **IN FLEET 1956–1972** |

BUILT: 1956 by Henry Robb Ltd., Leith.

SUBSEQUENT HISTORY: Sold Lineng Enterprises S.A., Panama, (Kie Hock Shipping (1971) Pte. Ltd., Singapore, Mgrs 1972 and renamed *Meladju* (Panama) 1972–78 (Malaysia) 1978–80). Sold Tay Chye Chuan, Port Kelang, 1977–78, Kamarado Sdn. Bhd., Labuan, 1978–80. Walek Sdn. Bhd., Port Kelang, (Kie Gwan Shipping M Sdn.Bhd., Port Kelang, Mgrs) 1980 and renamed *Kita* (Malaysia) 1980–85. Sold Paisi Shipping S.A., Singapore, 1985 and renamed *Sanua* (Honduras) 1985–86, *Paisi* (Honduras) 1986–87. Sold Thailand shipbreakers and arrived Sattahip for demolition 24/6/1987.

◄ *Similar in design to the* **Navua**, *the* **Kaimai** *ran trials in September 1956. Another 'soft nosed' coaster,* **Kaimai** *was a smaller general purpose vessel designed to carry coal, timber or general cargo, with a deadweight lifting capacity of 2100 tons. She was surplus to requirements before her economic life had ended, being sold in 1972 but spent another 15 years operating in the Malyasian/Singapore area*   BAIN-WRIGHT COLLECTION

| **KUMALLA** | **1865 GRT** | **IN FLEET 1956–1973** |

BUILT: 1956 by Henry Robb Ltd., Leith.

SUBSEQUENT HISTORY: Sold Hethking Steamships Pty. Ltd., Sydney, (Hetherington, Kingsbury Pty. Ltd., Sydney, Mgrs) 1973 and renamed *Cobargo* (Aust) 1973–78. Sold South Sea Freighters Ltd., Port Vila, (Wm. Martin and K.W. Trueman) 1978 and intended to be renamed *Jihad* (New Hebrides) 1978. Sold K.W. Trueman, Port Vila, 1978 and renamed *Bismarck Sea* (New Hebrides) 1978–82. Ownership reverted to South Sea Freighters Ltd., Port Vila, 1980 (same name). Sold Carthage Navigation Co. S.A., Panama, (Clew Enterprises Pte. Ltd., Singapore, Mgrs) 1982 and renamed *Avondale* (Pan) 1982, (Tonga) 1982–85. Sold Segment Holdings Ltd., Sydney, (Hetherington, Kingsbury Pty. Ltd., Sydney, Mgrs) 1982 (same name). Sailed Tauranga 30/10/1985 for Taiwan via Ponape, Caroline Islands. Arrived Kaohsiung for demolition by Chia Fu Steel Enterprises, 18/3/1986.

◄ *Specially designed for the carriage of pyritic ores from the shallow draft port of Strahan on the West Coast of Tasmania to Melbourne, the 1865-ton* **Kumalla** *was launched in Scotland on 8 August 1956. She was the first Union Company vessel to bear this name which means 'Father' in the Aboriginal language. Because the company had employed English migrants for the delivery voyage, Australian seamen boycotted the vessel when she arrived in Melbourne and it was several months before she could take up her scheduled running. Sold in 1973, she lasted for a further 15 years trading in the Pacific and Indian Oceans*   J.Y. FREEMAN

| **KORANUI** | **3722 GRT** | **IN FLEET 1956–1975** |

BUILT: 1956 by A. Stephen & Sons Ltd., Linthouse, Glasgow.

SUBSEQUENT HISTORY: Laid up Auckland, 12/12/1974. Sold Maldives Shipping Ltd., Male, 10/9/1975 and renamed *South Pacific* (Maldive Is.) 1975–77 (Panama) 1977–79. Transferred Southern Navigation Corp. S.A., Panama, 1977 (Maldives Shipping Ltd., Male, Mgrs) 1977. Renamed *Pride of Baghdad* (Pan) 1979–84 (same owners/mgrs). Sold Great Straits Navigation Co. S.A., Panama, (Island Cargo Shipping Agency Sdn. Bhd., Penang, Mgrs) 1984 and renamed *Kutub Star* (Pan) 1984. Sold Bangladesh shipbreakers and arrived Chittagong Roads for demolition 29/11/1984. Broken up 1985.

◄ **Koranui** *was yet another of the standard 5300-ton deadweight K class freighters built for the Trans Tasman trade. She was launched on 3 October 1956 and was mainly employed on the Australia – North Island services. More welding was used in construction of each vessel in this series as the shipyard developed more sophistication in these techniques. Improvements since the* **Komata** *was completed in 1947 saw the later ships gaining increased lifting capacity due to the greater use of welding*   BAIN-WRIGHT COLLECTION

As each of the standard K class ships were built, they incorporated new technology. The **Koraki** had a slightly wider beam than the others and was probably the first New Zealand registered vessel to have lifeboats made of fibre resin. She arrived at Auckland on her delivery voyage on 7 December 1957. Changed cargo handling practices saw her sold out of the fleet after only 18 years

MARINE PHOTOS

KONINI — 2007 GRT — IN FLEET 1957–1971

BUILT: 1957 by Henry Robb Ltd., Leith.

SUBSEQUENT HISTORY: Sold Guan Guan Shipping (Pte.) Ltd., Singapore, 1971 and renamed *King Tower* (Singapore) 1971–85. Ownership registered to King Line Pte. Ltd., Singapore, (Guan Guan Shipping (Pte.) Ltd., Singapore, Mgrs) 1976. Sold 21/1/1985 to National Shipbreakers Pte. Ltd., Singapore, and broken up Jurong.

◄ *Introduced to the New Zealand coastal service in August 1957,* **Konini** *was similar in size to* **Navua** *and* **Kaimai**. *They were smart-looking vessels but had short lives with the Union Company as the introduction of roll-on, roll-off ships made them redundant. Sold to Singapore owners in 1971,* **Konini** *saw another 14 years' service before being scrapped* BAIN-WRIGHT COLLECTION

KORAKI — 3790 GRT — IN FLEET 1957–1975

BUILT: 1957 by A. Stephen & Sons Ltd., Linthouse, Glasgow.

SUBSEQUENT HISTORY: Laid up Auckland, 1/1975. Sold Maldives Shipping Ltd., Male, 8/1975 and renamed *Maldive Ambassador* (Maldive Is.) 1975–84. Sold Northern Atolls Shipping Ltd., Male, (Maldives National Ship Management Ltd., Male, Mgrs) 1984 and renamed *Northern Sun* (Maldive Is.) 1984. Sold Pakistan shipbreakers and arrived Karachi for demolition 25/8/1984.

KOONYA — 1946 GRT — IN FLEET 1957–1971

BUILT: 1957 by Henry Robb Ltd., Leith.

SUBSEQUENT HISTORY: Sold Guan Guan Shipping (Pte.) Ltd., Singapore, 1971 and renamed *King Star* (Singapore) 1971–85. Ownership registered to King Line Pte. Ltd., Singapore, (Guan Guan Shipping (Pte.) Ltd., Singapore, Mgrs) 1975. Sold 21/1/1985 to National Shipbreakers Pte. Ltd., Singapore, and broken up Jurong.

◄ *The* **Koonya** *was a sister ship to* **Kumalla** *and was the 20th vessel built by Henry Robb Ltd. of Leith for the Union Company in 20 years.* **Koonya** *was designed for the carriage of ores, general and refrigerated cargoes from Tasmania to mainland Australia. After 14 years in the fleet she was sold to Singapore owners and traded out of that port for a further 14 years.* J.Y. FREEMAN

182 Union Fleet

| KATEA | 3790 GRT | IN FLEET 1958–1975 |

BUILT: 1958 by A. Stephen & Sons Ltd., Linthouse, Glasgow.

SUBSEQUENT HISTORY: Laid up Auckland, 12/4/1975. Sold Pac Trade Navigation Co., Monrovia, (Madrigal & Co. Inc., Manila, Mgrs) 11/9/1975 and renamed *Santa Ursula* (Pan) 1975–82. Sold Hsi Ying Enterprises Co. Ltd., Kaohsiung, shipbreakers, and arrived Kaohsiung for demolition 6/3/1982.

◀ *A sister to the* **Koraki** *and thirteenth in the class,* **Katea** *arrived on her delivery voyage on 28 July 1958. Improvements were continually made to the crew accommodation where each seafarer had his own cabin, complete with bunk, built-in settee and wardrobe. The floors in the accommodation were fully carpeted and accommodation was also provided for two cadets. In line with the increasing traffic across the Tasman in livestock, the ship was equipped with permanent stalls for eight horses* BAIN-WRIGHT COLLECTION

| TARAWERA | 2103 GRT | IN FLEET 1958–1974 |

BUILT: 1958 by Taikoo Dockyard & Engineering Co. of Hong Kong Ltd., Hong Kong.

SUBSEQUENT HISTORY: Laid up Auckland, 12/1973. Sold Maldives Shipping Ltd., Male, 1/7/1974 and renamed *Maldive Quest* (Maldive Is.) 1974–80. Sold Taiwan shipbreakers. Sailed Singapore after 2/4/1980 and arrived Kaohsiung for demolition prior to 3/5/1980.

◀ *Designed for the carriage of fruit, frozen meat and dairy produce,* **Tarawera** *was the first Union Company to be built by a Hong Kong shipbuilder. Launched on 23 April 1958 at the Taikoo Dockyard she had a capacity of 11,000 cubic feet of refrigerated space and also incorporated two deep freeze lockers for carrying quick frozen vegetables from New Zealand to the Pacific Islands and Australia. With the introduction of* **Tarawera,** *the company had the capacity to bring in fruit cargoes directly to South Island ports. She was sold in 1974* MARINE PHOTOS

| WAIKARE | 3839 GRT | IN FLEET 1958–1975 |

BUILT: 1958 by A. Stephen & Sons Ltd., Linthouse, Glasgow.

SUBSEQUENT HISTORY: Sold Maldives Shipping Ltd., Male, 1975 and renamed *Maldive Sailor* (Maldive Is.) 1975–77. In collision with tanker *Japan Daisy* (116,327 grt/1976) off Cape Comorin 19/6/1977 and abandoned sinking 20/6/1977 in position 08.24N – 76.42E on passage Karachi to Colombo.

◀ *To supplement the trade to Indonesia, Malaysia and India maintained by* **Wairata** *and* **Wairimu,** *the 14th motorship in the series of K class vessels was adapted for this service. This was the* **Waikare** *and following her arrival at Auckland in December 1958, a monthly service was introduced. She incorporated additional refrigerated capacity and the forward hold and tween deck was arranged for the carriage of flammable cargo. In 1965 she replaced the* **Waimea** *in the South Island–Melbourne trade and was sold 10 years later* BAIN-WRIGHT COLLECTION

184 *Union Fleet*

| **PATEENA** | **2099 GRT** | **IN FLEET 1958–1975** |

BUILT: 1958 by Henry Robb Ltd., Leith.

SUBSEQUENT HISTORY: Laid up Sydney 26/12/1974. Sold Maldives Shipping Ltd., Male, 10/6/1975 and renamed *Maldive Republic* (Maldive Is.) 1975–83. Sold Pakistan shipbreakers and arrived Gadani Beach for demolition 5/6/1983.

◀ *In 1958 and 1959, the Union Company introduced two new sister ships into the Australian coastal trade, the first being the* **Pateena***. With a deadweight capacity of 2120 tons she was somewhat smaller than the* **Kaitoa** *built by the same yard in 1956. In common with other vessels of that era, limited refrigerated space was provided. After only 17 years' service she was sold and broken up eight years later*   J.Y. FREEMAN

| **POOLTA** | **2085 GRT** | **IN FLEET 1959–1976** |

BUILT: 1959 by Henry Robb Ltd., Leith.

SUBSEQUENT HISTORY: Lengthened 18.29 metres and converted 1968 to unit load carrier by Taikoo Dockyard & Eng. Co. Ltd., of Hong Kong Ltd., Hong Kong. (new grt 2800) Sold Bulkships Container Pty. Ltd., Melbourne, (Associated Steamships Pty. Ltd., Melbourne, Mgrs) 1976–81. Sold H.K. Unit Trust (Hetherington, Kingsbury Pty. Ltd., Sydney, Mgrs) 1981–84. Transferred Segment Holdings Ltd., Tonga, (Warner Pacific Line, Tonga, Mgrs) 1984 and renamed *Kali* (Tonga) 1985–88. Sold Golden Arrow International Shipping Navigation & Transport Co., Sharjah, 1988 and renamed *Ali* (Cook Islands then United Arab Emirates) 1988–89. Sold Ocean Shipping Services Ltd., St. Vincent, (Tuscar Lloyds Inc., Dubai, Mgrs) 1989 and renamed *Mahan* (St Vincent & Grenadines) 1989–90. Sold Sentry Shipping Corp., Dubai, (Henderson Marine Consultants, Dubai, Mgrs) 1990 and renamed *Sublime* (St Vincent & Grenadines) 1990–92. Sold Elahi Shipping Ltd., St. Vincent (Nasser Ibrahimi Co., Dubai, Mgrs) 1992 and renamed *Blue Pearl* (St Vincent & Grenadines) 1992–95 (Under arrest Bombay 27/10/93–30/12/94). Renamed *Ocean Success* (same registry/owners/mgrs) 1995–99. Sold Indian shipbreakers and arrived 2/6/1999 for demolition at Alang.

◀ *Sister ship to the* **Pateena***, was the* **Poolta***. Launched on 10 March 1959, she was redundant within a few years as roll-on, roll-off vessels were progressively introduced. The Union Company decided to convert the* **Poolta** *into a unit load and container carrier and she was lengthened in Hong Kong in 1968. The company sold her in 1976 but she remained on the Australian coast for a further five years and since then had a variety of owners and operated out of Arabian Gulf ports as the* **Ocean Success** *until 1999.*   J.Y. FREEMAN

◀ *The illustration shows a lengthened* **Poolta** *with her five sets of union purchase derricks replaced by three cranes*
J.Y. FREEMAN

186   *Union Fleet*

| RISDON | 4125 GRT | IN FLEET 1959–1975 |

BUILT: 1959 by A. Stephen & Sons Ltd., Linthouse, Glasgow.

SUBSEQUENT HISTORY: Sold Maldives Shipping Ltd., Male, 1975 and renamed *Maldive Navigator* (Maldive Is.) 1975–76. Sold Sorysin Cia. Nav. S.A., Panama, (Gold Marine Co. Ltd., Piraeus, Mgrs) 1976 and renamed *Panagia Spiliani* (Greek) 1976–79 (Panama) 1979–84). Transferred Spiliani Shipping Co. S.A., Panama, 1979 (Gold Marine Co. Ltd., Piraeus, Mgrs 1979–80, Yannadis Brothers Shipping Co. S.A., Piraeus, Mgrs 1980–84). Sold Indian shipbreakers and arrived Bedi for demolition 6/6/1984.

◄ *The 4025-ton motorship* **Risdon** *was specially designed for the Australian services of the Union Company and was appropriately named, as for much of her time she was engaged in the carriage of zinc concentrates from the plant at Risdon, close to Hobart. The ship was designed to carry 5000 tons deadweight and her lines were similar to the K class vessels. With the completion of* **Risdon** *in 1959, the company owned 70 vessels and it marked the completion of the post war rebuilding programme. She was sold in 1975 as roll-on, roll-off vessels took over the conventional trades*

| NGAKUTA | 4576 GRT | IN FLEET 1962–1983 |

BUILT: 1962 by Caledon Shipbuilding & Engineering Co. Ltd., Dundee.

SUBSEQUENT HISTORY: Laid up Dunedin from 26/9/1982. Sold Giant Ocean Shipping S.A., Panama, (Hwa Bao Shipping Agency Co. Ltd., Taipeh, Mgrs) 5/1983 and renamed *Giant Treasure* (Pan) 1983–86. Sold Reach Shipping S.A., Panama & Taipeh, 1986 and renamed *Richer* (Pan) 1986–92. On passage Fancheng to Muara Harbour, took water in No. 2 hold after hatch covers ripped off in heavy weather, and abandoned by crew 23/10/1992 in position 10.32N – 112.06E.

◄ *When the 4576-ton motor ship* **Ngakuta** *arrived on the New Zealand coast in September 1962, she presented a totally new image for Union Company cargo vessels. She had six cranes replacing the standard union purchase derricks and with very wide hatches, the cranes could plumb any part of the entire hold. The hatch covers were hydraulically-operated steel covers. Rivets had also been eliminated with virtually the entire construction being welded. With engines and accommodation aft there was a clear forward deck area* I.J. FARQUHAR

| NGATORO | 4576 GRT | IN FLEET 1962–1976 |

BUILT: 1962 by Caledon Shipbuilding & Engineering Co. Ltd., Dundee.

SUBSEQUENT HISTORY: Laid up Wellington from 8/1975. Sold Florvik Compania Naviera S.A., Panama, (Kollintzas Marine Co. S.A., Piraeus, Mgrs) 1/1976 and renamed *Florentia* (Greek) 1976–78. Sold Ippocampus Maritime (Hellas) Ltd., Piraeus, 1978 and renamed *Kapetan Antonis* (Greek) 1978–81. Sold Eastern Queen Co. S.A., Piraeus, (Ippocampus Maritime (Hellas) Ltd., Piraeus, Mgrs) 1981 and renamed *Antony P* (Greek) 1981. Sold Fadel Shipping Co. S.A.R.L., Tripoli, (General United Trading & Shipping Co. S.A.R.L., Tripoli, Mgrs) 1981 and renamed *Fadel G* (Lebanon) 1981–96. Sold Indian shipbreakers, anchored off Alang 27/6/1996 and beached for demolition 2/7/1996.

◄ *Sister ship to the* **Ngakuta** *was the* **Ngatoro**, *which was launched in June 1962. Both ships were designed for the carriage of newsprint, pulp and timber from Mount Maunganui to Australian ports – principally Sydney and Melbourne. Whilst the Wellington office had designed the ships to its requirements, the major shipper of newsprint was not so enthusiastic, as the preferred method of shipping rolls of newsprint was stowing them on their ends rather than the bilge to prevent excessive damage. A few years after the first 'crane ships' were introduced, the Tasman Pulp and Paper Company built two specialised timber product carriers for its own use, which enabled them to handle the newsprint in the manner that company preferred. Despite this loss of cargo,* **Ngatoro** *and* **Ngakuta** *were successful vessels and had long lives after being sold by the company* BAIN-WRIGHT COLLECTION

188 *Union Fleet*

KAREPO   3222 GRT   IN FLEET 1964–1978

BUILT: 1964 by Taikoo Dockyard & Engineering Co. of Hong Kong Ltd., Hong Kong.

SUBSEQUENT HISTORY: Sold Atlantic Navigation (Pte.) Ltd., Singapore, 1978 and renamed *Atlantic Viking* (Singapore) 1978. Transferred Pacific Viking (Pte.) Ltd., Singapore, (Pacific Navigation Co. Pte. Ltd., Singapore, Mgrs) 1978 and renamed *Pacific Viking* (Singapore) 1978–86. Sold Thailand shipbreakers and arrived Rayong for demolition 9/12/1986.

◀ *As replacement vessels for old Trans Tasman tonnage, the company ordered two new ships from the Taikoo Dockyard in Hong Kong in early 1963 and the first of these vessels, the 3222-ton* **Karepo** *came into service in May 1964. She, too, had deck cranes with mechanically-operated hatch covers. She was driven by a single screw and was designed to operate at 12.5 knots – somewhat faster than the 'slow greens' of the 1940s and 50s.* **Karepo** *was sold out of the fleet after only 14 years service* R.D. SCOTT

WAITAKI   8726 GRT   IN FLEET 1964–1970

BUILT: 1954 by A. Stephen & Sons Ltd., Linthouse, Glasgow as *Whakatane* 1954–64.

PREVIOUS OWNERS: New Zealand Shipping Co. Ltd., London, 1954–64.

SUBSEQUENT HISTORY: Sold Cia. Maritime Ta Teh S.A., Panama, (Tung Lee Navigation Co. Ltd., Kaohsiung, Mgrs) 1970 and renamed *Successful Enterprise* (Panama) 1970–72. Sold Wan Lung Nav. Co. S.A., Panama, (Wan Tung Transportation Co. Ltd., Kaohsiung, Mgrs) 1972 and renamed *Wan Yu* (Panama) 1972–77. Transferred Truthful Shipping Co. S.A., Panama, (same mgrs) 1977 and renamed *Truthful* (Pan) 1977. Arrived Kaohsiung 10/5/1977 and following collision damage after typhoon 'Thelma' 24/7/1977 was subsequently broken up Kaohsiung with demolition commencing 11/1/1979.

◀ *To meet the growing demands for more refrigerated capacity on the service between New Zealand, Singapore, Malaysia, India and Sri Lanka, the Union Company, with the cooperation of shareholder P &O, took over the 8726-ton New Zealand Shipping Company motorship* **Whakatane** *on 6 May 1964 and renamed her* **Waitaki**. *This vessel had 90,000 cubic feet of refrigerated space. The 10-year old ship remained in this service for only six years until the company abandoned the trade as continuing losses were being incurred* BAIN-WRIGHT COLLECTION

SEAWAY QUEEN   2961 GRT   IN FLEET 1964–1975

BUILT: 1964 by Broken Hill Pty. Co. Ltd., Whyalla.

SUBSEQUENT HISTORY: Sold Trucape Pty. Ltd., Melbourne, (Associated Steamships Pty. Ltd., Melbourne, Mgrs) 1975–78, transferred to Bulkships Container Pty. Ltd., Melbourne, 1978 (same mgrs). Laid up Singapore 22/2/1979 and sold Seaways Shipping & Trading S.A., Piraeus, 1979. Resold Perkapalan Lautan Biru Sdn. Bhd., Kota Kinabalu, 1980 and renamed *Lautan Rani* (Malaysia) 1980–85. Sold Chinese shipbreakers and towed from Kota Kinabalu arriving Zhangjiang 21/4/1985 for demolition.

◀ *By the early 1960s cargo handling methods overseas were rapidly changing and in the short sea trades, lift on, lift off conventional cargo handling methods were being replaced by roll-on, roll-off vessels loading wheeled and also larger unitised cargoes using forklifts. The Whyalla shipyard of the Broken Hill Proprietary built two such specialist ships for the Union Company in 1964. The first of these was the* **Seaway Queen** *which entered service between Melbourne and Hobart in June 1964. She was the first Union Company vessel fitted with fin stabilisers and twin bow lateral thrusters as well as being the first stern door roll-on, roll-off ship in the fleet designed for the company's own Seafreighter cargo pallet and wheeled traffic. With an operating speed of 16.5 knots, the 2961 ton freighter was the fastest cargo ship on the Australian coast in 1964. Customer demand for the new cargo handling methods saw the ship replaced with larger vessels after only 11 years service* J.Y. FREEMAN

In 1965 the Union Company acquired another New Zealand Shipping Company vessel for its eastern service to run in conjunction with the **Waitaki**. *This was the* **Whangaroa**, *a sister ship, and she was renamed* **Wainui**. *She remained on the service for a little over four years until a dispute arose with the maritime unions when the Union Company engineer officers refused to accept motorman Robert Kidd as a member of the crew.* **Wainui** *was ready to sail from Auckland to Singapore when the dispute arose and she subsequently spent 141 days idle before she finally left manned at officer and engineer levels by Union Company shore personnel. She was sold on completion of discharge and the Union Company abandoned the eastern service commenced in 1887* BAIN-WRIGHT COLLECTION

| SEAWAY KING | 2961 GRT | IN FLEET 1964–1976 |

BUILT: 1964 by Broken Hill Pty. Co. Ltd., Whyalla.

SUBSEQUENT HISTORY: Transferred Best Shipping (Pte.) Ltd., Singapore, (Bulkships Ltd., Sydney, subsidiary, Thome & Co. Pte. Ltd., Singapore, Mgrs) 1976 and renamed *Sentosa Trader* (Singapore) 1977–78. Sold Zefyrus Maritime Co. S.A., Monrovia (Seaways Shipping & Trading Co. S.A., Piraeus, Mgrs) 1978 and renamed *Lucky Trader* (Greek) 1978–79. Sold Finda Transport Enterprises S.A., Athens, (N. Demetriades and M. Keusseoglou, Athens, Mgrs 1979–85, M Keusseoglou, Mgr 1985–86) and renamed *Ponte Negro* (Greek) 1979–86. Laid up Chalkis, Greece from 6/61984. Sold Greek shipbreakers and arrived Piraeus for demolition 14/8/1986.

◀ The second specialist roro ship was the **Seaway King** which made her maiden voyage from Sydney to Hobart on 1 September 1964. They had to be built in Australian shipyards as this was a condition for all vessels trading on the Australian coast. **Seaway King** left Sydney every Tuesday, arrived Hobart on Thursday, left on Friday and was back in Sydney on Sunday. While the stern doors handled wheeled or unitised cargoes the two ships also had four deck cranes to handle lift on lift off containers and other units. **Seaway King** was sold in 1976 and spent a further 10 years operating on other roll-on, roll-off services out of Singapore and later Mediterranean ports   J.Y. FREEMAN

| KARETU | 3222 GRT | IN FLEET 1964–1980 |

BUILT: 1964 by Taikoo Dockyard & Engineering Co. of Hong Kong Ltd., Hong Kong.

SUBSEQUENT HISTORY: Sold B.C.D. Shipping Pte. Ltd., Singapore, (Chuan Peng Kiat, Singapore, Mgr 1980–82, Pacific Navigation Co. Pte. Ltd., Singapore, Mgrs 1982–87) and renamed *Pacific Ocean* (Singapore) 1980–87. Sold Taiwan shipbreakers and sailed Keelung 15/7/1987 for demolition at Kaohsiung.

◀ The second Hong Kong-built cargo ship was the **Karetu,** which entered service in August 1964. The decision to build **Karetu** and **Karepo** in Hong Kong saved both money and time. The introduction of roll-on, roll-off ships and unit load cargoes saw the two vessels redundant in the Union Company fleet long before their economic life was over. They were both active for Singapore owners for several years after their disposal by the Union Company
   BAIN-WRIGHT COLLECTION

| WAINUI | 8573 GRT | IN FLEET 1965–1970 |

BUILT: 1955 by John Brown & Co. (Clydebank) Ltd., Clydebank, Glasgow as *Whangaroa*.

PREVIOUS OWNERS: New Zealand Shipping Co. Ltd., London, 1955–65.

SUBSEQUENT HISTORY: Sold British India Steam Navigation Co. Ltd., London, 1970 and renamed *Warina* (Br) 1970–71. Sold Stylianos C. Halkias, Piraeus, 1971 and registered to Admiti Shipping Co. Ltd., Famagusta, 1971, and renamed *Garoufalia* (Cyprus) 1971–72. Registered to Ganadera Sudamericana S.A., Chios, 1972 (same owner) and renamed *Dromeus* (Greek) 1972–73. Registry reverted to Admiti Shipping Co. Ltd., Famagusta, 1973 and renamed *Garoufalia* (Cyprus) 1973–74. Sold Tai Kien Industry Co. Ltd., Taiwan, shipbreakers and arrived Kaohsiung 19/3/1974 for demolition, which commenced 28/6/1974.

Sister ship to the **Ngahere,** *the* **Ngapara** *entered service in the middle of 1966. Named after a small inland community close to Oamaru, the school children of the Ngapara School took great interest in the ship and on occasion travelled to Port Chalmers to see it. She was sold after 20 years service and was finally broken up in China in 1993*

R.D. SCOTT

NGAHERE   4575 GRT   IN FLEET 1966–1987

BUILT: 1966 by Caledon Shipbuilding & Engineering Co. Ltd., Dundee.

SUBSEQUENT HISTORY: Sold Foojadi Shipping Co. Ltd., (Maldives National Ship Management Pty. Co. Ltd., Male) 1987 and renamed *Sea Horse* (Maldive Is.) 1987–99. Sold Indian shipbreakers and arrived Mumbai, Bombay for demolition 20/12/1999.

◄ *In November 1964 the company ordered two further 'crane ships' similar in design to* **Ngakuta** *and* **Ngatoro** *from the Caledon Shipbuilding Company, Dundee. The first, named* **Ngahere**, *arrived at Melbourne on on 29 April 1966. Although similar in design to the earlier ships, the new vessels carried two 10-ton cranes and four 5-ton cranes in order to cater for containers and larger unit loads. In October 1982 she became the largest ship to berth at Tarakohe, bringing a part cargo of gypsum. From April to June 1985 the vessel participated in 'Operation Hope', carrying a cargo of food and relief goods in support of famine relief in Ethiopia. The cargo was donated by the people of New Zealand and she loaded at main New Zealand ports for Sudan. She remained in service for 21 years before being sold in 1987 to Maldivian owners who were still operating the vessel in eastern waters 12 years later*   J.Y. FREEMAN

NGAPARA   4575 GRT   IN FLEET 1966–1986

BUILT: 1966 by Caledon Shipbuilding & Engineering Co. Ltd., Dundee.

SUBSEQUENT HISTORY: Laid up Lyttelton from 12/5/1986. Sold Reach Shipping S.A., Panama & Taipei, 10/1986 and renamed *Kent Brilliant* (Pan) 1986–93. Following loss of rudder north of Philippines, vessel towed to Keelung 14/4/1993. Sold and renamed *Financier* (Pan) 1993. No repairs effected and vessel towed out 15/5/1993 by tug *Huajen* and arrived Huangpu for demolition 18/5/1993.

WAHINE   8944 GRT   IN FLEET 1966–1968

BUILT: 1966 by Fairfield Shipbuilding & Engineering Co. Ltd., Govan.

SUBSEQUENT HISTORY: Grounded on Barrett's Reef, entrance to Wellington Harbour in gale 10/4/1968, refloated, drifted into harbour and foundered off Steeple Rock on passage Lyttelton to Wellington. Subsequently declared constructive total loss 9/5/1968. Wreck removed by United Salvage Pty. Ltd., Melbourne, between 10/1968–9/1973.

◄ *The momentum in the development of roll-on, roll-off services in the 1960s developed apace and to provide a running mate for the converted* **Maori**, *the Union Company ordered another specialist roll-on, roll-off ship for the Lyttelton-Wellington express service. This was the* **Wahine**, *which was launched on 14 July 1966. With accommodation for 931 cabin passengers and space for 200 cars and trailers, she was the largest express steamer yet built for the service. She was powered by turbo electric machinery developing 18,000 shaft horse power to give a speed of 22 knots. Stabilisers were also fitted. She entered service in August 1966 but on 10 April 1968 she tragically sank in heavy weather at the entrance to Wellington Harbour with the loss of 51 lives*   N.J. KIRBY

194 *Union Fleet*

Steamers and Motorships

HAWEA — 2268 GRT — IN FLEET 1967–1976

BUILT: 1967 by Taikoo Dockyard & Engineering Co. of Hong Kong Ltd., Hong Kong.

SUBSEQUENT HISTORY: Sold New Zealand Ministry of Transport, Wellington (The Shipping Corporation of New Zealand Ltd., Wellington, Mgrs) 1976 and renamed *Coastal Ranger* (New Zealand) 1976–79. Sold Faros Maritime Co. S.A., Monrovia, (Seaways Shipping & Trading Co. S.A., Piraeus, Mgrs) 1979 and renamed *Iniochos Express II* (Greek) 1979–85. Ownership transferred to Iniochos Shipping Co. S.A., Piraeus, 1980 (Seaways Shipping & Trading Co. S.A., Piraeus, Mgrs 1980) (same name). Sold Seastar Navigation Co. Ltd., Piraeus, 1984 (same name). Sold Brodospas, Yugoslav shipbreakers, and left Piraeus 16/6/1985 in tow for Split, Yugoslavia for demolition.

◄ *The move to convert the New Zealand coastal trade to roll-on, roll-off shipping came in February 1966 when the Union Company let a contract to the Taikoo Dockyard in Hong Kong for a specialist roro ship for a new weekly service between Auckland, Lyttelton and Dunedin. The vessel was designed to handle the standard Seafreighter collapsible units, stowed two high in the hold and loaded by large forklifts. The ship, named* **Hawea**, *also had a 15-ton crane to handle larger container and pallet loads on deck or in the lower container hold. After nine years,* **Hawea** *was sold to the New Zealand Ministry of Transport and for a short time ran in the Lyttelton-Wellington cargo service when the passenger service terminated. She was sold a little over two years later*   BAIN-WRIGHT COLLECTION

TAVEUNI — 2808 GRT — IN FLEET 1968–1972

BUILT: 1945 by Aalborg Vaerft A/S, Aalborg, Denmark (launched 1940 but not completed until 6/1945) as *Argentinean Reefer* (Denmark) 1945–68.

PREVIOUS OWNERS: Rederiet "Ocean" A/S, Copenhagen (J. Lauritzen, Mgrs) 1945–68.

SUBSEQUENT HISTORY: Sold Wan Lee S.S. Co. S.A. Panama, 1972 and renamed *Wan Lee* (Panama) 1972–73. Resold Chou's Iron & Steel Corporation, Taiwan shipbreakers and arrived Kaohsiung for demolition 23/1/1973 with work undertaken 23/4 to 7/5/1973.

◄ *With the withdrawal of the* **Matua** *from the Pacific Islands service in 1968, the Union Company purchased the fully refrigerated vessel* **Argentinian Reefer** *as a replacement. Although launched in 1940 the ship had not been completed until 1945 so she was 23 years old when acquired. Renamed* **Taveuni** *(a slight variation of* **Taviuni**, *the name of an earlier vessel in the fleet, but reflective of the present day spelling) she entered service in mid 1968. A serious copra fire in 1970 caused extensive damage and saw her under repair for nearly three months. High running costs, out of date handling equipment and a decline in the volume of fruit available saw her sold in 1972*

MAHENO — 4510 GRT — IN FLEET 1969–1976

BUILT: 1969 by Caledon Shipbuilding & Engineering Co. Ltd., Dundee.

SUBSEQUENT HISTORY: Sold Thames Marine Ltd. S.A., Panama, (A.G. Societe de Gestion Maritime Socigemar, Zurich, Mgrs 1976–79, Orconsult S.A., Zurich, Mgrs 1979–82, Orconsult Shipping Co. Ltd., Zurich, Mgrs 1982–85) 1976 and renamed *Jolly Giallo* (Panama) 1976–80, *African Trader* (Panama) 1980–85. Sold Oyster Shipping Ltd., Gibraltar, (Vlasov Group, Monto Carlo, Mgrs) 1985 and renamed *June Lady* (Bahamas) 1985–87, *Olbios* (Italian) 1987, *June Lady* (Bahamas) 1987. Sold Naviera Interoceangas S.A., (N.I.S.A.), Santiago, 1987 and renamed *Tierra Del Fuego* (Chile) 1987–91. Sold Compagnia Navigazione del Tirreno (CONATIR) S.p.A., Trapani, 1991 and renamed *Carla E* (Italian) 1991– (Operating Mediterranean – Leghorn/Trapani from 1991)

◄ *Following the success of the roll-on, roll-off services in Australia, the Union Company ordered two specialist roro ships to operate on a fortnightly service from Auckland, and Wellington to Sydney and Melbourne. The first of the new ships was launched on 11 July 1968 but did not leave the shipyard until 20 April 1969 due to engine breakdowns on trials. She was named* **Maheno** *and her design incorporated many new ideas. The accommodation and navigating bridge was right forward, and she had twin funnels. Unitised cargo (mainly carried on the Seafreighter base) entered the ship through a stern door and was distributed over three decks through the use of 30-ton capacity 'scissor' lifts. On her introduction, the company reduced ocean freight by about 17%.* **Maheno** *sailed for Sydney on 27 May 1969 but the rapid growth of the ISO 20 ft container saw her replaced in only seven years as larger ships were introduced*
BAIN-WRIGHT COLLECTION

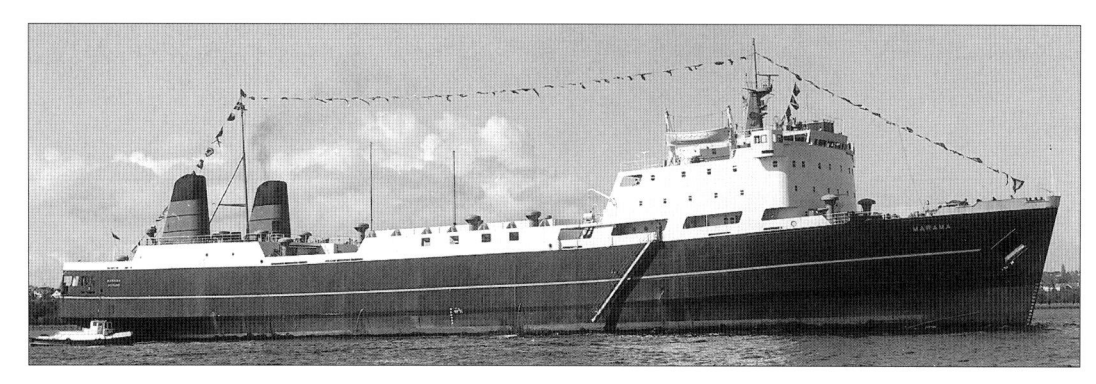

Shipyard industrial problems also delayed the completion of the **Marama,** *the sister ship of* **Maheno.** *The ship was originally due for delivery in November 1968. Even the launching ceremony was thwarted with the sponsor christening the ship but industrial action prevented the launch. It was not until 23 September 1969 that* **Marama** *sailed on her first voyage to Melbourne. An identical sister to* **Maheno,** *she had a service speed of 16.5 knots, bow thrusters and anti-rolling flume tank stabilisers. She was sold and chartered back for five years from 1976 to 1981 but remained on the Tasman service as well as voyages to the Pacific Islands. Back under company ownership in 1981, she was finally sold for demolition in 1985* BAIN-WRIGHT COLLECTION

Following the tragic loss of the **Wahine,** *the company ordered a replacement vessel. The* **Rangatira** *entered the Wellington-Lyttelton express service on 28 March 1972. Originally due for completion in November 1971, continual shipyard delays saw the vessel being sent from the builder's yards in Newcastle to Southampton for final fitting out. The largest vessel ever employed in the inter-island service,* **Rangatira** *accommodated 733 passengers and over 200 cars. Propulsion was again turbo-electric, generating 20,500-shaft horsepower for a maximum speed of 22.5 knots. The growth of air travel and competition from the roll-on, roll-off rail ferries between Picton and Wellington saw a continual decline in passengers. Operating costs just kept rising and the New Zealand Government chartered the ship from 1974 to maintain the service. In the 12 months to 31 January 1976 the service lost $3.7 million; it ceased 15 September 1976. Since then,* **Rangatira,** *under various guises has twice been employed as an accommodation ship, saw service in the Falklands War and after operating spasmodically in a passenger service between Italy and Greece since 1986, has been laid up at Naples since August 1995* N.J. KIRBY

MARAMA 4510 GRT IN FLEET 1969–1976 & 1981–1985

BUILT: 1969 by Caledon Shipbuilding & Engineering Co. Ltd., Dundee.

SUBSEQUENT HISTORY: Sold Ascot Shipping Co. Ltd., Wellington, 1976 (Union Company, managers and charterers). Re-purchased by Union Company 1981. Sold Trident Transportation Co. S.A., Panama, 1985 and renamed *Marada* (Panama) 1985. Sold Taiwan shipbreakers and arrived Kaohsiung for demolition 23/3/1985.

WANAKA 2769 GRT IN FLEET 1970 – 1976

BUILT: 1970 by Taikoo Dockyard & Engineering Co. of Hong Kong Ltd., Hong Kong.

SUBSEQUENT HISTORY: Laid up Dunedin from 1/3/1975. Sold Sealanes Transport Corporation, Monrovia (Seaways Shipping & Trading Co. S.A., Piraeus, Mgrs) 3/1976 and renamed *Rata Hills* (Greek) 1976–78. Registry transferred to Iniochos Shipping Ltd., Piraeus, 1978 (same mgrs) and renamed *Iniochos Express* (Greek) 1978–80. Under charter to B.A.I.S.A. Brittany Ferries (Bretagne-Angleterre-Irlande), Roscoff, France and renamed *Breizh-Izel* (France) 1980–89 and registered to Seaways Transport Group, Roscoff, 1980–83 and to Sofigepar S.A., Roscoff, 1983–89 (Denholm Ship Management (Isle of Man) Ltd., Douglas, Mgrs 1988–89) Sold Seatruck Services Ltd., Nicosia, (Marlines S.A., Piraeus, Mgrs) 1989 and renamed *Duchess M* (Cyprus) 1989–00 . Registry transferred to Marelite Marine Co. Ltd., Limassol, 1991–00 (same name/mgrs). Renamed *Balbek* 2000. (Trading Igoumenitsa/Bari 7/2000 but laid up Eleusis Bay near Piraeus 12/9/2000)

◀ *The success of the coastal roro service with* **Hawea** *saw the company order a further vessel from the Taikoo Dockyard in Hong Kong. The new ship was named* **Wanaka** *and entered service in April 1970 between Auckland, Wellington and Dunedin, providing South Island shippers an opportunity for transhipment to Australia via the two northern ports. Slightly larger than* **Hawea**, **Wanaka** *was the first ship in the company to be fitted with a bulbous bow. She also had stabilisers and a bow thruster. The growth of road and rail transport in New Zealand coupled with the inability of sea transport to provide only weekly services between coastal ports saw the* **Wanaka** *sold in 1976.*

RANGATIRA 9387 GRT IN FLEET 1972–1986

BUILT: 1972 by Swan Hunter Shipbuilders Ltd., Walker Shipyard, Newcastle.

SUBSEQUENT HISTORY: Ownership registered to Union Steam Ship Company (U.K.) Ltd., London, 1972–1986. Vessel chartered to New Zealand Ministry of Transport from 1/7/1974–76 as interisland service under Government subsidy. Concluded Lyttelton/Wellington service 15/9/1976. Left Wellington for Falmouth 17/9/1976 and arrived there to lay up 17/10/1976. Chartered to Sea Truck Trading A/S, Stavanger, and employed as accommodation ship at Loch Kishorn, Scotland. (Sailed Falmouth, arrived Loch Kishorn 14/3/1977). Subsequently chartered to British Petroleum for 4 years and arrived Sullum Voe, Shetland Islands, for use as accommodation ship 2/10/1978. Completed charter and returned to lay up Falmouth 5/7/1981. Chartered by British Government (Blue Star Ship Management Ltd., London, Mgrs) 24/5/1982 for service in Falkland Islands. Sailed Devonport 19/6/1982 and arrived Port Stanley 11/7/1982. Returned Devonport 18/10/1983, subsequently refitted Harland & Wolff Ltd., Belfast. Returned to lay up, Falmouth 30/3/1984. Sold Searoyal Ferries Ltd., Nicosia, (Marlines S.A., Piraeus, Mgrs) 1986 and towed Falmouth/Piraeus by tug *Vigen Supplier* 3/11/1986–20/11/1986. Renamed *Queen M* (Cyprus 1986–89, Panama 1989–90). Sold Alimar Shipping Co. Ltd., Malta, (Alimar S.R.L., Naples, Mgrs) 1990 and renamed *Carlo R* (Malta) 1990– (Arrived Naples 16/8/1995 and still there under arrest 18/7/2000)

One of the supplementary roro vessels purchased for the Trans Tasman trade was one of the most unattractive vessels ever owned by the company. She was one of three ships built in the Netherlands for the Swedish Stena Line and was to be named **Stena Shipper.** *She was intended to be chartered but the ship had to be sold to the Union Company to allow a New Zealand crew to be employed, as Swedish seafarers claimed the right to crew chartered Swedish vessels. She was taken over at Rotterdam on 15 February 1974 and renamed* **Union Wellington.** *She operated on the Tasman for only two years. With her bridge front and accommodation virtually overlooking the bow, she would have given the crew some 'exciting' experiences in heavy weather. Her trim always suggested she was 'down by the head'. Despite her unusual appearance she was obviously successful, as she was in active service in European waters for a further 19 years*
BAIN-WRIGHT COLLECTION

The negotiations for the sale of the Union Company from P & O to Australian and New Zealand interests in 1970/71 delayed the ordering of new tonnage and it was not until 1975 that a replacement vessel for **Seaway Queen** *could be completed.* **Seaway Prince**, *built at Whyalla, had a deadweight capacity of 4216 tonnes and incorporated stabilisers, a bow thruster and her stern door was 36 feet wide. She was revolutionary in that she was propelled by a heavy duty gas turbine engine driving a generator producing electricity for the electric motors coupled to each propellor shaft. The high construction costs of building in Australia were somewhat offset by a $9 million Government subsidy* J.Y. FREEMAN

UNION WELLINGTON 2638 GRT IN FLEET 1973–1976

BUILT: 1973 by A. Vuijk & Zonen, Capelle. Launched as *Stena Shipper* for Stena A/B Gothenburg. Sold on completion to Union Company.

SUBSEQUENT HISTORY: Laid up Wellington 25/11/1975. Sold Arghiris Navigation Co. S.A., Piraeus, 1976 and renamed *Alpha Express* (Greek) 1977–79. Lengthened 27 metres by Werft Nobiskrug, Rendsburg 11/11/76–26/1/1977. Following owners' collapse, vessel re-purchased by Stena A/B, Gothenburg 1980 and renamed *Stena Shipper* (Br) 1980. Registered Northern Coasters Ltd., London, (Triport Ferries Management Lt., London, Mgrs) 1980 and renamed *Speedlink Vanguard* (Br) 1980–87. Returned to Stena Line 3/87 and renamed *Caribe Express* (Br) 1987–88, *Stena Shipper* (Br) 1988, *Kirk Shipper* (Br) 1988–89. Registered to Northern Coasters Ltd., Georgetown, (Northern Marine Management (Cyprus) Ltd., Mgrs) 1987–89. Registered Marine Investments Ltd., (Stena A/B, Mgrs) 1989 and renamed *Normandie Shipper* (Br) 1989–92 (Bahamas) 1992–93, (French) 1993–99. Registered to Stena Ferries Ltd., London, 1992–93, B.A.I.S.A. Brittany Ferries (Bretagne-Angleterre-Irland). Laid up in Caen Canal 1995–1999. Sold Bonavista Shipping Corp., Nassau (Adecom Ship Management, Ontario) 1999 and renamed *Bonavista* (Bahamas) 1999–. (Arrived Swinoujscie, Poland 5/4/2000).

SEAWAY PRINCE 4174 GRT IN FLEET 1975–1985

BUILT: 1975 by Broken Hill Pty. Co. Ltd., Whyalla.

SUBSEQUENT HISTORY: Ownership registered to Union Steam Ship Company of Australia Pty. Ltd., Melbourne, 1979–85, Union Steam Ship Company (U.K.) Ltd., London, 1985. Laid up Melbourne, 25/11/83–26/12/1985. Sold and delivered Melbourne, 26/12/1985 to Huang Ta Enterprise Co. Ltd., Taiwan, on behalf Ging Ya Enterprise Co. Ltd., Kaohsiung. Left Melbourne, 3/1/1986 in tandem tow with *Seaway Princess* by tug *Tiburon 1* and arrived Kaohsiung for demolition 14/3/1986.

200 *Union Fleet*

| SEAWAY PRINCESS | 4189 GRT | IN FLEET 1976–1985 |

BUILT: 1976 by Broken Hill Pty. Co. Ltd., Whyalla.

SUBSEQUENT HISTORY: Ownership registered to Union Steam Ship Company of Australia Pty. Ltd., Melbourne, 1979–85, Union Steam Ship Company (U.K.) Ltd., London, 1985. Laid up Melbourne, 23/9/1983–26/12/1985. Sold and delivered Melbourne, 26/12/1985 to Huang Ta Enterprise Co. Ltd., Taiwan, on behalf Ging Ya Enterprise Co. Ltd., Kaohsiung. Left Melbourne, 3/1/1986 in tandem tow with *Seaway Prince* by tug *Tiburon 1* and arrived Kaohsiung for demolition 18/3/1986.

◀ *Sister ship to* **Seaway Prince**, *was the* **Seaway Princess**, *completed a few months later. The decision to power the ships with fuel-guzzling gas turbine engines was a bold move but the phenomenal increases in fuel prices only a few years after they entered service made them totally uneconomic to operate. They were laid up from 1983 and never worked again, being towed in tandem to the breaker's yard in Taiwan in 1986* J.Y. FREEMAN

| UNION ROTORUA | 23962 GRT | IN FLEET 1976–1998 |

BUILT: 1976 by Broken Hill Pty. Co. Ltd., Whyalla. (Stabilizers fitted Singapore 10/1976). (Ownership registered to Union Shipping New Zealand Ltd., 1988–98).

SUBSEQUENT HISTORY: Sold Ruby Enterprises Inc., (Rederij Gebr. Wijsmuller B.V., Mgrs) 1998 and renamed *Rotorua* (St. Vincent & Grenadines) 1998. Sailed Auckland, 13/5/1998 for demolition by Indian shipbreakers. Following departure from Singapore 18/6/1998, returned to port 19/7/1998 where gas turbines, generators and electrical equipment removed. Left Singapore 18/9/1998 and anchored Batu Ampar, Indonesia 18/9/1998. Sold Indian shipbreakers. Sailed Batu Ampar 12/1/1999 and arrived Alang 29/1/1999 in tow of tug *Britoil* (1984, 879grt).

◀ *Surging forestry cargoes from Mount Maunganui saw the company order two more large gas turbine ships. The first was launched at Whyalla in January 1976 and named* **Union Rotorua**. *Equipped with a bow visor ramp and an angled port side stern quarter ramp, the new ships incorporated the cargo lifts and other handling features of* **Union Melbourne** *but on a larger scale. The gas turbine-powered electrical machinery generated 21,800-brake horsepower for a speed of 20 knots. The 23,962 ton* **Union Rotorua** *entered service at the end of 1976. During the collapse of electric power supplies to the Auckland central business district in 1998, she was used to supply 12 megawatts of electric power for several weeks. She was sold later that year* N.J. KIRBY

◀ *During 1993-95 the deck configuration of both* **Union Rotorua** *and* **Union Rotoiti** *was changed to enable the ships to carry more ISO containers. The main deck superstructure was cut back to allow space for another 80 containers and the foredeck pedestal was cleared to fit in 50 to 60 extra containers. The illustration shows the alterations* N.J. KIRBY

The Union Company management cast envious eyes at the volume of increased trade between New Zealand and Australia to Singapore and Malaysia, a service terminated in 1970. In May 1973 it chartered the 9352-tonne **Ocean Crest** *and renamed her* **Union Aotearoa**. *She was intended to run in a joint service with the Dutch-owned Royal Interocean Lines between Australian and New Zealand ports to Bangkok, Port Kelang and Singapore, with calls at Indonesian ports if required.* **Union Aotearoa** *had made four round voyages when she was urgently needed to supplement the Trans Tasman services and in August 1974 she lifted a record newsprint cargo of 6200 tonnes plus 800 tonnes of kraft pulp from Mount Maunganui to Australia. To suit financing purposes, the company exercised their option to purchase the ship in 1977. She was sold in August 1978 but in the interim period she lay idle in Singapore* N.J. KIRBY

| UNION AOTEAROA | 9352 GRT | IN FLEET 1977–1978 |

BUILT: 1973 by Warnowerft Warnemunde VEB, Rostock-Warnemunde and originally intended to be named *Ocean Crest*.

PREVIOUS OWNERS: Deep Sea Shipping Co. Ltd., London, 1973. Gannel Shipping Co. Ltd., London, (Maritime Carriers N.Z. Ltd., Auckland, Mgrs) 1973–77. (Union Company charterers 1973–77).

SUBSEQUENT HISTORY: Laid up Singapore 20/3/1977. Sold Forsyth Shipping Pte. Ltd., Singapore, (Union Company control) and renamed *Golden Harvest* (Singapore) 8/1978 for bareboat charter to Guan Guan Shipping Pte. Ltd., Singapore, but resold 9/1978 to Peoples Republic of China, Beijing and placed under China Ocean Shipping Company (COSCO), Shanghai, and renamed *Xing Cheng* (China) 1978–96. Under Dalian Ocean Shipping Company (COSCO), Dalian) 1992–96. Sold Mortimer Shipping Corp., Belize and renamed *Ada* (Belize) 1996. Sold Golden Arrow Shipping, Honduras 1997 and renamed *Golden Arrow II* (Honduras) 1997. Sold Indian shipbreakers and arrived Alang for demolition 18/10/1997.

| UNION ROTOITI | 23971 GRT | IN FLEET 1977–1999 |

BUILT: 1977 by Broken Hill Pty.Co. Ltd., Whyalla. (Stabilisers fitted Brisbane 6–7/1977). (Converted from gas turbine to diesel propulsion at Newcastle. N.S.W. between 12/1985 and 6/1986).

SUBSEQUENT HISTORY: (Ownership registered Union Shipping New Zealand Ltd., 1988–91. Canterbury Shipping Co. Ltd., 1991–93, Union Shipping New Zealand Ltd., 1993–99). Sold Anzdl Ltd., (Anglo-Eastern Ship Management Ltd., Hong Kong, Mgrs) 1999 and renamed *Rotoiti* (Bermuda) 1999– (Still operating Trans-Tasman 7/2000).

◄ *The second 24,000 tonne gas turbine ship built at Whyalla was the* **Union Rotoiti**. *She arrived at Auckland on her maiden voyage on 23 July 1977. The subsequent horrendous fuel costs for the gas turbine vessels saw her converted at Newcastle, New South Wales between December 1985 and June 1986, to medium speed diesel engines burning 50% less fuel. The illustration shows her after her conversion to diesel power with the gas turbine house abaft the funnel removed* J.Y. FREEMAN

◄ **Union Rotoiti** *in 1995 showing the effects of the structural alterations to the decks to allow for the carriage of further ISO containers* N.J. KIRBY

In 1981, the Union Company decided to replace the conventional coaster **Titoki,** *then on the run from Onehunga to Nelson, with a specialist container ship. It acquired the one-year-old* **Sunny Karina,** *which could carry 150 – 20 foot containers. Renamed* **Union Nelson**, *she commenced 14-day round trips between Onehunga, Nelson, Lyttelton and New Plymouth in March 1982. A little over three years later she was withdrawn due to intense competition from road and rail, declining cargo volumes and high costs. She was subsequently employed under Union Company control around Pacific Island ports until she heeled over and sank at Suva in 1991*   N.J. KIRBY

| HOLMDALE | 911 GRT | IN FLEET 1981–1991 |

BUILT: 1961 by Bodewes Scheepswerven N.V., Martinshoek as *Holmdale* 1961–1991.

PREVIOUS OWNERS: Holm Shipping Co. Ltd., Wellington, 1961–81.

SUBSEQUENT HISTORY: (Union Company, Mgrs 1972–1981). (Ownership registered to Union Shipping New Zealand Ltd., 1988–91). Sold Celtic Pacific Shipping Ltd., Avatiu, Cook Islands 1991 and renamed *Celtic Kiwi* (Cook Islands) 1991. Vessel abandoned in listing condition and subsequently sank 27/10/1991 about 180 miles north, northwest of North Cape, New Zealand, on passage Auckland to Norfolk Island.

◂ *The small 911 tonne coaster* **Holmdale** *had been managed by the Union Company since 1972 and she had been engaged in the service to the Chatham Islands from 1968. She had been built in Holland in 1961 for the Holm Shipping Company of Wellington. The company purchased the ship in 1981 and she continued on the Chatham Island service until September 1990 when the New Zealand Government withdrew the operating subsidy. She was subsequently sold in 1991 and foundered at sea the same year* N.J. KIRBY

| UNION NELSON | 3023 GRT | IN FLEET 1981–1991 |

BUILT: 1980 by Dong Hae Shipbuilding Co. Ltd., Ulsan as *Sunny Karina* (Liberia) 1980–81.

PREVIOUS OWNERS: Sunny Karina Tramp Corp., Monrovia (Aquarius Seereederi Edgar Leicher, Hamburg, Mgrs) 1980–81.

SUBSEQUENT HISTORY: Ownership registered Broadbank Nominees Ltd., Auckland, 1981–86. Under Union Steam Ship Company of N.Z. Ltd., Wellington, 1986–1991 and renamed *Capricornia* (Tonga) 1986–89, (New Zealand) 1989–90. Renamed *Polynesian Link* (New Zealand) 1990–91. Chartered to Fathom Fisheries Ltd., Tonga, (Warner Pacific Line) and subsequently sub-chartered to Rarotonga Line Ltd., Avatiu (Translink Pacific Shipping Ltd., Avatiu, Mgrs) 1990–91. During loading at Suva 12/10/1991, heeled over and sank at berth. Salvindo Towage & Salvage Pte. Ltd., Singapore, removed accommodation section with sheerlegs *Perkasa 11* and hull cut in three sections and removed 1–2/1992.

| TAIKO (OIL TANKER) | 21187 GRT | IN FLEET 1984–1999 |

BUILT: 1984 by Mitsubishi Heavy Industries Ltd., Nagasaki. (Intended to be named *Tara* but launched 24/12/1983 un-named. Delivered 30/5/1984 as *Taiko* and registered Hong Kong, 30/6/1984, Wellington, 9/10/1984.

SUBSEQUENT HISTORY: (Vessel on long term charter to New Zealand Oil Consortium now known as Coastal Tankers Limited, Wellington). Sold Coastal Tankers Limited, Wellington, 1999 and ownership registered to Penagree No 2 Ltd., (same name and registry)

◂ *Since 1965 the Union Company had managed the chartered tankers delivering petroleum products from the Marsden Point refinery to the main ports. It decided to build its own tanker and charter it back to the New Zealand Oil Consortium. An order was placed with a Nagasaki shipyard in December 1982. The ship was built in two halves and joined together in a floating dock. The company intended to use the name* **Tara** *but that had been taken by a small pleasure craft and she was named* **Taiko** *instead. Although registered on 30 May 1984, she did not reach New Zealand until 2 October of that year because of industrial problems over crewing the vessel. Although the Union Company lost the management contract for the coastal tankers in 1994,* **Taiko** *remains in this trade* N.J. KIRBY

To handle bulk parcels in the trans Tasman trade and sugar from Fiji, the company took the 12,259-tonnes Norwegian bulk carrier **Columbia** *on 10-year time charter in 1974 and renamed her* **Union Auckland.***. When her charter expired in 1984 it was financially expedient to purchase the vessel and she remained in service until sold for demolition in 1997. Originally equipped with five 5 tonne shipboard cranes, these could not handle large modern grabs, so from 1989 the four forward crane jibs were removed, making her a gearless bulk carrier* BAIN-WRIGHT COLLECTION

The massive capital outlay required for the Australian-built roro ships and the related equipment and shore terminals, saw the company take a number of vessels on long term charter. Two of these were ships built in Norway to a modified design employed by the Tor Line of Sweden. The first ship, **Union Hobart,** *entered service in August 1976, running between South Island New Zealand ports and Melbourne. She was transferred to the Sydney-Hobart service in 1984 and renamed* **Seaway Hobart.** *At the end of the time charter in 1988, the vessel was purchased by the company and she remained in the fleet for another five years* N.J. KIRBY

UNION AUCKLAND   12559 GRT   IN FLEET 1984–1997

BUILT: 1970 by Fredrikstad Mek. Verksted, A/S, Fredrikstad as *Columbia* (Norway) 1970–74.

PREVIOUS OWNERS: Reidar Rods Rederi A/S, Tonsberg 1970–74. Wigmore Ltd., Bermuda (A.J. Chandris, Piraeus, Mgrs) 1974 and renamed *Union Auckland* (Br) 1974. (Union Company time charterers 1974–1984).

SUBSEQUENT HISTORY: (New Zealand registry from 26/6/1985) (Ownership registered to Union Shipping New Zealand Ltd., 1988–97). Sold Ruby Enterprises Inc (Rederij Gebr. Wijsmuller B.V., Mgrs) 1997 and renamed *Lars* (St. Vincent & Grenadines) 1997. Sold Indian shipbreakers and ran ashore Alang for demolition 13/11/1997.

SEAWAY HOBART   4376 GRT   IN FLEET 1988–1993

BUILT: 1976 by Framnaes Mek.Vaerksted A/S, Sandefjord, for Whitminster Co. Ltd., Hamilton, (A.J. Chandris, Piraeus, Mgr) for time charter to Union Company as *Union Hobart* (New Zealand) 1976–84, *Seaway Hobart* (New Zealand), 1984–88.

SUBSEQUENT HISTORY: (Ownership registered to Union Steam Ship Co. of Australia Pty. Ltd., Melbourne, 1988–90. Union Shipping Australia Pty. Ltd., Melbourne, 1990–93.) Sold Sontak Shipping Company Ltd., Limassol, (A.K.Ventouris Inc., Athens, Mgrs) 1993 and renamed *Seaway 1* (Cyprus) 1993. Converted to passenger/car ferry and renamed *Agia Methodia* (Cyprus) 1994–95 (same owners/mgrs). Sold Icemare Shipping Co. S.A., Nassau, 1995 and renamed *Euromantique* (Bahamas) 1995–99. Sold Maritime Company of Lesvos S.A., Mytilene, Greece (NEL Lines, Mgrs) 1999 and renamed *Taxiarchis* (Greece) 1999– (Operating out of Piraeus 7/2000).

SEAWAY MELBOURNE   4376 GRT   IN FLEET 1989–1992

BUILT: 1977 by Framnaes Mek.Vaerksted A/S, Sandefjord for Lulworth & Co. Ltd., Hamilton, (A.J. Chandris, Piraeus, Mgr) for time charter to Union Company as *Union Lyttelton* (New Zealand) 1977–83, *Seaway Melbourne* (New Zealand) 1983–89.

SUBSEQUENT HISTORY: (Ownership registered to Union Steam Ship Co. of Australia Pty. Ltd., Melbourne, 1989–90. Union Shipping Australia Pty. Ltd., Melbourne, 1990–92). Laid up Melbourne, 17/4/1992. Sold to Fast Trader Co., Valetta, 1992 and renamed *Seaway* (Malta) 1992. Sold Demline Egypt for Maritime Transport, Alexandria, (John Khapat & Co. (DEM Line), Beirut, Mgrs) 1992 and renamed *Fast Trader* (Malta) 1992–93 (Egypt) 1993– (Trading Mediterranean 7/2000.)

◀ *Sister ship of the* **Union Hobart** *was the* **Union Lyttelton,** *which entered service in 1977. Her career followed a similar pattern to* **Union Hobart,** *with her transferring to the Melbourne-Hobart service in 1983. She was renamed* **Seaway Melbourne** *until she was withdrawn in April 1992 and sold for trading in the Mediterranean Sea a few months later. She, too, was purchased by the Union Company when her 10-year charter expired in 1989. In the years preceding the withdrawal of both* **Seaway Hobart** *and* **Seaway Melbourne,** *the yellow line on the upper half of their green hulls was removed* N.J. KIRBY

The greater demand for ISO container space in the Trans Tasman roro vessels, which were designed around the smaller Seafreighter module, saw the Union Company charter a multi-purpose bulker in 1986 and rename her **Union Endeavour**. *Suitable for pallet loads, packaged steel, and timber packs, the ship could handle 1024 containers. She was self-sustaining with six 25 tonne cranes. Throughout her time with the company she had a corn coloured hull instead of the usual bronze green. The advent of the* **Union Endeavour**, *made the link spans at the various ports redundant. She was purchased in 1989 and sold in 1991*   J.Y. FREEMAN

The experience gained with the lift-on, lift-off multi purpose **Union Endeavour** *saw the company revert in 1991 to a purely roll-on, roll-off fleet. The 14,000 tonne, 15-year-old motorship* **Kagoro** *was purchased. Briefly renamed* **Rost** *for Union Shipping Group financing purposes, she was renamed* **Union Rotoma** *in 1991. With a stern quarter ramp, the vessel had a TEU container capacity of 1467. She also had a 40 tonne crane on deck. On her first voyage in April 1991,* **Union Rotoma** *was manned by a crew of only 19, representing the efforts of months and months of negotiations by the company with maritime union representatives*   J.Y. FREEMAN

UNION ENDEAVOUR   13483 GRT   IN FLEET 1989–1991

BUILT: 1982 by VEB Mathias-Thesen-Werft, Wismar as *Dagmar Reeckmann* (East German) 1982, (Liberia) 1982–83.

PREVIOUS OWNERS: Halstead Shipping Corp.Ltd., Monrovia (F. Laeisz, Hamburg, Mgrs 1982, F.Laeisz Schiffahrtsge M.B.H. & Co, Mgrs 1982–89) and renamed *Norasia Dagmar* (Liberia) 1983–85, *Dagmar Reeckmann* (Liberia) 1985–86. Transferred Halstead Shipping (Bermuda) Ltd., Hamilton, 1986 and renamed *Union Endeavour* (New Zealand) 1986–91. (Under charter to Union Company 1986–89).

SUBSEQUENT HISTORY: (Ownership registered to Union Shipping New Zealand Ltd., 1989–91). Sold Jade Co. Inc., Panama, (Nicos Vernicos-Eugenides, Piraeus, Mgrs) 1991 and renamed *Penelope 11* (Pan) 1991– (Trading South American ports to Europe 7/2000.)

UNION ROTOMA   13979 GRT   IN FLEET 1991–1999

PREVIOUS OWNERS: Compagnie Generale Maritime, Paris 1976–88. Renamed *CGM Rostand* (French) 1987–88, *PAD Australia* (French) 1988–89 (Panama) 1989. Sold Burma Navigation Corp.,Yangon, 1988–89. Sold Kagoro Ltd., Nassau, (Acomarit Seervices Maritimes S.A., Geneva 1989 and renamed *Kagoro* (Bahamas) 1989–90.(Isle of Man) 1990–91. Under Kagoro Ltd., Douglas, (Celtic Pacific Shipping Ltd., Douglas, Mgrs on behalf Union Company) 1990–91 and renamed *Rost* (Isle of Man) 1991. Sold Corisande Ltd., Douglas, (same mgrs/registry) 1991.

SUBSEQUENT HISTORY: (Ownership registered to Union Shipping New Zealand Ltd., 1991–1999). (Gross tonnage increased to 29,040 1995). Sold Anzdl Ltd, (Anglo-Eastern Ship Management Ltd, Hong Kong, Ltd. Mgrs) 1999 and renamed *Rotoma* (Bermuda) 1999– (Still operating Trans-Tasman 7/2000).

PART TWO

Subsidiary and Associated Companies, Sailing Vessels and Hulks

Subsidiary and Associated Companies

Abel Tasman Shipping Co. Pty. Limited, Melbourne

Abel Tasman Shipping Co. Pty. Ltd. was formed 1/9/1972 to take over the assets of H.C.S. Coasters Pty. Ltd., Melbourne – a company first registered 9/8/1933 by H.C. Sleigh Ltd., Melbourne, for the purpose of operating a trans-Tasman cargo service. Three years later on 12/6/1936 a new H.C.S. Coasters Pty. Ltd. was registered with the Union Company, through nominees, being the beneficial owner. Ships employed were the *Abel Tasman* – 2047 tons (1933–36), *James Cook* – 2181 tons (1935–53), *Matthew Flinders* – 2235 tons (1938–57) and *Abel Tasman* – 2681 tons (1958–72). The ships remained managed by H.C. Sleigh Ltd., Melbourne, until September 1972.

Abel Tasman Shipping Co. Pty. Ltd. was a fully owned subsidiary of the Union Company and until its sale in 1975 the only ship registered under the company name retained the colours of H.C.S. Coasters Pty. Ltd. The company was no longer active from 28/6/1979. Then it was renamed Union Steam Ship Company of Australia Pty. Ltd. on 29/6/1979. Ownership of the *Seaway Prince* and *Seaway Princess* was transferred to this company between 1979 and 1985.

ABEL TASMAN	2681 GRT	IN FLEET 1972–1975

BUILT: 1957 by Hall, Russell & Co., Ltd. Aberdeen.
SUBSEQUENT HISTORY: Sold Guan Guan Shipping (Pte.) Ltd. Singapore, 1975 and renamed *Golden Globe* (Singapore) 1975–82 (Panama) 1982–84. Sold Safinatus Salem Shipping (Pte.) Ltd., Singapore, 1984 and renamed *Sam Ju* (Panama) 1984–85. Sold Azim Shipping Co (Pte.)

The last ship built for the Union Company subsidiary, H.C.S. Coasters Pty. Ltd. of Melbourne was the 2681-ton **Abel Tasman** *in 1957. She was a specialist timber carrier with two large clear holds and derricks with a lifting capacity of 7.5 tons. She spent 18 years under Union Company control and a further 14 years under various owners in eastern waters* BAIN-WRIGHT COLLECTION

Ltd., Singapore, 1985 (Bayanihan Shipping (Pte.) Ltd., Singapore, Mgrs) and renamed *Azim 1* 1985. Sold Amora Holdings Inc., Panama (Hind Shipping Agencies, Bombay, Mgrs) 1985 and renamed *Alfalah* 1985, *Alsarah* 1985, *Alba III* (1985–89 (all Panama registry). Arrested by Bangladesh Navy 23/12/1985 in Chittagong Outer Anchorage (for alleged smuggling) on passage Singapore to Chittagong. Released 1989 and sold to Mariners Bangladesh Ltd. for demolition at Begum Dockyards, Sadarghat and beached in position 7/12/1989 with work commencing 7/2/1990.

Canadian Australasian Line, Vancouver

On 2/7/1931 the Canadian Australasian Line Limited was formed in Vancouver. The Canadian Pacific Railway Company purchased a half interest in the new line with the Union Company for £500,000. The Union Company vessels *Aorangi* and *Niagara* were transferred to the company (full details of the ships appear in the main fleet list). Four cargo ships purchased from the Canadian Government – *Waikawa*, *Waitomo*, *Wairuna* and *Waihemo*, were also briefly registered under the ownership of Canadian Australasian Line from 1946–47. The services under this company were terminated from 8/6/1953 when the *Aorangi* arrived in Sydney on her last voyage from Vancouver to Australia and New Zealand.

Canterbury Shipping Company Limited

See Pacifica Shipping Company Ltd., Christchurch.

Wm. Holyman and Sons Pty. Limited, Launceston

This company was established by Captain William Holyman, who arrived in Tasmania in 1854. He acquired an interest in his first ship in 1861 and subsequently expanded the business with other vessels operating out of Tasmanian ports. Initially this was in partnership with his sons or others but on 13/10/1904 two joint stock companies were formed – Wm. Holyman & Sons Ltd. and Holymans Limited. In that year the Union Company and Huddart Parker Limited of Melbourne each acquired a third share in the Holyman companies and the Union Company sold its *Wareatea* to the company.

In April 1921 the parent company became known as Wm. Holyman and Sons Pty. Limited and in September 1924 there was a capital reconstruction of the group. The Union Company and Huddart Parker Ltd. then each held 25% of the capital, with the Holyman family interests holding the remaining 50%. The Union Company subsequently acquired the Huddart Parker interest in 1962. During re-organisation of the Union Company interests, following the sale by P & O, the shares in Holymans, were disposed of to Trucape Pty. Limited of Melbourne. This company was registered on 9/11/1973 with a capital of $A10,000. Trucape shares were equally owned by N.Z. Maritime Holdings Ltd., Auckland and Bulkships Ltd. of Melbourne. By 1975 Wm. Holyman and Sons Pty. Limited had a paid up share capital of $A1,150,000 and of this, 82% was owned by Trucape and the remainder by James Holyman Pty. Ltd. The Union Company interests in Trucape Pty. Ltd. were sold to Bulkships Limited 22/9/1978.

The company sold its remaining ship – *William Holyman* – in 1975 and then chartered the *Mary Holyman* (2577 tons – built 1971 and owned by Wm. Brandts (Leasing) Ltd., Newcastle 1971–82 and T.N.T. Bulkships Operations Pty Ltd. from 1982 until 1988. (Last voyage Devonport to Melbourne 5/1987)

WILLIAM HOLYMAN	1975 GRT	IN FLEET 1961–1975

BUILT: 1961 by N.S.W. Government Engineering and Shipbuilding Undertaking, Newcastle.
SUBSEQUENT HISTORY: Sold Maldives Shipping Ltd., Male, and renamed *Maldive Swift* (Maldive

Islands) 1975–82. Arrived Khorramshar 14/9/1980. Damaged during Iran/Iraq conflict 5/10/1980, 7/10/1980 and again 9/10/1980. Subsequently declared compromised total loss 5/1982.

Indo Pacific Shipping Company Limited, London

In 1929, the Union Company formed a London subsidiary concern, the Indo Pacific Shipping Company Limited, in order to operate vessels in the Indian service using Asian crews. The *Leitrim* was transferred to this company and renamed *Narbada*. In 1936 the *Limerick* was also transferred. (Full details of the ships appear in the main fleet list). The Indo Pacific Shipping Co.Ltd. ceased as shipowners on the sale of *Narbada* in 1947.

Livestock International Limited, Wellington

This company was originally registered as E. Hopkinson (1966) Ltd., Wellington on 31/10/1966 and was renamed Livestock International Ltd., on 7/7/1972. The Union Company acquired a 50% interest (3000 – one dollar shares) on 25/7/1978 with the remaining 50% shareholding held by Freightways Holdings Ltd., Auckland. This company was wound up by board resolution on 22/12/1992. The company had been set up for the export of livestock overseas.

G. McLatchie and Company Limited, Christchurch

This company was registered at Christchurch in March 1913 to take over the coal and firewood business of George McLatchie. At that time, 50% of the shares were owned by H.J. Beswick of Christchurch, son-in-law of Sir James Mills. On 18/8/1930, Union Company nominees owned 80% of the paid up capital and from 24/10/1939 this was increased to 68,498 shares from a total of 68,500. The company was dissolved on 18/12/1973.

Mercantile Investments Limited, Wellington

For the purposes of investing and assisting with the capital development of smaller air and shipping companies mainly owned or controlled by localised interests, the Union Company formed Land and Mortgage Securities Limited, Wellington on 17/10/1928. It was wound up 11/3/1936 and superseded by Mercantile Investments Limited of Wellington, which was incorporated on the same day.

Prior to the establishment of these companies, the Union Company had made significant investments in a number of smaller New Zealand shipping companies. These investments were handled by nominees on behalf of the Union Company in order to ensure complete secrecy. They gave the Union Company an essential element of control over operations and future expansion of the companies and because of the secret nature of the holdings, the public in general were not aware of the extent of the Union Company monopoly in the majority of shipping services operating around the New Zealand coast.

The first of these arrangements dated from November 1905 when the Union Company obtained 50% of the shareholding of the Canterbury Steam Shipping Company Limited of Christchurch. Similar investments of 25% each were made in the Invercargill Shipping Company of Dunedin and the Wairau Steam Ship Co. Ltd. of Wellington in 1907. A 50% share was obtained in the Anchor Shipping and Foundry Co. Ltd. of Nelson in 1908 and in the same year the Union Company acquired 50% of the shares in Ferdinand Holm's Maoriland Steamship Co. Ltd. of Wellington. In October 1912 a 25% share was obtained in Napier-based Richardson and Co. Ltd.

The company was also involved with the Gisborne Sheepfarmers' Frozen Meat & Mercantile Co. Ltd. and contributed the major share of the purchase costs of its ships *Margaret W* in 1935 and *Turihaua* in 1948. The Anchor Shipping & Foundry Company vessel *Totara* (421 tons gross – built 1924), which entered the Anchor Line fleet in 1926, was paid for by the Union Company. Anchor remained the nominal owner, as *Totara* was under the tonnage allowed in Union Company agreements with the various maritime unions. Although *Port Waikato* and *Port Tauranga* were not formally transferred to the Union Company fleet until 1947, most of the vessels operated by Captain A.F. Watchlin had been owned by the Union Company from 27 September 1934. At that time Captain Watchlin accepted an offer to purchase *Port Waikato* and *Port Whangarei* with him retaining a 10% interest in the former. The *Port Tauranga*, built in 1937, was paid for by the Union Company and the subsequent vessel, intended to be named *Port Underwood*, was also to be financed by it.

By the 1950s the Union Company held a controlling interest (either indirectly through nominees or through Mercantile Investments Ltd.) in Anchor Shipping and Foundry Co. Ltd. of Nelson, the Canterbury Steam Shipping Co. Ltd. of Christchurch, Holm Shipping Co. Ltd. of Wellington and Richardson and Co. Ltd. of Napier. In 1964 the Union Company purchased the shares held by minority interests in Richardson and Co. Ltd. and the Canterbury Steam Shipping Co. Ltd. All four concerns were independently managed but from 1/10/1969 the ships of Canterbury Steam and Richardsons were bareboat chartered to Holm Shipping Company Limited and painted in Holm colours. This firm managed the vessels of all three companies and the Union Company took over the agency for the ships at ports where Holm Shipping did not have its own office. The Anchor Company continued to operate independently until 1973.

From 1/3/1972 all the ships then managed by Holm Shipping Co. Ltd. came directly under the management of the Union Company and registered ownerships of the Canterbury and Richardson vessels were transferred to the Holm Shipping Co., Ltd. Although the vessels retained Holm Shipping colours, they were operated from that day as if they were Union Company vessels. In December 1973, the name of Anchor Shipping and Foundry Co. Ltd. was changed to Anchor Dorman Ltd. – incorporating the interests of Dorman Engineering Co. Ltd. of Nelson, which the Union Company had acquired in 1969.

Canterbury Steam and Richardsons went into voluntary liquidation and were wound up on 6/12/1978 and 25/11/1978 respectively. Mercantile Investments was itself dissolved 28/5/1981. Anchor Dorman was operated as Anchor Shipping (shipping) and Anchor Dorman (engineering) but from 31/3/1982 the former company was renamed Union Maritime Services Ltd. and the Anchor Dorman engineering interests were sold to the Perry Dines Corporation Ltd., New Plymouth, on 31/3/1984. With the sale of the *Holmdale* to the Union Company in 1981, the Holm Shipping Co. Ltd. ceased as shipowners and the company was subsequently sold and renamed Super Luggage Stores Ltd. in 1982.

Particulars of the vessels taken over from their respective interests from 1/3/1972 were as follows:

Anchor Shipping and Foundry Company Limited, Nelson

PURIRI	1248 GRT	IN FLEET 1972–1974

BUILT: 1948 by Henry Robb Ltd., Leith.

SUBSEQUENT HISTORY: Sold Maldives Shipping Ltd., Male, 1974 and renamed *Maldive Pilot* (Maldive Islands) 1974–75. Sold Power Shipping (Pte.) Ltd., Singapore, (Navitrade (Pte.) Ltd., Singapore, Mgrs) 1975 and renamed *Yellow River* (Singapore) 1975–79. Sold Ya Chou Steel Manufacturing Co. Ltd., Kaohsiung, and delivered for demolition 16/12/1979.

Amongst the coasters the Union Company managed from 1972 was the Anchor Shipping and Foundry vessel **Titoki**. *She was sold in 1982 after a 24-year career on the New Zealand coast. In later years she ran to Cocos Island in the Indian Ocean and finally ended her working days when she was arrested for smuggling in Madras in 1986* BAIN-WRIGHT COLLECTION

| TITOKI | 855 GRT | IN FLEET 1972–1982 |

BUILT: 1958 by E.J. Smit & Zoon's Scheepswerven N.V., Westerbroek, Holland.
SUBSEQUENT HISTORY: Sold Tropic Island Shipping Co. Pte. Ltd., Singapore (Thome & Co., Pte. Ltd., Mgrs.) 1982 and renamed *Wild Rover* (Panama) 1982–83. Sold Vertom Scheepvaart en Handel Maatschappij N.V., Rotterdam, and registered ownership to Barretto Shipping & Trading Co., (Pte.) Ltd., Singapore, 1983 (same name/registry) Under management John Clunies Ross, Cocos Islands 1983–84 (same registered owners/name/registry). Sold Trans American International (Pelorus Shipping Co. Pte. Ltd., Singapore, Mgrs) 1984 and renamed *Varuna* (Panama) 1984–85. Sold Golden Pearl Shipping Co. Ltd., Valletta, 1985 and renamed *Golden Pearl* (Malta) 1985–86. Sold Intercity Shipping Co. Ltd., Valletta, 1986 and renamed *Inter City 1* (Malta). Seized by Customs and Coastguard authorities off Madras Harbour entrance 16/12/1986 for smuggling. Subsequently sold Indian shipbreakers and arrived Mangalore for demolition 7/10/1987.

| TOTARA | 855 GRT | IN FLEET 1972–1978 |

BUILT: 1957 by E.J. Smit & Zoon's Scheepswerven N.V., Westerbroek, Holland.
SUBSEQUENT HISTORY: Sold Ruby Marine Ltd., Singapore, (Pacific Navigation Co. Pte. Ltd., Singapore, Mgrs) 1978 and renamed *Pacific Bold* (Singapore) 1978–87. Sold Island Enterprises (Pte.) Ltd., Male, 1987 and renamed *Antares* (Maldive Islands) 1987–90. Sold Island Trade & Travel Pte. Ltd., Male, 1990 and renamed *Sygnus* (Maldive Islands) 1990–91. Sold M/S Mahaal Tours of Maldives 1991 and renamed *Riviheli* (Maldive Islands) 1991. Sold Indian shipbreakers (Reported 7/2000 but likely sometime prior to that date). Idle at Male in 1993.

The Canterbury Steam Shipping Company Limited, Christchurch

| SQUALL | 817 GRT | IN FLEET 1972–1973 |

BUILT: 1956 by James Lamont & Co. Ltd., Port Glasgow
SUBSEQUENT HISTORY: Sold King Line S.A., Panama (Guan Guan Shipping (Pte.) Ltd., Singapore, Mgrs) 1973 and renamed *King Tiger* (Panama) 1973–74. Transferred Guan Guan Shipping (Pte.) Ltd., Singapore, 1974 (same name but Singapore registry). Renamed *Golden Summer* (Singapore) 1984 (same owners). Sold White Shipping & Trading Pte. Ltd., Singapore, 1/8/1984 and broken up Singapore.

| STORM | 931 GRT | IN FLEET 1972–1975 |

BUILT: 1960 by Scott & Sons, (Bowling) Ltd., Bowling, Glasgow.

SUBSEQUENT HISTORY: Sold Crossworld Management & Brokerage (H.K.) Ltd., Hong Kong, (Crossworld Navigational Services (S) Pte. Ltd., Singapore, Mgrs) 1975 and renamed *Surabaya Fortune* (Singapore) 1975–77. Sold Pacific International Lines Pte. Ltd., Singapore, 1977 and renamed *Kota Perwira* (Singapore) 1977–84. Sold Sabah South East Asia Investment Corp., Panama, 1984 (same name but Panama registry). Sold Thai Boon Roong Trading (S) Pte. Ltd., Singapore, 1984 (same name). Arrested Madras 23/6/1986 for smuggling gold bars and other contraband. Sold by auction 11/1986 to Johan Fidel, Madras. Sprang leak and partially sank 1/9/1987 in Madras outer harbour and effectively constructive total loss. Sold Indian shipbreakers 5/1988.

Holm Shipping Company Limited, Wellington

| HOLMBURN | 845 GRT | IN FLEET 1972–1975 |

BUILT: 1957 by Bodewes Scheepswerven N.V., Martenshoek.

SUBSEQUENT HISTORY: Sold Guan Guan Shipping (Pte.) Ltd., Singapore, 1975 and renamed *Golden Summer* (Singapore) 1975–83. Sold National Shipbreakers Pte. Ltd., Singapore, and delivered Jurong for demolition 20/12/1983.

| HOLMDALE | 911 GRT | IN FLEET 1972–1981 |

BUILT: 1961 by Bodewes Scheepswereven N.V., Martenshoek.

SUBSEQUENT HISTORY: Ownership transferred to Union Steam Ship Company of N.Z. Ltd. 1981 (see main fleet list page 205)

| HOLMLEA | 1053 GRT | IN FLEET 1972–1975 |

BUILT: 1967 by Hong Kong & Whampoa Dock Co., Ltd., Kowloon, Hong Kong, as *Seaway Princess* (N.Z.) Northern Steam Ship Co. Ltd., Auckland, 1967–69. Holm Shipping Co. Ltd., Wellington, 1969–72.

SUBSEQUENT HISTORY: Sold A.M.A.L. S.p.A., Messina 1975 and renamed *Annarita Seconda* (Italy) 1975–78, *Gabbiano* (Italy) 1978–83 (same owners). Sold Mediterranea Marittima S. p. A. di Nav., Genoa (Soc. Co-operative di Nav. Garibaldi S.R.L., Genoa, Mgrs) 1983–89 (same name). Sold Italian shipbreakers, Eurofer S.p.A. and demolition began at San Giorgio di Nogaro, Italy, 2/11/1989.

| HOLMPARK | 600 GRT | IN FLEET 1972–1972 |

BUILT: 1953 by G. Renck Jnr., Komm. Ges., Harburg as *Commandant Milliasseau* (French) 1953–65.

PREVIOUS OWNERS: Compagnie Generale Transatlantique, Paris 1953–65. N.V. Redwijs, Netherlands, 1965 and renamed *Command* (Dutch) 1965. Holm Shipping Co., Ltd., Wellington, 1965 and renamed *Holmpark* (N.Z.) 1965–72.

SUBSEQUENT HISTORY: On charter to United Salvage Pty. Ltd., Melbourne, 1968–72 and sold same company 1972–74. Sold Hiap Seng Shipping and Trading Co. (Pte.) Ltd., Singapore, 1974 and renamed *Holmi* (Singapore) 1974–79. Sold Raebin Mas Shipping S. A., Bangkok, 1979 and renamed *Good Year* (Thailand) 1979–87. Sold Soo Hai Fong Shipping, Songkla, 1987 and renamed *Hadyai Union 1* (Thailand) 1987–88. Arrived Port Moresby 2/2/1988, later declared unseaworthy, abandoned by owners and subsequently scuttled by port authority 4.5 miles south of Basalisk Passage off Port Moresby 21/11/1988.

| HOLMWOOD | 7976 GRT | IN FLEET 1972–1972 |

BUILT: 1953 by Bodewes Scheepswerven N.V., Martenshoek.

SUBSEQUENT HISTORY: Sold King Line S.A., Panama (Guan Guan Shipping (Pte.) Ltd., Singapore, Mgrs) 1972 and renamed *King Fish* (Panama) 1972–75. Transferred Guan Guan Shipping (Pte.) Ltd. (same name but Singapore registry) 1975–84. Sold Pioneer Shipping Co., Male, (Seaward Shipping & Trading Co. (S) Pte. Ltd., Male, Mgrs) 1984 and renamed *Pioneer Elite* (Maldive Islands) 1984–85. Sold Molasses Trading & Export Co., Pakistan and demolition commenced Gadani Beach 23/7/1985.

Richardson and Company Limited, Napier

| PARERA | 823 GRT | IN FLEET 1972–1975 |

BUILT: 1957 by George Brown & Co (Marine) Ltd., Greenock.

SUBSEQUENT HISTORY: Sold King Line S.A., Panama, (Guan Guan Shipping (Pte.) Ltd., Singapore, Mgrs) 1975 and renamed *King Lake* (Panama) 1975. Transferred to Guan Guan Shipping (Pte.) Ltd., Singapore, 1975 (same name but Singapore registry 1975–85). Sold Nan Wah Enterprise S.A., Panama, 1985 and renamed *Kin Lake* (Panama) 1985. Went aground 12/4/1985 at Tankan Shan, 12 miles south of Hong Kong and wrecked.

| PATEKE | 800 GRT | IN FLEET 1972–1972 |

BUILT: 1954 by Jac. Bodewes Scheepsbouwwerf "Hoogezand", Hoogezand.

SUBSEQUENT HISTORY: Sold Pacific International Lines (Pte.) Ltd., Singapore, 1972 and renamed *Kota Gembira* (Singapore) 1972–78. Sold Malaysian Shipping Corporation Sdn., Bhd., Kuala Lumpur, (Pacific International Lines (Pte.) Ltd., Singapore, Mgrs) 1978. Renamed *Kota Intan* (Malaysia) 1978–82. Sold Syrikat Perkapalan Pacific Utara Sdn, Bhd., Penang, (Uni-Ocean Lines Pte., Ltd., Singapore, Mgrs) 1982 and renamed *Gembira 11* (Malaysia) 1982–83. Arrived Bangkok 9/3/1983 from Kota Kinabalu. Laid up due persistent machinery breakdowns and later sold for demolition in Thailand.

| PUKEKO | 1020 GRT | IN FLEET 1972–1975 |

BUILT: 1961 by James Lamont & Co. Ltd., Port Glasgow.

SUBSEQUENT HISTORY: Ownership transferred to Anchor Dorman Limited, Nelson, 23/4/1974. Sold Crossworld Management and Brokerage (H.K.) Ltd., Hong Kong, (Crossworld Naviga-

The Scottish-built, Richardson Company coaster **Parera** *came under Union Company management in 1972. She was sold to Singapore owners after 18 years on the New Zealand coast and was finally wrecked south of Hong Kong in 1986* BAIN-WRIGHT COLLECTION

tional Services (S) Pte. Ltd., Singapore, Mgrs) 1975 and renamed *Sirdhana Fortune* (Singapore) 1975–82. Sold Asia Marine Services Co. WLL, Kuwait (Almouaket Shipping & Trading Co. WLL., Kuwait, Mgrs) 1982 and renamed *Almoussa* (Kuwait) 1982–87. Ownership registered to Almouaket Shipping & Trading Co. WLL., Kuwait, 1986–87. Sold Delta Maritime Co. S.A.E., Cairo, 1987 and renamed *Almoussa D* (Egypt) 1987–88. Reported on fire 17/10/1988 off Mokha, Yemen and abandoned drifting 18/10/1988 in position 14.07N – 42.50E. Sank west north west of Zubair Island 20/10/1988.

John Mill and Company Limited, Dunedin

This company was formed by John Mill at Port Chalmers in 1866 and was incorporated on 26/10/1908. As shipping agents, stevedores, coal merchants and later wool dumpers, the company became one of the largest of its kind in New Zealand, with branches at Bluff, Oamaru, Timaru and Wellington. John Mill died in 1926 and the company was purchased by the Union Company on 23/9/1926. It continued to operate as John Mill and Company and in 1951 the remaining assets, which mainly included wool stores and wool dumping presses, were sold to the New Zealand Shipping Co. Ltd., another P & O Group company. It merged these interests with its own wool dumping facilities and John Mill and Co. Ltd. went into voluntary liquidation in 1952 and was subsequently wound up 17/11/1953.

New Zealand Offshore Services Limited, New Plymouth

In order to participate in the management and crewing of vessels involved in the energy projects in the exploration of oil and gas finds, principally off the Taranaki coast, New Zealand Offshore Services Ltd. was registered 25/8/1977 with a capital of $50,000. The Union Company held 30,000 shares, with Australian Offshore Services (a division of P & O Australia Pty. Ltd.) holding the balance of 20,000 shares. The 40% held by Australian Offshore Services was acquired by Union Company in July 1991. Company sold in management buyout 12/2/99.

The company operated from New Plymouth and employed specialist staff experienced in the management of support vessels involved with oil exploration, offshore construction platforms and the servicing of such platforms.

A list of vessels and rigs which the company crewed or managed follows and prior to the formation of the company, the Union Company itself had been involved in the crewing of some oil service vessels and these included the following:

Name	Built	Gross Tonnes	Type	Date under Union Company/NZOFS
SYDNEY TIDE	1969	685	Supply tug	1975
ASIAN MOON	1975	449	Supply tug	1975
LADY VILMA	1973	987	Supply tug	1975/76
NORTHERN TIDE	1973	769	Supply tug	1975/76
BETTY	1970	189	Supply tug	1976
KAREN TIDE	1967	487	Supply tug	1975/76
MISTER FRED	1975	155	Supply tug	1975/77
AUSTRAL TIDE	1968	663	Supply tug	1976
MISTER MARSHALL D	1975	152	Supply tug	1976
MAERSK TRANSPORTER	1974	832	Supply tug	1977
OSA OSTEND	1976	1186	Supply tug	1977
KILDARE	1973	1391	Dive support	1977
LADY VERA	1974	987	Supply tug	1977
MISTER NELSON	1975	359	Supply tug	1976/77

Name	Built	Gross Tonnes	Type	Date under Union Line/NZOFS
PACIFIC INSTALLER	1978	2646	Crane ship	1979
BLUE WHALE	1955	16378	Crane ship	1976/78

Since 1980, New Zealand Offshore Services both crewed and managed the following vessels:

Name	Built	Gross Tonnes	Type	Date
SEDCO 445	1971	6667	Drill ship	1980/81
LADY RACHEL	1973	967	Supply tug	1980/81
LADY VILMA	1973	987	Supply tug	1981/82
WESTERN ODYSSEY	1980	825	Seismic survey	1982/84
TOANUI	1983	1701	Supply tug	1983/84
TAKAPU	1983	1701	Supply tug	1983/84
KODIAK 1	1983	455	Supply tug	1983/84
KODIAK 11	1983	455	Supply tug	1983/84
DIAMOND M EPOCH	1977	5830	Drill platform	1984/85
ATLAS VAN DIEMEN	1982	1179	Supply tug	1984/85
LADY PENELOPE	1982	1239	Supply tug	1984/85
BLUE NABILLA	1984	200	Seismic survey	1984/85
TENDER SEARCHER	1975	498	Supply tug	1985
RAVENSTURM	1977	1175	Supply tug	1985
ZAPATA ARCTIC	1984	10731	Drilling rig	1985
GRANT MARINER	1982	652	Seismic survey	1985/86
PACIFIC SHOGUN	1982	1475	Supply tug	1986
SEAWAY SANDPIPER	1971	13095	Pipe burying	1986
LADY PENELOPE	1982	1239	Supply tug	1986
WESTERN ODYSSEY	1980	825	Seismic survey	1986
LADY LORRAINE	1982	1179	Supply tug	1987
LADY VERA	1974	987	Supply tug	1987
WESTERN PACIFIC	1980	825	Seismic survey	1987
SMIT-LLOYD 104	1973	1294	Supply tug	1987/89
SMIT-LLOYD 109	1974	1292	Supply tug	1987/88
SMIT-LLOYD 111	1972	1292	Supply tug	1987/88
SMIT-LLOYD 105	1973	1292	Supply tug	1986/88
SMIT-LLOYD 106	1973	1294	Supply tug	1987/88
WESTERN ORIENT	1981	779	Seismic survey	1987
OMEGA 803	1976	499	Anchor tug	1987
SEAHORSE 11	1976	3457	Dive support	1988
WESTERN ORIENT	1981	779	Seismic survey	1989
STENA WELLSERVICER	1989	9158	Dive support	1991/92
SEDCO 702	1973	7931	Drilling rig	1992/94
CSO VENTURER	1981	8300	Dive support	1996

Ocean Bulk Limited/Union Shipping Bulk Limited

Registered 4 March 1997, Ocean Bulk Limited was set up as a joint venture between Union Shipping New Zealand Ltd. and Ocean Towing & Salvage (Cook Island) Ltd. to barge low grade coal from Westport, initially to Port Kembla, New South Wales and other destinations as required, State coal exporter, Solid Energy, being the coal supplier. Initial capital was $300,000 of which each party held 50%.

The company acquired the 131-metre barge *Hawaii* from Crowley Maritime Corporation, San Francisco. Built in 1970 and modified in 1990, the barge had a gross tonnage of 6377 tonnes and a maximum deadweight capacity of 15,500 tonnes. Delivered to Ocean Bulk Ltd. at Astoria, Oregon in March 1997, the barge was renamed *Ocean Bulk 1* and arrived in Nelson 7 June 1997 in tow of the tug *Raumanga*.

A tug, *Anglian Warrior* (1978 – 557 gt) was purchased to tow the barge. She was renamed *Frederick Brown* and left Lowestoft on 19 April 1997, arriving in Nelson 7 June 1997. The vessels left Westport 9 July 1997 with the first shipment for Port Kembla (arrived 18 July). An additional tug was needed to assist with the handling of the barge at Westport and the *Parahaki* (1963 – 375 gt), renamed *Alfred Brown*, was supplied by Ocean Towage & Salvage (Cook Island) Ltd.

On 17 November 1997 *Ocean Bulk 1* lifted 10,630 tonnes of coal from Westport for Port Kembla – the largest individual cargo ever to be shipped from a West Coast port. On 1 February 1998, *Ocean Bulk 1* arrived at Suva with the first shipment of 10,600 tonnes of coal from Westport.

On 9/7/1998, Union Shipping purchased the Ocean Towing shares and the company became wholly owned. On 13/10/1998 a new company, Union Shipping Bulk Limited, was formed for the purpose of acquiring the assets of Ocean Bulk Limited. The tug *Frederick Brown* was renamed *Karamea*. The Tasmanian tug *Gawler* which arrived Westport 30/9/1998 on charter to the company was purchased 3/8/1999. Union Shipping Bulk Ltd. came under management of Milburn New Zealand Limited, Westport from 1/9/1999. On 23/6/2000 Solid Energy Ltd., and Union Shipping Bulk Ltd., announced the termination of the contract to barge coal from Westport.

Vessels owned by Union Shipping Bulk Limited:

KARAMEA	557 GRT	IN FLEET 1998–

BUILT: 1978 by Schps & Ghbw v/h Jonker & Stans, Holland as *Schotland* (Netherlands) 1978–87.
PREVIOUS OWNERS: Sleepboot Maatschappij "Schotland" (B.V. Skua and Wm. Muller, Mgrs), Terneuzen 1978–84. Scheepvaart Maatschappiji Ewout b.v. POR Rotterdam, 1984–85. Goliath Towage and Salvage Co. v.v. Rotterdam, 1985–87. Blue Gulf Trading Co. W.L.L., Kuwait 1987 and renamed *Hilal 2* (Kuwait) 1987–90. Mercator Shipping Co. Ltd., Nassau (Nassau Towing Ltd., mgrs) 1990 and renamed *Scaldia* (Bahamas) 1990–93. Sold Al-Jazeera Shipping Co. W.L.L., Manama, Bahrain, 1993 and renamed *Samson* (Bahrain) 1993–95. Klyne Tugs (Lowestoft) Ltd., Kingston, 1995 and renamed *Anglian Warrior* (St. V &G) 1995–97.
SUBSEQUENT HISTORY: Sold Ocean Bulk Ltd., Auckland, renamed *Frederick Brown* (New Zealand) 1997–98. Sold Union Shipping Bulk Ltd., Auckland, 1998 and renamed *Karamea* (New Zealand) 1998–. Laid up Lyttelton from 6/7/2000.

GAWLER	216 GRT	IN FLEET 1998–

BUILT: 1967 by Adelaide Ship Construction Pty. Ltd., Port Adelaide.
PREVIOUS OWNERS: Marine Board of Devonport, Tasmania, 1967–99 (later Devonport Marine Board and Port of Devonport Authority).
SUBSEQUENT HISTORY: On charter to Union Shipping Bulk Ltd. 9/1998 to 8/1999 and then sold to the company 1999 (same name). Laid up Lyttelton from 10/8/2000.

OCEAN BULK 1	6379 GRT	IN FLEET 1998–

BUILT: 1970 by Kelso Marine Inc., Galveston, as *Hawaii* (USA) 1970–97.
PREVIOUS OWNERS: Bankers Trust Co., (as trustee) New York, 1970–79. Hilo Transportation &

Terminal Co. Inc., Hilo, Hawaii, 1979–89. The Harbor Tug & Barge Company, San Francisco, 1989–92 (Crowley Towing & Transportation Co., mgrs – Crowley Maritime Corp. subsidiary). Crowley Marine Services Inc., San Francisco, 1992–97.
SUBSEQUENT HISTORY: Sold Ocean Bulk Ltd., Auckland 1997 and renamed *Ocean Bulk 1* (New Zealand) 1997. Sold Union Shipping Bulk Ltd., Auckland, 1998– (same name). (Laid up Lyttelton from 6/7/2000).

Pacifica Shipping Company Limited, Christchurch

Pacifica Shipping Company Ltd., Christchurch, was registered 26/2/1982 by Christchurch entrepreneur, R. Brooke McKenzie, for the purpose of running a scheduled roll-on, roll-off cargo service between Lyttelton and Wellington.

The Union Company became involved 16/6/1983 through a subsidiary – South Seas Shipping Ltd., Auckland, registered on 6/5/1983 – with a 24.9% holding of the capital of Pacifica. This was increased to 57.4% by 21/8/1984. In 1985 the Union Company decided to sell its interest due to the perilous financial state of the company and Skeggs Foods Ltd. of Dunedin (whose principal, C.G. Skeggs, was a director of the Union Company) acquired those assets it required to continue the business. Skeggs interests assumed control from 7/11/1985 and registered a new company, Pacifica Shipping (1985) Limited, in Dunedin on 10/2/1986.

Of the two ships operated by Pacifica, the *Spirit of Competition* was taken over by the new company but the original vessel in the service, *Spirit of Free Enterprise*, which had been laid up in Wellington from 4/11/1985, remained under Union Company control until delivered to Consort Shipping Line Limited, of Suva, Fiji on 17/7/1986. The Union Company retained a 50% interest in the new registered owners of the vessel – SOFE Shipping Enterprises Ltd. of Suva, with the balance of the shares held equally between Wong Shipping Co. Ltd., Suva and Inter Ports Shipping Corporation Ltd., Suva. The 50% interest held by the Union Company was relinquished in 1988.

The original Pacifica Shipping Company Limited, as a subsidiary of the Union Company, was renamed Canterbury Shipping Co. Ltd. on 23/4/1986.

SPIRIT OF FREE ENTERPRISE 1204 GRT	IN FLEET **1983–1986**

BUILT: 1968 by Soc. Nouvelle des At. & Ch. du Havre, Le Havre as *Sealord Contender* (Br) 1968–69.
PREVIOUS OWNERS: Sealord Shipping Co. Ltd., London 1968–69 (Marine and Industrial Developments Ltd., Thames Line, Mgrs). Cardigan Shipping Co. Ltd., London, (Blandford Shipping Co. Ltd., London, Mgrs) 1969–74 and renamed *Bravo Contender* (Br) 1969–74. Societe Navale Caennaise S.A., Marseilles (Anct. G. Lamy & Cie., Marseilles, Mgrs) 1974–79 and renamed *Daphne* (Fr) 1974–82. Societe Navale Caennaise (SNC) Anct G Lamy & Cie., Marseilles, 1979–82 (same name). Balmoral Shipping Line S.A., Panama 1982 and renamed *Irish Shamrock* (Pan) 1982–86.
SUBSEQUENT HISTORY: Operated under bareboat charter by Pacifica Shipping Co., Ltd., Christchurch and renamed *Spirit of Free Enterprise* (Pan) 1983–86. Laid up Wellington from 4/11/1985. Sold SOFE Shipping Enterprises Ltd., Suva (Wong's Shipping Co., Ltd., Suva, Mgrs) 1986–95 (Same name). Ownership transferred Consort Shipping Co. Ltd., Suva 1995 and renamed *Sofe* (Fiji) 1995– (Still operating in Fijian waters 7/2000).

SPIRIT OF COMPETITION 1600 GRT	IN FLEET **1985–**

BUILT: 1977 by Niigata Engineering Co. Ltd., Niigata as *Marina* (Fr) 1977–80.
PREVIOUS OWNERS: Societe pour le Development du Cabotage 'SODECA', Marseilles (Agence

Maritime De L'Ouest, Paimpol, Mgrs) 1977–80. Levkas Shipping Co.S.A., Panama 1980 and renamed *Marina I* (Pan) 1980–82. Re-possessed by Societe pour le Development du Cabotage 'SODECA' 1982 and renamed *Marina* (Fr) 1982–85.

SUBSEQUENT HISTORY: Registered to Bimac Ltd., Hamilton, Bermuda 1985 and bareboat chartered to Pacifica Shipping Co. Ltd., Christchurch 1985. Renamed *Spirit of Competition* (Bermuda 1985, New Zealand 1985) and later sold 1985 to Pacifica Shipping (1985) Ltd., Dunedin 1985–. Ownership transferred Southern Star Shipping (1985) Ltd., Mgrs) 1998 (same name but Antigua and Barbuda registry). (Still operating New Zealand inter-island services 7/2000).

Smokeless Fuel Company Limited, Christchurch

Formed in Christchurch on 15/8/1933 as Smokeless Fuel and Briquettes (Canterbury) Limited, the company was a subsidiary of G. McLatchie & Co. Ltd., long established Christchurch coal merchants. The name was changed to Smokeless Fuel Co. Ltd. on 14/7/1949 and remained a wholly owned subsidiary of the Union Company until wound up 6/12/1978.

Tasmanian Steamers Proprietary Limited, Melbourne

On 22 December 1921 the Union Company, in conjunction with Huddart Parker Limited of Melbourne, formed Tasmanian Steamers Pty Ltd., Melbourne to run a joint passenger and cargo service between Melbourne and Tasmania. The *Loongana* and *Oonah* of the Union Company and the *Nairana* of Huddart Parker were transferred to the new company which commenced operations on 1/1/1922. The 50% shareholding held by Huddart Parker Ltd. was acquired by the Union Company in December 1961. The company was placed in voluntary liquidation 5/5/1983 and was finally dissolved 22/5/1984. The fleet list of this company was as follows:

LOONGANA	2448 GRT	IN FLEET 1922–1936

Details of career in Union Company fleet list – Page 73.

OONAH	1694 GRT	IN FLEET 1922–1935

Details of career in Union Company fleet list – Page 49.

NAIRANA	3042 GRT	IN FLEET 1922–1950

BUILT: 1917 by Wm. Denny & Bros., Dumbarton, for Huddart Parker Ltd., Melbourne.
PREVIOUS OWNERS: Requisitioned by British Admiralty and converted for use as seaplane carrier HMS *Nairana*. Reverted to owners and refitted Devonport Dockyard 1920.
SUBSEQUENT HISTORY: Laid up Melbourne 1948 and sold Melbourne shipbreakers (Wm. Mussell Pty. Ltd.) 1950. Broke moorings in gale and blown ashore 18/2/1951. Remains removed 1953/54 by order of Melbourne Harbor Trust.

TAROONA	4286 GRT	IN FLEET 1935–1959

BUILT: 1935 by A. Stephen & Sons Ltd., Linthouse, Glasgow.
SUBSEQUENT HISTORY: Sold Typaldos Bros. Steam Ship Co. Piraeus. 1959 and renamed *Hellas* (Greek) 1959–1989. Registered ownership transferred to Aegean Steam Navigation Typaldos Bros. Ltd., Piraeus 1963. Laid up Kynossoura, later near Elefsina, Piraeus from 1967. Following collapse of Typaldos Bros. group 1970, vessel eventually sold by National Bank of Greece (as creditors) to Nigdeliler Hurdacilik ve Makina Ticaret S.A., Turkey and arrived Aliaga in tow 23/5/1989 for demolition.

The 3042-ton passenger ferry **Nairana** *was built in 1917 for Huddart Parker Ltd of Melbourne and was transferred to Tasmanian Steamers Proprietary Ltd. in 1922. Designed for the Melbourne-Launceston service she had accommodation for 450 passengers and was powered by steam turbines for a speed of 20.5 knots. On completion she served as a hangar ship for aircraft and did not enter her designed service until 1920* ALLAN C. GREEN

The **Taroona** *was built for Tasmanian Steamers Pty. Ltd – the company jointly-owned by Huddart Parker Ltd and the Union Company. She entered service on the Melbourne–Launceston passenger service in 1935. During World War 2 she was employed as a fast troop transport and over four years carried 93,482 troops. She was sold to Mediterranean owners in 1959* ALLAN C. GREEN

Following her release from war service in 1946, **Taroona**'s *extensive refit, saw her two squat funnels being replaced by one taller funnel, somewhat destroying her attractive lines*

The last vessel owned by Tasmanian Steamers Pty. Ltd. was the cargo vessel **Tatana***, which was built in Scotland in 1955. On her sale in 1970 the company ceased as shipowners*   J.Y. FREEMAN

| TATANA | 1396 GRT | IN FLEET 1955–1970 |

BUILT: 1955 by Ardrossan Dockyard Co. Ltd., Ardrossan.
SUBSEQUENT HISTORY: Sold Express Navigation (Pte.) Ltd., Singapore (Unique Shipping & Trading Co. Pte. Ltd., Singapore, Mgrs) 1970 and renamed *Bonawind* (Singapore) 1970–72. Sold Oceania (Liberia) Inc., Monrovia (Asafridel (Hong Kong) Ltd., Mgrs) 1972 and renamed *Pisang Tembaga* (Liberia) 1972–74. Sold P.T. Astri Lines, Belawan, 1974 (same name but Indonesian registry). Vessel arrived Belawan 12/1984 and subsequently broken up (in accordance with Indonesian Government policy that vessels over 25 years of age must be decommissioned).

Tasman Union Limited, Wellington

Tasman Union Ltd. was registered 1//11/1971, the company being formerly known as the Kaipara Steam Ship Company Ltd. of Auckland. Formed on 28/11/1930 the Kaipara Steam Ship Company was essentially a "dormant" company in 1971 and was owned by Fletcher Holdings Limited of Auckland. It was into Tasman Union Limited that the P & O ordinary shares of the Union Company were transferred with N.Z. Maritime Holdings Ltd. and T.N.T. Shipping N.Z. Ltd. each holding 50% of the initial $12,000,000 capital. Tasman Union was therefore the "holding company" of the joint Australian and New Zealand interests which acquired the Union Company from P & O Steam Navigation Company of London. Since 1971 the capital was increased to $24,000,000. Tasman Union Ltd. was renamed Union Shipping Group Ltd. on 26/3/1980 prior to a major restructuring of the company from 1/4/1980.

N.Z. Maritime Holdings Ltd. was registered in Auckland 6/9/1971 with a nominal capital of $12,000,000. This was increased to $15,000,000 on 29/10/1975. Initially a number of New Zealand companies held shares in N.Z. Maritime Holdings but by August 1986, Brierley Investments Limited had completed the purchase of the shares held by these investors and the Union Shipping Group was then jointly owned by Brierley Investments and T.N.T. Effective 1/1/1991, South Pacific Passenger Services Ltd., a dormant company within the Union Shipping Group Ltd., was sold to the two shareholders and all the investments in subsidiaries held by the Union Shipping Group Ltd. were then sold to South Pacific Passenger Services Ltd.

At the same time South Pacific Passenger Services Ltd. changed its name to Union Shipping Group Ltd. and the former Union Shipping Group was renamed Union Corporate Services Ltd. The capital of the new Union Shipping Group Ltd. was reduced to $1,000,000.

T.N.T. Shipping N.Z. Ltd. was originally registered in Christchurch as Piesse Transport Ltd. This concern was taken over by T.N.T. in 1971 and the name was changed to T.N.T. Shipping N.Z. Ltd. on 4/10/1971 and registry transferred to Auckland. Capital was increased on 22/10/1971 from $12,000 to $4,000,000 with Thomas Nationwide Transport Limited (T.N.T.) holding 1,966,000 shares and Bulkships Ltd., the remaining 2,034,000 shares. By 1973, all the shares were held by T.N.T. Shipping & Development Pty. Ltd. except one in the name of Associated Steamships Pty Ltd. On 25/2/1975 the capital was increased to $10,000,000. Following the acquisition of T.N.T. in October 1996 by Dutch group K.P.N., Brierley Investments Ltd. exercised its pre-emptive rights and purchased T.N.T. Shipping (N.Z.) Ltd., subsequently changing its name to BIL Maritime Holdings Ltd. BIL Maritime Holdings Ltd was renamed Union Shipping Group Ltd. on 28/7/1997 (the former Union Shipping Group Ltd being renamed Holyman (New Zealand) Ltd.)

Union Direct Line

Brierley Investments Limited, owner of the Union Shipping Group, sold 100% of its trans-Tasman cargo operations to the Brierley subsidiary company, Australian Consolidated Industries Ltd. (A.C.I.L.) Sydney for $US18,000,000. In turn A.C.I.L. purchased 50% of the Australian New Zealand Direct Line (A.N.Z.D.L.) from Groupe Bollore Technologies of Paris for $US30,900,000 and sold 50% of the trans-Tasman cargo business to Group Bollore Technologies for $US9,000,000. Union Direct Line was established to operate an integrated trans-Tasman cargo service between Auckland, Sydney and Melbourne incorporating the three Union Line roll-on, roll-off ships time chartered to Union Direct Line and the seven Transpacific vessels of A.N.Z.D.L. – *Direct Condor, Direct Currawong, Direct Eagle, Direct Falcon, Direct Kea, Direct Kiwi* and *Direct Kookaburra*. Under the marketing name of Union Direct Line, managed from Auckland with its ultimate Head Office in Long Beach, California, the new venture commenced operations from 1/3/1997. CP Ships acquired Union Direct Line in September 1998.

Union Steam Ship Company (U.K.) Limited, London

This company was registered in London in 1971 to cover particular corporate and charter requirements. It was the registered owner of *Rangatira* from 1972 to 1986 (in order to protect the 20% British Government shipbuilding grant) as well as the *Seaway Prince* and *Seaway Princess* from 28/6/1985 until their sale 26/12/1985. It was also used as bareboat charterer of *Union South Pacific* from 1973–78. Union Steam Ship Company (U.K.) Limited was owned by the individual shareholders – T.N.T.(U.K.) and N.Z. Maritime Holdings Ltd.

Sailing Ships

The Union Company owned quite a number of sailing ships but many of these were purchased as coal storage hulks, or even after one or two commercial voyages, were intended for conversion to hulks. A few, however, were in commercial service on regular trading.

The *Sophia R Luhrs*, *Edwin Bassett* and *Genevie M Tucker* were all acquired when the Union Company purchased the ships of the Black Diamond Line (Captain W.R. Williams), Wellington in 1885. In 1908 the line bought the *Dartford* and *Loch Lomond* and it was proposed that the more suitable of the two ships be converted for service as a sail training ship. However, with the loss of *Loch Lomond* on its first voyage, the company converted the *Dartford*. In the latter part of World War 1, the *Dartford*, *Gladbrook* and *Ilma*, which were then in service as coal hulks, were refitted for trading as sailing ships. The company's final involvement with a

In 1908 the Union Company purchased the sailing barque **Dartford** *and fitted her out as a sail training ship for 12 cadets (increased to 36 cadets in 1911). She served in this role for four years. Already 31 years old when purchased by the Union Company,* **Dartford** *became a coal hulk at Auckland from 1921*

ALEXANDER TURNBULL LIBRARY

sailing ship came in 1942 with the management of the captured Finnish barque *Pamir* from 1942 to 1948. Details of the sailing ships owned by the Union Company and employed on commercial voyages were as follows:

| SOPHIA R LUHRS | 661 GRT | IN FLEET 1885–1888 |

BUILT: 1874 by W.R. Sawyer, Millbridge, Maine, U.S.A.
PREVIOUS OWNERS: John Zittlosen, Maine, 1874–78. Black Diamond Line (W.R. Williams), Wellington, 1878–85.
SUBSEQUENT HISTORY: Following entry into Kaipara Harbour 5/6/1888, vessel dragged her anchors, went ashore on the North Spit and became a total loss.

| EDWIN BASSETT | 398 GRT | IN FLEET 1885–1885 |

BUILT: 1866 by Walshaw, Sunderland.
PREVIOUS OWNERS: H. Bassett, North Shields 1866–72. S.J. Lindsay, Melbourne 1872–73. Black Diamond Line (W.R. Williams), Wellington, 1873–85.
SUBSEQUENT HISTORY: With little wind, vessel drifted ashore, four miles south of West Wanganui Inlet 31/8/1885 and was totally wrecked.

| GENEVIE M TUCKER | 519 GRT | IN FLEET 1885–1888 |

BUILT: 1870 by Wm. A. Curtis Portland, Maine, U.S.A.
PREVIOUS OWNERS: J.B. Curtis, B.J. Willard, F.G. Cummings and others, Portland, Maine, 1870–79 Black Diamond Line (W.R. Williams) Wellington 1879–85.
SUBSEQUENT HISTORY: Sold Brunner Coal Company, Greymouth (Martin Kennedy) 1888–89. Sold Ferdinand Holm, Wellington 1889–01. Sold H.W. Henderson, Sydney, 1901–02. Sold Westport Coal Co. Ltd., Dunedin, 1902 and converted to coal hulk 1902. Remains eventually scuttled as breakwater at Waiaro, 4 miles north of Colville, Auckland 23/10/1926.

| DARTFORD | 1312 GRT | IN FLEET 1908–1946 |

BUILT: 1877 by Mounsey & Foster, Sunderland.
PREVIOUS OWNERS: John T Morton, London 1877–1883. G. Traill & Sons, London, 1883–1900. D. Corsar & Sons, London, 1900–08.
SUBSEQUENT HISTORY: Fitted out as sail training ship 1908–12. Converted to coal hulk, Wellington 1912. Re-rigged as sailing barque 1918. Converted to coal hulk at Auckland 8/1921. Hull beached Rangitoto Island 25/7/1946.

| LOCH LOMOND | 1249 GRT | IN FLEET 1908–1908 |

BUILT: 1870 by J.G. Lawrie, Whiteinch, Glasgow.
PREVIOUS OWNERS: Glasgow Shipping Co., Glasgow, (Aitken, Lilburn & Co., Mgrs) 1870–08.
SUBSEQUENT HISTORY: Sailed from Newcastle, N.S.W. 16/7/1908 for Lyttelton and went missing. (Believed to have foundered about 16/9/1908 off the north west coast of the North Island).

| GLADBROOK | 1112 GRT | IN FLEET 1911–1945 |

BUILT: 1877 by R. & J. Evans & Co. Liverpool, as *County of Anglesea*.
PREVIOUS OWNERS: W. Thomas & Co., Liverpool, 1877–05. O. Pettersen & V. Gustafson & Co. (V. Gustafson, Mgr) Mariehamn 1905–08. O. Pettersen, Mariehamn, 1908–11.
SUBSEQUENT HISTORY: Converted to coal hulk at Auckland 1911. Re-rigged as sailing barque 1918–21. Renamed *Gladbrook* 1918. Converted to coal hulk at Suva 1921, transferred to Auckland 1924. Dismantled 1945 and hull beached Rangitoto Island 19/12/1945.

The Union Company was using the 26 year-old barquentine **Ilma** *as a coal hulk at Hobart from 1911 and with wartime shipping losses reducing the number of vessels available to maintain its regular Pacific routes, she was re-rigged as a barquentine in 1917. After a few voyages she reverted to being a coal hulk and then in 1922 was converted into a coal bunkering barge using a large grab, to effect discharge* KINNEAR

ILMA	345 GRT	IN FLEET **1911–1937**

BUILT: 1885 by Grangemouth Dockyard Co., Grangemouth.
PREVIOUS OWNERS: F. Klem, Christiania, 1885–92. British & Mexican Shipping Co. Ltd., (W.C. Jarvis & Sons, Mgrs) Liverpool, 1892–03. G.T. Niccol, Auckland, 1903–04. E.J. Chrisp, Gisborne, 1904–07. Transferred to Ship Ilma Co. Ltd., Gisborne, (E.J. Chrisp, Mgr) 1907–08. Reverted to G.T. Niccol, Auckland 1908–10. E.D. Pike & Co. Ltd., Sydney, 1910–11.
SUBSEQUENT HISTORY: Converted to coal hulk at Hobart 1911. Re-rigged Wellington as sailing barque 1917. Converted to coal hulk at Auckland 1919 and to coal bunkering elevator at Wellington 1922. Hull scuttled in Cook Strait 11/2/1937.

Chartered, Part Owned and Managed Vessels

Under this heading are some of the ships whose names are commonly linked with the Union Company – either as managers, part owners or charterers. Since its inception, over 260 vessels were chartered by the company either to supplement existing services or as temporary replacements for vessels lost. The vessels chartered also included a number of oil tankers. The list that follows covers ships managed but includes only a few of the more well known charters – the latter included to dispel any doubt that the ships were only chartered and not owned by the Union Company.

AMOKURA	19867 GRT	IN FLEET 1978–1993

BUILT: 1976

Union Company managers for B.P. New Zealand Ltd. Vessel engaged in carriage of petroleum products from Marsden Point oil refinery around New Zealand ports. Chartered on behalf of N.Z. Oil Consortium. Owned by Marsden Point Tankers Ltd., Nova Scotia (Papachristidis Maritime Inc., Montreal, Mgrs).

ARAMOANA	4160 GRT	IN FLEET 1962–1971

BUILT: 1962

Union Company managers and employed as rail ferry between Picton and Wellington. Owned by New Zealand Government (Railways Department).

ARANUI	4542 GRT	IN FLEET 1966–1971

BUILT: 1966

Union Company managers and employed as rail ferry between Picton and Wellington. Owned by New Zealand Government (Railways Department).

The 19867 ton tanker **Amokura** *was managed by the Union Company for the 15 years she was employed distributing petroleum products around the New Zealand coast*   BAIN-WRIGHT COLLECTION

Following the completion of the Marsden Point oil refinery at Whangarei, the **Athelviscount** *was the first tanker chartered for the carriage of petroleum products around the country. The Union Company was appointed manager for the vessel, which was on the coast for 13 years*   M.E.D. DOWNES

The 1658-ton collier **Balls Head** *was employed between Newcastle and the Balls Head storage depot in Sydney from 1921 to 1932. She was owned by a Sydney company in which the Union Company had a financial interest*

During World War 2, the 1793-ton steamer **Baltannic** *was requisitioned from the United Baltic Corporation of London to centralise refrigerated cargoes from the smaller ports to the main New Zealand ports for export. The illustration shows the vessel under wartime rig*   RNZAF

Chartered, Part Owned and Managed Vessels

| ARAWA | 5026 GRT | IN FLEET 1894–1895 |

BUILT: 1884

Under charter to the Union Company for two Pacific voyages. Owned by Shaw Savill & Albion Co. Ltd., London.

| ATHELVISCOUNT | 12778 GRT | IN FLEET 1965–1978 |

BUILT: 1961

Under Union Company manager for B.P. New Zealand Ltd. Vessel engaged in the carriage of petroleum products from Marsden Point oil refinery around New Zealand ports. Chartered on behalf of N.Z. Oil Consortium. Owned by Athel Line Ltd., Liverpool.

| AWAHOU | 407 GRT | IN FLEET 1912–1917 |

BUILT: 1912

Union Company held 25% interest, the remaining shares held by Levin & Co. Ltd., Wellington.

| BALLS HEAD | 1658 GRT | IN FLEET 1921–1932 |

BUILT: 1911

Union Company manager for the owners – Coal & Bunkering Co. Ltd., Sydney.

| BALTANNIC | 1793 GRT | IN FLEET 1940–1946 |

BUILT: 1913

Managed by the the Union Company and principally employed in carrying refrigerated cargo from smaller ports to main ports in New Zealand. Owned by United Baltic Corporation Ltd., London.

| BALTRAFFIC | 3297 GRT | IN FLEET 1940–1946 |

BUILT: 1918

Managed by the Union Company and principally employed in carrying refrigerated cargo from smaller ports to main ports in New Zealand. Owned by United Baltic Corporation Ltd., London.

| DUNEDIN | 3166 GRT | IN FLEET 1978–1981 |

BUILT: 1972

Union Company charterer and employed on trans-Tasman service. Owned by Deep Sea Shipping Co. Ltd., (Maritime Carriers N.Z. Ltd., Auckland, Mgrs). This vessel was also chartered as the *Union New Zealand* 1972–78.

Another United Baltic Corporation vessel, **Baltraffic** *was on the New Zealand coast as a refrigerated feeder vessel from 1941–1946* RNZAF

On charter from a subsidiary company of the Union Company parent, P & O, the tanker **Erne** *was employed on coastal distribution of petroleum products between 1970 and 1984*   BAIN-WRIGHT COLLECTION

The 13,315-ton tanker **Hamilton** *was managed by the Union Company during the eight years she spent distributing petroleum products from the Marsden Point refinery around the New Zealand coast*
A. DUNCAN

ERNE	14244 GRT	IN FLEET **1970–1984**

BUILT: 1962
Union Company manager for B.P. New Zealand Ltd. Vessel engaged in the carriage of petroleum products from Marsden Point refinery around New Zealand ports. Chartered on behalf of N.Z. Oil Consortium. Owned by Trident Tankers Ltd., London (P & O S.N. Co., London, Mgrs) 1970–73. Ownership registered to P & O Steam Navigation Company, London 1973–84.

GOLDEN AGE	113 GRT	IN FLEET **1875–1884**

BUILT: 1862
Owned by the Harbour Steam Company consortium, Dunedin 1863–84 but not transferred to the Union Company 1875, although managed by the company from that date. Employed on occasional excursions Otago Harbour 1875–76 and then laid up until broken up Port Chalmers 8/1884.

HAMILTON	13315 GRT	IN FLEET **1967–1975**

BUILT: 1960
Union Company manager for B.P. New Zealand Ltd. Vessel engaged in carriage of petroleum products from Marsden Point refinery around New Zealand ports. Chartered on behalf of New Zealand Oil Consortium. Owned by Hamilton Shipping Co. Ltd., (Evan Thomas Radcliffe & Co. Ltd., Cardiff, Mgrs).

The Union Company had a 25% interest in the small coaster **Himitangi**, *which traded out of Wellington, mainly to Foxton and Blenheim for Levin & Co., of Wellington*   J. DICKIE ALEXANDER TURNBULL LIBRARY

The Union Company managed the coastal tanker **Kotuku** *for the first 19 years she was on the New Zealand coast*   I.J. FARQUHAR

| HIMITANGI | 323 GRT | IN FLEET 1899–1911 |

BUILT: 1899

The Union Company held 25% interest, the remaining shares being held by Levin & Co. Ltd., Wellington.

| KOPUTAI | 158 GRT | IN FLEET 1876–1883 |

BUILT: 1876

Built by T. Wingate & Co., Whiteinch, Glasgow under Union Company supervision and employed as a harbour paddle tug, Otago Harbour. Ownership transferred to Otago Towing Co. Ltd., (James Mills, Mgr) 9/1877. Vessel continued to be managed by Union Company until 1883.

| KOTUKU | 16221 GRT | IN FLEET 1975–1994 |

BUILT: 1975

Union Company managers for B.P. New Zealand Ltd., later Coastal Tankers Ltd., Wellington. Vessels employed in the carriage of petroleum products from Marsden Point refinery around New Zealand ports. Initially chartered for 15 years jointly by B.P. New Zealand Ltd. and Shell Oil

N.Z. Ltd., on behalf New Zealand Oil Consortium. *Kotuku* owned by Hellenic Overseas Shipping Ltd., Cayman Islands 1975–76, Wellington Tankers Ltd. 1976–94 and *Kuaka* by British West Indies Navigation Ltd., Cayman Islands 1975–76, Auckland Tankers Ltd., 1976–94 (Papachristidis Co. Ltd., Montreal, managing owners for both tankers from 1975).

| KUAKA | 16221 GRT | IN FLEET 1975–1994 |

BUILT: 1975
See for *Kotuku*.

| LUHESAND | 1673 GRT | IN FLEET 1972–1978 |

BUILT: 1967
Union Company charterers from Omega Reefer Services, Limassol, Cyprus. Vessel employed on Pacific Island service and had previously been time chartered by Holm Shipping Co. Ltd., Wellington 1969–72. Owned by Reefer Services Ltd., Famagusta.

| MARRAWAH | 600 GRT | IN FLEET 1910–1910 |

BUILT: 1910
Built for Wm Holyman & Sons Ltd. but briefly registered 26/8/1910 to 30/10/1910 to the Union Company for financing purposes.

| MAUI POMARE | 1203 GRT | IN FLEET 1942–1960 |

BUILT: 1928
Union Company manager and employed on Pacific Island trade mainly from Auckland. Owned by New Zealand Government (Department of Island Territories – formerly Pacific Islands Administration Department).

| MOANA ROA | 2893 GRT | IN FLEET 1960–1974 |

BUILT: 1960
SUBSEQUENT HISTORY: As for *Maui Pomare*.

| NGAHERE | 1090 GRT | IN FLEET 1922–1924 |

BUILT: 1908
Under charter to the Union Company until wrecked on Grey River bar 12/5/1924 outward bound Greymouth for Wellington. Owned by Mann, George & Co. Ltd., London on behalf of the Union Company. (*Ngakuta* and *Ngatoro* also chartered from 1922 – see main fleet list pages 147/149).

| PAMIR | 2799 GRT | IN FLEET 1942–1948 |

BUILT: 1905
The Union Company managed the barque from 1/2/1942 as agents for the Crown (following her seizure in Wellington as Prize of war on 3/8/1941) until handed back to Finland 12/11/1948 in Wellington. Owned by Gustaf Erikson, Mariehamn, Finland.

| PLUCKY | 81 GRT | IN FLEET 1880–1883 |

BUILT: 1880
Built by Wm. Denny & Bros., Dumbarton, under Union Company supervision and employed as harbour tug, Otago Harbour. Owned by Otago Towing Co. Ltd., Dunedin (James Mills, Mgr) 1880–1883.

One of three Blackball Coal Company colliers taken by the Union Company on charter in 1922, **Ngahere**, *shown here in 1912 after leaving Westport, was wrecked on the Greymouth bar in 1924, as a result of the Greymouth harbour master not supplying the correct information on the state of the bar*   S. RAWSON

Seized as a prize of war in Wellington in 1941, the Finnish barque **Pamir** *was managed by the Union Company throughout the war years and made nine voyages across the Pacific and one to London in 1948. The sail training available in* **Pamir** *was keenly sought by many New Zealanders*

| RAPUHIA | 2615 GRT | IN FLEET 1984–1992 |

BUILT: 1964

Union Company manager for Government of New Zealand (Department of Scientific and Industrial Research).

| RED PINE | 364 GRT | IN FLEET 1912–1913 |

BUILT: 1912

Union Company part owner. Vessel traded out of Greymouth until wrecked off Cape Stephens 7/3/1913 on passage Greymouth to Wellington. Owned by The Pine Steamship Co. of Westland Ltd., Greymouth.

| SAMSON | 124 GRT | IN FLEET 1875–1878 |

BUILT: 1854

Owned by Harbour Steam Company, Dunedin consortium 1872–1878 but not transferred to Union Company in 1875 although managed by the company 1875–1878. Employed in Dunedin – Oamaru trade.

| TASMAN ENTERPRISE | 5578 GRT | IN FLEET 1977–1988 |

BUILT: 1977

Union Company responsible for technical management and crewing to Tasman Pulp & Paper Co. Ltd., Auckland, for a period of 10 years and both vessels employed in the carriage of forestry cargoes from Mount Maunganui to Australian ports (and for a limited period to Lyttelton and Dunedin between 1983–1989). *Tasman Enterprise* owned by Forestry Shippers Ltd., Auckland, 1977–1979, Tasman Pulp & Paper Co. Ltd., Auckland, 1979–1988. *Tasman Venture* owned by Development Finance Corporation of N.Z. Ltd., Wellington 1977–1988, Tasman Pulp & Paper Co. Ltd., Auckland, 1988.

| TASMAN VENTURE | 5561 GRT | IN FLEET 1977–1988 |

BUILT: 1977

As for *Tasman Enterprise*.

| TOTARA | 2800 GRT | IN FLEET 1982–1983 |

BUILT: 1979

Union Company took over balance of charter period following collapse of Waitaki Container Line.

One of two identical side-loading specialist newsprint and timber carriers built for the Tasman Pulp and Paper Company, **Tasman Venture** *was crewed by Union Company personnel from 1977–1988* N.J. KIRBY

Chartered, Part Owned and Managed Vessels

| WAITAKI | 3165 GRT | IN FLEET 1983–1985 |

BUILT: 1972

As for *Totara*. (*Waitaki* was also chartered as *Union Australia* 1972–1977).

| UNION AOTEAROA | 6732 GRT | IN FLEET 1973–1977 |

BUILT: 1972

Union Company charterers from Maritime Carriers (N.Z.) Ltd., Auckland for a period of 4 years. Vessel was purchased by Union Company on completion of charter (see main fleet list page 203). Owned by Gannel Shipping Co. Ltd., London, subsidiary of Maritime Carriers (N.Z.) Ltd.

| UNION AUCKLAND | 12782 GRT | IN FLEET 1974–1984 |

BUILT: 1969

Union Company charterer for 10 years, following which vessel was purchased by the company (see main fleet list – page 207). Owned by Wigmore Ltd., Bermuda (Evgenia Investment Co. S.A., Piraeus (A.J. Chandris, Mgr) 1974–1984.

| UNION AUSTRALIA | 3166 GRT | IN FLEET 1972–1977 |

BUILT: 1972

Union Company charterer from Maritime Carriers (N.Z.) Ltd., Auckland. Owned by Deep Sea Shipping Co. Ltd., Bermuda, subsidiary of Maritime Carriers (N.Z.) Ltd.

| UNION NEW ZEALAND | 3166 GRT | IN FLEET 1972–1978 |

BUILT: 1972

As for *Union Australia*.

| UNION TRANS TASMAN | 3166 GRT | IN FLEET 1973–1977 |

BUILT: 1973

As for *Union Australia*.

| UNION DUNEDIN | 6300 GRT | IN FLEET 1983–1986 |

BUILT: 1978

Union Company charterer and employed on Trans-Tasman service. Owned by Progress Shipping Co. Ltd., Bermuda (International Cruises S.A. (D.J. Chandris), Piraeus, Mgrs).

One of three identical Camit class vessels chartered by the Union Compay for the Trans Tasman trade, **Union Australia***, came into the Trans Tasman service direct from the builder's yard and was on charter from 1972 to 1977 and again as* **Waitaki** *from 1983 to 1985*

The second Camit class bulker was the **Union New Zealand.** *Originally chartered for 10 years, the Union Company had an option to terminate the fixtures after five years, which it did* J.Y. FREEMAN

Union Trans Tasman, *the third of the 5100-ton bulk carriers chartered for the Trans Tasman services, was in the Union Company fleet from 1973 to 1977* BAIN-WRIGHT COLLECTION

Chartered by the Union Company as a supplementary roll-on, roll-off vessel for the Trans Tasman service, the **TFL Progress** *was renamed* **Union Dunedin** *and was under charter between 1983 and 1986. She was withdrawn when the linkspans in the Union Company terminals became redundant and the company rationalised its Tasman services with the Shipping Corporation of New Zealand and the Australian National Line*
N.J. KIRBY

Union Hobart *was the first of the two Scandinavian roll-on, roll-off vessels chartered for the South Island Trans Tasman trade from 1976. They were later purchased by the company* BAIN-WRIGHT COLLECTION

Union Melbourne *was a new German-built roll-on, roll-off ship that was delivered on a five-year charter to the Union Company on 5 September 1975. She was withdrawn due to lack of cargo on the Tasman service in May 1978 and was twice sub-chartered by the Union Company to other operators in Europe before being re-delivered to her owners in September 1980* D.N. BRIGHAM

UNION HOBART	4376 GRT	IN FLEET 1976–1988

BUILT: 1976

Union Company charterer for trans-Tasman service 1976–1984, then renamed *Seaway Hobart* and employed Tasmanian services 1984–1988. Vessel purchased by the Union Company 1988 (see main fleet list – page 207) Owned by Whitminster Co. Ltd., London (A.J. Chandris, Piraeus, Mgr) 1976–1988.

UNION LYTTELTON	4376 GRT	IN FLEET 1977–1989

BUILT: 1977

Union Company charterer for Trans-Tasman service 1977–1983 and then renamed *Seaway Melbourne* and employed Tasmanian services 1983–1989. Vessel purchased by the Union Company 1989 (see main fleet list page 207). Owned by Lulworth Co. Ltd., London (A.J. Chandris, Piraeus, Mgr) 1977–1989.

UNION MELBOURNE	4043 GRT	IN FLEET 1975–1980

BUILT: 1975

Union Company charterer for Trans-Tasman service for period of 5 years but vessel subsequently re-chartered 1978 by P & O Steam Navigation Co., London, for service Fleetwood-Belfast until redelivered to owners 2/9/1980. Owned by Northern Coasters Ltd., London (Sten A. Olsson, Gothenburg subsidiary).

In 1972 the Union Company chartered **Union South Pacific**. *This ship had a stern ramp and her own gantry crane travelled along the deck to position containers in the holds or on deck. The ship had a capacity for 77 ISO containers and operated from Auckland to Suva, Pago Pago, Apia and Nukualofa on a 14 day voyage. She entered service in May 1973 and was re-delivered in Singapore in March 1978* N.J. KIRBY

Union Sydney *was chartered by the Union Company from Lauritzen Line of Copenhagen. for the Trans Tasman roll-on, roll-off services between 1974 and 1977. A year previous, the vessel, then known as* **Mont Laurier**, *had caught fire on 13 January 1973 and was almost completely gutted. Abandoned by her owners, she was salved and rebuilt in Finland and re-entered service as* **Leena Dan** *before being taken over by the Union Company* N.J. KIRBY

| UNION SOUTH PACIFIC | 1594 GRT | IN FLEET 1973–1978 |

BUILT: 1972
Union Company charterer for Pacific Island service for period of 5 years. Owned by Sea Containers Chartering Ltd., London (James B. Sherwood, Mgr).

| UNION SYDNEY | 4752 GRT | IN FLEET 1974–1977 |

BUILT: 1972
Union Company charterer for Trans-Tasman service for period of 3 years. Owned by Odin Shipping Ltd., London (J. Lauritzen, Copenhagen, Mgrs).

| UNION SYDNEY | 6299 GRT | IN FLEET 1983–1986 |

BUILT: 1978
Union Company charterer for Trans-Tasman service. Owned by Prosperity Shipping Co. Ltd., Bermuda (International Cruises S.A. (A.J. Chandris), Piraeus, Mgrs).

The Union Company chartered a second **Union Sydney** *in 1983. She was a sister to* **Union Dunedin**, *both vessels having a stern ramp as well as forward starboard shoulder-slewing ramp. She entered service on the Tasman in September 1983 and was re-delivered back to her Greek owners in September 1986*   N.J. KIRBY

To supplement their Tasman and Pacific Ocean passenger services, the Union Company took the twin screw passenger ship **Willochra** *on bare boat charter in 1913. She was one of three sister ships built for the Adelaide Steam Ship Company. She served as a troopship during World War 1 and was returned to her Australian owners in 1919*   DE MAUS

WILLOCHRA	7784 GRT	IN FLEET **1913–1919**

BUILT: 1913
Under charter to the Union Company 1913 -1914 then requisitioned by British Government 1914 -1919, still operated by Union Company. Owned by Adelaide Steamship Co. Ltd., Adelaide.

ZEALANDIA	6660 GRT	IN FLEET **1910–1913**

BUILT: 1910
Under charter to Union Company for Trans-Pacific service. Owned by Huddart Parker Ltd., Melbourne.

Coal and Oil Storage Hulks

The following vessels have been omitted from the main fleet list because they were principally in service as coal storage hulks, oil storage vessels and the like. Some of these ships may have undertaken commercial voyages, however, before being hulked. This list of sundry vessels owned by the Union Company is probably far from complete.

Vessel	Built	Acquired	Remarks/Fate
ADDERLEY	1888	1910	Coal hulk at Wellington converted to oil storage hulk 1920/21. Scuttled off Baring Head, Cook Strait 28/11/1947.
ADVANCE	1885	1896	Lighter at Strahan. Broken up 10/1925.
ALARM	1854	1877	Hulk at Port Chalmers. Broken up 1910.
ALBION	1866	1885	Hulk at Wellington. Scuttled Cook Strait 9/9/1913.
ALDEBARAN	1869	1912	Hulk at Hobart. Sold 13/4/1948 and beached as breakwater at Dunalley, near Hobart.
ALFRED HAWLEY	1860	1900	Hulk at Launceston and later Devonport. Sold for breaking up 1/1927.
AMOKURA	1889	1940	Hulk at Wellington. Sold 3/1953 and towed Kenepuru Sound, Marlborough for use as storeship and jetty. Broken up 1955.
ANNE AND JANE	1836	1885	Hulk at Wellington. Destroyed by fire 14/4/1898.
ANNIE BOW	1869	1900	Hulk at Hobart. Sunk alongside wharf 22/3/1924 and destroyed by explosives 4/1924.
ARAWATA	1875	1878	See main fleet list page 11.
BELLE ISLE	1857	1893	Dismantled at Lyttelton 1923 and beached Quail Island, Lyttelton Harbour.
BELLA MARIA	1840	1885	Sold G. Niccol, Auckland 1896 and broken up Drunken (now Islington) Bay, Rangitoto 1896.
BLACKWALL	1858	1922	Coal hulk Wellington. Condemned 1923. Sold and left Wellington 5/11/923 in tow for Wairau Bar to be used as breakwater. Tow abandoned and vessel beached Port Underwood, Marlborough Sounds 5/11/1923.
BROXTON	1920	1922	Hulk Port Chalmers. Partially dismantled and hull placed as dry dock fairway, Port Chalmers 30/6/1926. Remains buried in reclamation 1976.
CABERFEIDH	1864	1891	Hulk at Auckland.
CALIFORNIA			Broken up Deborah Bay, Port Chalmers about 1902.
CANTERO	1844	1881	Hulk at Auckland. Condemned 10/1883. Sold 1885.

Coal and Oil Storage Hulks

Vessel	Built	Acquired	Remarks/Fate
CLANSMAN	1879	1912	Hulk at Papeete.
COMMERZIENRATH RODBERTUS	1878	1896	Hulk at Hobart, later at Devonport. Broken up 12/1926.
COROMANDEL	1875	1922	Scuttled off Turakirae Heads, Cook Strait 31/3/1933.
CINCINNATTI			Hulk at Port Chalmers – Broken up and burnt 4/5/1910.
C. TOBIAS	1886	1905	Hulk at Wellington. Sold for breaking up 2/1920.
DARTFORD	1877	1908	See Sailing Ships – page 229.
DELAWARE	1848	1879	Hulk at Port Chalmers. Sold New Zealand Government 5/1881. Burnt out Dunedin 4/5/1930.
DEVONPORT	1878	1907	Hulk at Wellington. Scuttled Cook Strait 14/8/1913.
DILPUSSUND	1864	1906	Hulk at Wellington. Broken up Evans Bay, 1933.
DON JUAN	1857	1877	Broken up Port Chalmers and hull sunk Deborah Bay, Port Chalmers about 1902.
ELSINORE	1866	1894	Destroyed by fire at Levuka, 24/9/1895.
ELINOR VERNON	1876	1922	Hulk at Auckland. Burnt at Rangitoto Island 21/6/1928.
EMPREZA	1865	1910	Hulk at Port Chalmers. Sunk off Taiaroa Head 24/6/1948.
ESPERANCE	1884	1900	Lighter in Tasmania.
FAITHFUL	1864	1885	Lighter – Broken up Port Chalmers.
FANTOME	1901	1926	Hulk at Devonport, Tasmania. Sold 9/1953 to Australian Aluminium Production Commission.
FELICITAS	1874	1905	Hulk at Port Chalmers. Broken up 8/1932.
FLORA	1882	1891	See main fleet list – page 47.
FLEETWING		1899	Hulk at Suva.
GANYMEDE	1868	1912	Hulk at Wellington. Sold 1934 and towed Nelson for demolition.
GAZELLE	1837	1885	Hulk at Wellington. Scuttled in Palliser Bay 3/12/1907.
GLADBROOK	1877	1911	See Sailing Ships – page 229.
GYDA		1898	Hulk at Papeete.
HELEN DENNY	1866	1928	Hulk at Wellington, Lyttelton and Auckland. Scuttled off Cuvier Island 26/4/1948.
HELENE	1880	1902	Hulk at Auckland. Dismantled and burnt at Pine Island, Auckland 16/10/1924.
HENBURY			Hulk at Port Chalmers.
HINUPAHI	1947	1947	Oil fuel lighter at Wellington. Sold B.P. New Zealand Ltd., 1975–85. Sold N. Colley, Auckland and towed 15/1/1986 to Kaipara.
HINUWAI	1936	1936	Oil fuel lighter at Wellington. Sold United Salvage Pty Ltd. 1968 for use with *Wahine* salvage. Renamed *Nuwa*. Sold 1971 and renamed *David C Ette*. Sold 1987 to Sea Tow Ltd. and renamed *Sea Tow 14*. Sold 1990 to Marstel Terminals Ltd. and renamed *Estoril Hauler*.
HINUWAKA	1944	1944	Oil fuel lighter at Auckland. Sold B.P. New Zealand Ltd. 1975.
ILMA	1885	1911	See sailing ships page 230.
JESSIE CRAIG	1876	1944	Hulk at Hobart. Donated Tasmanian Government 1953 and sunk as breakwater, New Harbour, south west Tasmania 1/1954.

The oil barge **Hinuwai,** *which was built as a bunkering barge to Union Company requirements, following her launch at Wellington in September 1936*

Vessel	Built	Acquired	Remarks/Fate
JOHN AND WINTHROP	1876	1924	Hulk at Launceston. Demolished by explosives behind Tamar Island, Launceston 13/11/1939.
JOHN KNOX	1852	1888	Hulk at Auckland. Sold G. Niccol, Auckland 1896 and broken up Drunken (now Islington) Bay, Rangitoto 1896.
KAKAPO	1901	1903	See main fleet list – page 71.
KILLARNEY	1869	1897	Hulk at Auckland. Dismantled and burnt, Pine Island, Auckland 11/1924.
LAIRA	1870	1898	Hulk at Port Chalmers. Sold Captain Gibbons, Port Chalmers 1900.
LA PLATA	1863	1903	Hulk at Lyttelton. Dismantled 7/1927 and sunk at Quail Island, Lyttelton, 13/10/1927.
LASS OF GAWLER	1862	1891	Hulk at Hobart. Sold 1908.
LILLA	1886	1914	See *Opihi* – main fleet list – page 117.
LOTA	1861	1884	Hulk at Lyttelton. Broken up 1935.
LUTTERWORTH	1868	1906	Hulk at Wellington. Scuttled in Cook Strait 26/6/1950.
M.A.DORAN	1875	1899	Hulk at Auckland. Beached Waiheke Island and broken up 4/1914.
MARIE	1869	1887	Sold Westport Coal Co Ltd., Dunedin for use as coal hulk at Lyttelton. Beached and destroyed Purau Bay 1913.
MAY	1869	1898	Purchased by Union Line 8/10/1898 for conversion to coal hulk but resold 1/11/1898 to J. Harrison and J.W. Paton, Aratapu.

A Wellington scene in August 1904 with the Union Company collier **Rosamond** *lying alongside the coal hulk* **Arawata** *as the 12,000 ton steamer* **Ionic** *takes her coal bunkers for the return passage to the United Kingdom*

S.H. RAWSON

Vessel	Built	Acquired	Remarks/Fate
MAYFLOWER	1868	1922	Sold Anchor Shipping & Foundry Co. Ltd. Nelson 31/7/1923.
MELBOURNE	1892	1925	Purchased 8/4/1925 from Tasmanian Government (with *Poolta*) but resold 16/4/1925 to Comptoirs Francois des Nouvelle Hebrides, Noumea for conversion to storage hulk.
MENSHIKOFF	1847	1891	Hulk at Lyttelton. Towed to Purau Bay 6/1906, dismantled and burnt.
MIKADO	1868	1891	Hulk at Suva. Destroyed by fire 27/10/1916.
ML 400	1942	1947	Former New Zealand Navy Fairmile launch purchased in damaged condition 18/4/1947 and resold 15/5/1947.
NELSON	1809	1898	Hulk at Sydney, Launceston then Hobart. Sold for breaking up 18/8/1920 and demolished Shag Bay, River Derwent.
NEPTUNE	1867	1886	Hulk at Auckland. Sunk at moorings 27/10/1898 and broken up 1899.
NONPAREIL			Hulk at Port Chalmers.
OCCIDENT	1889	1901	Hulk at Wellington. Scuttled in Cook Strait 22/3/1949.
OSCEOLA	1864	1884	Hulk at Wellington. Scuttled off Palliser Bay 9/10/1912.
ONYX	1864	1908	Hulk at Auckland. Scuttled off Cuvier Island 11/10/1925.
OTTOLINA	1870	1891	Hulk at Wellington. Scuttled in Cook Strait 1/11/1905.
PHILIPPINE	1860	1891	Hulk at Hobart and Launceston. Broken up and burnt at Legana, Tamar River, Tasmania.

Vessel	Built	Acquired	Remarks/Fate
PHOENIX	1867	1896	Hulk at Strahan.
PLANTER	1857	1891	Hulk at Hobart.
POLLY	1879	1908	Hulk at Auckland. Burnt at Rangitoto Island 22/6/1928.
PRINCE OF WALES	1850	1906	Hulk at Wellington. Broken up East Bay, Queen Charlotte Sound 1941.
PROPONTIS	1844	1891	Hulk at Hobart. Sold 1901.
PORT WHANGAREI	1906	1944	Purchased 21/11/1944 but resold 24/11/1944 to Holm Shipping Co. Ltd., Wellington.
RAKANOA	1896	1896	See main fleet list – page 53.
RETRIEVER	1881	1920	Hulk at Auckland. Dismantled 1923 and remains blown up Herald Island, Auckland (about) 30/6/1950.
ROSAMOND	1884	1888	See main fleet list – page 39.
ROTHESAY BAY	1877	1921	Hulk at Wellington, later Auckland. Broken up Orakei 4 – 7/1936.
SAMPSON	1864	1878	Hulk at Melbourne. Sold Wm Howard Smith & Sons Ltd., Melbourne 1884.
ST KILDA	1861	1888	Hulk at Wellington. Broken up 1900.
SELWYN CRAIG	1868	1911	Hulk at Auckland. Foundered off Chelsea 5/10/1919 and blown up as she lay 2/1922.
S.F. HERSEY	1865	1891	Hulk at Melbourne, Hobart and Launceston. Sold Melbourne Steam Ship Co. Ltd., Melbourne 29/1/1914.
SILVER CLOUD	1874	1908	Hulk at Hobart. Broken up 1932.
SIR HARRY SMITH		1878	Hulk at Melbourne. Sold Huddart Parker Ltd., Melbourne 1884.
SOLGRAN	1885	1911	Hulk at Wellington. Scuttled in Cook Strait 8/4/1926.
SUNLIGHT		1901	Hulk at Suva. Scuttled outside Suva harbour 6/1916.
THISTLE		1887	Hulk at Suva.
TRUSTY	1864		Lighter at Napier. Wrecked Napier 2/12/1914.
WAI-ITI	1891	1922	Hulk at Lyttelton. Sunk Starvation Bay, just south of Port Levy, Lyttelton 30/10/1935.
WEATHERSFIELD	1865	1908	Hulk at Suva. Scuttled off Suva 18/2/1928.
WILLIAM MANSON	1872	1897	Hulk at Wellington. Burnt at Ward Island, 24/5/1939.
WISEMAN	1895	1897	Hulk at Levuka.
WOODLARK	1832	1879	Hulk at Wellington. Scuttled in Palliser Bay 26/10/1906.
WOOSUNG	1863	1896	Hulk at Suva. Broken up Suva by 1926.
ZELATEUR	1892	1907	Hulk at Launceston. Demolished by explosives behind Pig Island, Tamar River 1/12/1932.

Harbour Launches, Passenger Tenders

This list of launches and tenders is probably not complete and also excludes the vessels *Boojum*, *Pilot*, *Pioneer*, *Snark*, *Waihi* and *Tuatea*, which are listed in the main fleet list.

Vessel	Built	Tons	In Fleet	Remarks/Fate
APARIMA			1906	Launch.
AROHA				Launch – sold 1905.
ATUA	1948		1951	Launch Apia.
AUTE			1923	Launch Apia.
AUTE			1946	Launch Apia – formerly ex *Mo'o*.
AVARUA	1927		1927	Launch Rarotonga.
EAGLE			1901	Launch Strahan-sold 1904.
FLORENCE				Launch – sold 1899.
GARELOCH			1884	Launch Wellington.
GERALDINE				Launch Port Chalmers.
HARTFORD				Launch Strahan.
HINEMOA	1898		1907	Launch Suva-sold 1939.
KAA-ANA				Launch Strahan.
KATE	1884		1884	Launch Port Chalmers.
KATHLEEN	1876		1899	Launch Strahan.
KILLARA	1925		1947	Launch ex S.S. *Monowai* based Sydney.
KOKIRI	1908		1908	Launch ex S.S. *Makura* based Sydney – sold 1947.
LOWANA	1915		1915	Launch Strahan.
MAHENO	1905		1905	Launch ex S.S. *Maheno* based Port Chalmers and Lyttelton – sold 1949.
MANUKA	1903			Launch ex S.S. *Manuka* based Lyttelton and Wellington – sold 1941.
MAORI	1909		1909	Launch Sydney – sold 1948.
MAORI			1946	Launch Apia formerly ex *Pili*. Broken up 1957.
MAVORO				Launch Auckland.
MOANA	1961		1964	Launch Apia 1964–67, Suva 1967.
POTIKI	1911	31	1911	Launch Sydney – sold 1953.
PRINCE				Launch Wellington – sold 1932.
RANADI	1939		1939	Launch Suva. Sunk and sold 1974.
SEILOSA			1955	Launch Apia.
TAKUVAINE	1926		1936	Launch Rarotonga.
VAEA			1946	Launch Apia – formerly ex *Oli*.
WAMMERA			1881	Launch Wellington.
WYONG	1948		1948	Launch Sydney – sold 1960.

Appendices

There goes the last parking space for 176 miles

The Steamer Express vessel 'Maori' is more than a floating hotel that carries you nearly 200 miles while you relax and sleep. It is a floating car park. On her huge parking deck a large number of vehicles can be carried secure and safe. When the vessel berths at 7.00 a.m. the first cars are ashore within two minutes— the decks are cleared in short time. Car rates start as low as $11.50. This is the service you should use. It operates each way between WELLINGTON and LYTTELTON — on a regular timetable.

Book with any office or agent of
Union Steam Ship Co. of New Zealand Limited

SE 68 S 2

An advertisement for the Inter-island express service following the conversion of the **Maori** *to a roll-on, roll-off ship in December 1965*

Company Colour Scheme, Motto and Coat of Arms

HULL Bronze Green with yellow band and red boot-topping.
Note – The boot-topping was originally pink 1875–1948.
The yellow band was thinner than the band applied in recent years. It was discontinued with the Australian Seaway ships from 1987, *Union Rotoma* had no yellow band at all from 1991, *Union Auckland* abandoned hers from the mid 1980s and *Union Rotorua* and *Union Rotoiti* lost the yellow band from 1993.

UPPERWORKS White

MASTS, SAMSON POSTS, DERRICKS, CRANES Buff (except for the deck cranes on *Ngatoro*, *Ngakuta*, *Karepo*, *Karetu*, *Ngahere* and *Ngapara* which were painted white)

FUNNEL Red with black top, two thin black bands on red.
Note – Some of the early ships, such as *Rotomahana, Paloona, Maitai, Wainui, Moeraki, Moura, Pukaki, Talune, Pateena, Ovalau, Monowai* (1890) and *Wakatipu* all had three black bands on their funnel collars while at one time *Mararoa* had four bands. *Monowai* (1925) only had one band for a period.

Following the purchase of the Black Diamond Line in 1885, the hull colours of the purely cargo carriers were left as black with an orange – buff upperworks although the exact colour scheme varied from ship to ship. The passenger ships in the fleet as well as tugs *Natone* and *Terawhiti* (but not the more recent tugs *Tapuhi* and *Taioma*) continued to be painted in the normal colours. In 1960 the company reverted to painting all the ships with the bronze green hull and white colour scheme as detailed above. Vessels of the Blackball Coal Company and R.S.Lamb & Co. Ltd. retained their own funnel colours for some time after being purchased by the Union Company. The tankers *Otokia* and *Orowaiti* were painted in Wm Cory & Sons Ltd., colours (black funnel with white band and black diamond on the white band and black hull with red boot-topping) Following the absorption of the remaining Richardson and Holm Shipping vessels into the Union Company services and management in 1972, the vessels were painted in Holm colours (grey hull, green funnel with black top) and even during the period of her ownership under Union Company from 1981–90, *Holmdale* was painted in Holm colours. *Taiko* was always painted in the colours of Coastal Tankers Ltd. For the period of her charter 1986–89 and ownership 1989–91 *Union Endeavour* had a corn-coloured hull.

Over the years a number of ships on special services have been painted differently. Some of the ships on the Pacific Island services have had white hulls instead of green. These included *Southern Cross* (1896–1901), *Mawhera* (1901–02), *Waitemata* (one voyage only in 1910), *Waipahi* (1927–36), *Matua* (1936–49) and *Navua* (1955–58). Apart from the periods stated these ships were painted in the black or bronze green colours applicable. Between 1948–1949 the Trans Pacific liner *Aorangi* was given a white hull with green band and dark green boot-topping.

Manapouri, which for a short time from 1909

ran under a subsidised service between Australia and Fiji was painted in the colours of the Australasian United Steam Navigation Co. Ltd. (grey hull, black funnel with two white bands). Between 1928–30 the *Moeraki* also ran on this service and although she had a grey hull, the Union Line funnel marking was retained.

These notes are applicable to peace time services only, as during World Wars 1 and 2, ships were painted in accordance with the wartime role they each filled.

Company Motto and Coat of Arms

PER MARE PER CAELUM (By Sea By Air)

The Company's earlier motto EN AVANT (Forward) was superseded by a new motto in 1940.

The armoral bearings of the Union Steam Ship Company of N.Z. Ltd. were granted by the British Kings of Arms, London on 16/10/1940. The symbolism of the Coat of Arms is as follows:

ARMS – On a blue field, a silver chevron having two cheronels red and black, the colours of the company, in the upper portion of the shield two wings displayed, typifying the air interests of the company, and in the lower portion of the shield a galley with sails set and flagged red, on six wavy bars coloured alternately blue and silver, representing the sea and the sea services of the company.

MANTLING – Blue and silver

CREST – On a wreath of blue and silver, a demi-lion rampant gold, with a red tongue, holding in his paws a standard with the house flag of the Company, red having a small Union Jack in the centre surrounded by the letters U S S Co.

SUPPORTERS – On either side, and supporting the shield, a carved Maori panel coloured dark red, representing Tangaroa, the Maori Sea – God who guards the great sea of Kiwa, the Pacific Ocean.

The whole stands on a golden ribbon, with the motto *Per Mare, Per Caelum*. On the ribbon on either side of the motto are three wavy lines representing the sea.

Personalia
Union Steam Ship Company of N. Z. Ltd., 1875–1980
Union Shipping Group Limited, 1980–2000

DIRECTORS

J. Mills	1875 – 1936
(Kt. 1907, K.C.M.G 1909)	
G. McLean	1875 – 1906
(Kt. 1909)	
J.R. Jones	1875 – 1903
H. McNeil	1875 – 1885
H. Tewsley	1875 – 1879
E.B. Cargill	1875 – 1877
	1883 – 1903
J. Cargill	1877 – 1903
A.W. Morris	1879 – 1910
J.M. Ritchie	1885 – 1912
A. Lee Smith	1903 – 1915
J Roberts	1903 – 1931
(C.M.G. 1891, Kt. 1920)	
A. Cameron	1906 – 1909
C. Holdsworth	1909 – 1934
(Kt. 1926)	
D.A. Aiken	1915 – 1934
A.W. Wheeler	1932 – 1934
C.W. Rattray	1913 – 1938
G.R. Ritchie	1910 – 1955
C.G. White	1917 – 1966
(O.B.E. 1946)	
N.S. Falla	1934 – 1945
(C.M.G., D.S.O., V.D. 1914–18)	
A.F. Roberts	1934 – 1961
(C.B.E. 1918, K.B.E. 1926)	
W. Green	1934 – 1942
J.N. Greenland	1939 – 1956
(O.B.E. 1946)	
M.B. Miller	1945 – 1968
H.H. Dobie	1955 – 1971
J. Grierson	1957 – 1964
(C.B.E. 1954)	
L.M. Wright	1957 – 1967
(Kt. 1957)	
A.N. Leslie	1961 – 1962
F.K. Macfarlane	1962 – 1973
P.B. Marshall	1964 – 1971
(C.B.E. 1965)	
A.T. Waugh	1966 – 1971
I.T. Cook	1968 – 1971
B.S. Cole	1968 – 1971
G. Hunter	1971 – 1971
R.T.M. Rose	1971 – 1971
E.H.P. Abeles	1972 – 1992
(Kt 1992)	
J.R. Cribb	1972 – 1997
(O.B.E. 1972)	
O.T. Hannigan	1972 – 1993
J.B. Horrocks	1972 – 1993
(C.B.E. 1981)	
M.H. Kjar	1972 – 1974
R.A. Owens	1972 – 1983
(C.B.E. 1991)	1986 – 1988
R.H. Pettigrew	1972 – 1991
(Kt. 1982)	
W.I. Potter	1972 – 1988
(Kt. 1962)	
R.H. Smythe	1972 – 1981
(K.B.E. 1971)	
C.G. Skeggs	1972 – 1986
(Kt. 1987)	
B.J. Godfrey	1974 – 1983
W.J. Sandman	1981 – 1986
R.A. Brierley	1983 – 1987
(Kt. 1988)	
K.M. Forsyth	1983 – 1986

255

T.J.N. Beyer	1987 – 1993
S.J. Cushing	1987 – 1997
(C.M.G. 1993, K.N.Z.M. 1998)	
R.H. Fisher	1987 – 1988
D.C. Shelton	1987 – 1987
R.J. Hoy	1987 –
J.W. Holdsworth	1988 – 1991
J.S. Beattie	1991 – 1994
J.M. Green	1992 – 1999
P.J. Rowe	1992 – 1997
J.N. Keegan	1979 – 1993
W.M. Loewenthal	1994 – 1997
G.C. Gibbard	1997 – 1997
I.C. Newman	1997 – 2000
A. Amarsi	2000 –
M.A. Weston	2000 –

CHAIRMEN

G. McLean	1875 – 1906
(Kt. 1909)	
J. Mills	1906 – 1936
(Kt. 1907, K.C.M.G. 1909)	
N.S. Falla	1936 – 1945
(C.M.G., D.S.O., V.D. 1914–1918)	
G.R. Ritchie	1945 – 1955
M.B. Miller	1955 – 1958
H.H. Dobie	1958 – 1963
F.K. Macfarlane	1963 – 1971
E.H.P. Abeles	1972 – 1988
(Kt. 1972)	
R.J. Hoy	1988 –

MANAGING DIRECTORS

J. Mills	1875 – 1913
(Kt. 1907, K.C.M.G. 1909)	
C. Holdsworth	1914 – 1930
(Kt. 1926)	
D.A. Aiken	1931 – 1934
N.S. Falla	1934 – 1945
(C.M.G., D.S.O., V.D. 1914–1918)	
J.N. Greenland	1945 – 1950
(O.B.E. 1946)	
M.B. Miller	1950 – 1958
H.H. Dobie	1958 – 1963
F.K. Macfarlane	1963 – 1973
J.N. Keegan	1979 – 1990
J.E. Bryant	1997 – 1997
I.C. Newman	1997 – 1999

GENERAL MANAGERS

C. Holdsworth	1898 – 1914
(Kt. 1926)	
D. Aiken	1914 – 1930
A.W. Wheeler	1931 – 1934
N.S. Falla	1934 – 1934
(C.M.G., D.S.O., V.D. 1914–1918)	
J.W. Matthewson	1934 – 1936
J.N. Greenland	1936 – 1945
(O.B.E. 1946)	
M.B. Miller	1945 – 1950
H.H. Dobie	1950 – 1958
A.N. Leslie	1958 – 1962
F.K. Macfarlane	1962 – 1963
B.S. Cole	1972 – 1979
D.C. Jury	1980 – 1984

(D. C. Jury was Chief General Manager for the company and following various restructuring from 1980, divisional managers were appointed. On the retirement of J.N. Keegan as Managing Director in 1990, overall management of the company came under the Chairman R.J. Hoy, until the appointment of J.E. Bryant as Chief Executive Officer 1993–1997.

SECRETARIES

T.W. Whitson	1891 – 1911
C.H. Hughes	1911 – 1916
S.K. Sleigh	1917 – 1932
C.T. Jarvis	1932 – 1950
G.R. Edmonds	1950 – 1971
P.R. Bremford	1971 – 1978
P.E. Maxwell	1978 – 1987
R.G. Offwood	1987 – 1993
W.R. Holdsworth	1993 – 1998

CHIEF MARINE SUPERINTENDENTS

A. Cameron	1878 – 1906
R. Strang	1906 – 1915
C. McDonald	1914 – 1923
P.J. Foster	1923 – 1930
V.G. Webb (O.B.E. 1952)	1930 – 1953
E.J. McClellan	1953 – 1959
A.C. Crosbie	1959 – 1969
J.F. Collins	1969 – 1977

CHIEF SUPERINTENDING ENGINEERS

J. Darling	1875 – 1878

J Cook	1878 – 1903
W. Smart	1903 – 1920
J. Smith	1920 – 1934
R.L. Gillies	1934 – 1946
A.L. Gatland	1946 – 1952
R.A. Stables	1952 – 1976

With a reducing fleet, the titles of Chief Marine Superintendent and Chief Superintending Engineer were not used after 1977 and 1976 respectively. The marine operations of the company came under V.L. Kilgour as Fleet Manager from 1974–84 and D.E. McPherson, Engineer Superintendent in 1977, became Technical Manager and subsequently in 1984, General Manager of the Fleet Division (Fleet Division was renamed Marine Division in 1988).

An advertisement for the 1885 cruise to the West Coast Sounds by the **Tarawera**

Acknowledgements

The research for *Union Fleet* began just short of 50 years ago and a list of the ships and their fates was produced in stencilled form in 1951. The two previous editions were published through the assistance of the N.Z. Ship and Marine Society in 1968 and 1976 respectively. This latest edition updates the data to the present and also refines and enhances some of the earlier information. More of the Union Company's own records have become more publicly available in the last 20 years and the efforts of other specialist researchers worldwide have assisted in tracing more accurate fates of a number of vessels, particularly vessels sold for service in the Far East.

In undertaking this research to provide a concise source of reference to the ramifications of the Union Steam Ship Company over the past 125 years I have been assisted by many fellow researchers and archivists around the world. The accuracy sought could not have been obtained without their help and dedication. Two most prominent have been the late J.A. Henry, who made a tremendous contribution through his lifetime employment with the company and his keen interest to seek out information from company records and staff. The other is Nigel J. Kirby of Lyttelton, whose analytical approach and attention to detail has been extremely helpful in checking established data and fates of vessels in the post World War 2 period. I must also express appreciation to several others who could not have been more helpful and have always been ready to assist with queries or to volunteer information. They are the late Professor E.K. Haviland of Baltimore, W.A. Laxon of Auckland, A. McMillan of Dunedin and the late W.G. Volum of Melbourne.

Throughout this project I have also welcomed the support and assistance of the company and over the past 30 years I have been grateful to G.R. Edmonds, D.A.Graham, P.R. Bremford, P.E. Maxwell R.G. Offwood, W.R. Holdsworth and latterly A.G. Pickering for the courtesies they have extended by checking my many queries and also offering suggestions to ensure correct presentation. Mr D.K. Richards of New Zealand Offshore Services Ltd. was also helpful in providing information on the vessels that company has been involved with since its inception. Union Company records sourced have included the vast amount of company archives held by the Hocken Library, Dunedin, *Annual Reports*, the histories of 1925, 1940 and the *Pocket Guides* from 1900 to 1968. The recent company magazines *Under Way* produced from 1967 to 1972, 1973 to 1984 and *Linkspan* from 1984 to 1988 have also been useful sources of reference.

I have been grateful for the support given by the New Zealand Ship and Marine Society of Wellington and the ready assistance provided by their publications editor, Dr. Gavin McLean.

As this project has extended over such a long period, it is difficult to enumerate in full, the many maritime enthusiasts and researchers who have assisted but I would particularly like to thank the following:

R.B. Applebee, Searsport, Maine; G.V. Broom, Auckland; D.C.E. Burrell, P.E. Cundall, Sydney; Alan B. Deitsch, New York; Howard W. Dick, Melbourne; Reece Discombe, Port Vila; J.Y. Freeman, Sydney; F.J. Hermans, Antwerp; David W. Johnson, Auckland; A.L. Kirk, Wanganui; N.J. McDonald, Baltimore; R.J. McDougall, Wellington; N.L. McKellar, Tamworth; S.J. Mallard, Dunedin;

T.A. Miles, Sydney; Ronald Parsons, Adelaide; Captain Michael Pryce, Wellington; Wm. A. Schell, Holbrook, Maine; T.S. Stevens, Melbourne; R.J. Tompkins, Sydney; E.H. Wallcott, Wellington; Eric Wharton, Auckland and D. Wright, Port Chalmers.

Whilst every endeavour has been made to achieve a high degree of accuracy with the information presented, the data is by no means infallible and any additional particulars or corrections would be welcomed and can be sent to me at P O Box 92, Dunedin.

Illustrations

Unless otherwise acknowledged, all the illustrations have come from the author's collection. Many have also been supplied by current ship photographers and their assistance is very much appreciated. The principal contributors, other than the author, are as follows:

Bain-Wright Collection – Photographs taken in Otago Harbour by J. Garry Bain from 1968 and Doug Wright from 1950.

J.Y. Freeman – Photographs taken in Adelaide 1947-1961 and Sydney from 1961.

N.J. Kirby – Photographs mainly taken in Lyttelton from 1960.

Where it has been possible to identify the original photographer his name has been put at the end of the caption. Most of the early prints have come from the following photographers:

Burton Brothers – Photographed throughout New Zealand between 1868–1916

David de Maus – Photographer at Port Chalmers 1867–1925

John Dickie – Photographer at Wellington circa 1910–1930

Edward Fluck – Ship photographer at Adelaide circa 1920–1938

Allan C. Green – Photographed ships in the port of Melbourne circa 1900–1954

Douglas Jones – Lyttelton ship photographer circa 1920–1957

William Livermore – Photographer at Sydney circa 1894–1924

Sydney Rawson – Amateur photographer in Dunedin circa 1901–1916

James Ring – Photographer at Greymouth circa 1880–1910

Many of the early glass plates and original prints used are now held in archives, museums and libraries in Australia and New Zealand and several illustrations have come from the collections in the Alexander Turnbull Library in Wellington and the Hocken Library in Dunedin. The availability of these prints has been very helpful in obtaining a photographic coverage of virtually all the ships owned by the company since its inception. Sincere thanks are extended to the archives and individual photographers who have kindly provided illustrations.

Reference Sources and Bibliography

NEWSPAPERS/CLASSIFICATION SOCIETIES/GOVERNMENT RECORDS CONSULTED

American Bureau of Shipping, Auckland, Manila and New York
Archives Office of Tasmania, Hobart
British Merchant Shipping (Losses) World War 1
British Merchant Vessels Lost or Damaged by Enemy Action during World War 2
Campbeltown Courier Ltd., Campbeltown
Companies Offices, Auckland, Christchurch, Dunedin, London and Wellington
Die Norske Veritas, Oslo
Evening Star, Dunedin
H.M. Customs Registers, Auckland, Christchurch, Dunedin, Hobart, Melbourne, Sydney and Wellington
Japan Maritime Science Foundation, Tokyo
Japanese Naval & Merchant Shipping Losses during World War 11
Lloyd's Agents, Kirkwall, Madras, Manila and Port Kelang
Lloyd's Confidential Indexes 1972–1992
Lloyd's Register of Shipping – Register Books from 1850–1999
Lloyd's Register of Shipping surveyors, Dunedin, Istanbul, London, Manila and Piraeus
Lloyd's Shipping Indexes 1976–2000
Marine Department, Hong Kong
Mercantile Navy Lists 1889–1963
Ministry of Defence, London
Nippon Kaiji Kyokai, Tokyo
Otago Daily Times, Dunedin
Otago Witness, Dunedin
Public Record Office, London
Registrar General of Shipping and Seamen, Cardiff
Register of Ships registered in New Zealand – 1840–1950 – Compiled by Dr. M.N. Watt, Dunedin
Ships of the Royal Navy – Statement of Losses during the Second World War 1939–1945
H.J. West handwritten notes from Otago newspapers 1858–1939

ARCHIVES/LIBRARIES/MAGAZINES

Australasian Shipping Record – Journal of the Australasian Maritime Historical Society, Adelaide
Australian National University, Canberra
Baltic Exchange, London
Belgian Shiplover – Journal of the Belgian Nautical Research Association
Central Library, Newcastle
Corporation of Dundee, Dundee
Denny Bros. records, University of Glasgow, Glasgow
Dunedin Public Library (Newspaper Card Index)
Fairplay Publications Ltd., London
General Assembly Library, Wellington
Greenock Public Library, Greenock
The Log – Journal of the Nautical Association of Australia Inc, Melbourne
Hocken Library, Dunedin (Union Steam Ship Company of N.Z. Ltd. archives)
Mitchell Library, Glasgow
National Archives, Auckland, Dunedin and Wellington
National Library of Australia, Canberra
National Library, Singapore
Newcastle Upon Tyne City Libraries, Newcastle
New Zealand Marine News – Journal of the N.Z. Ship and Marine Society Inc, Wellington
Orcadian, Kirkwall

References, Sources and Bibliography

Otago Settlers Museum (J.J. Mallard card index)
Royal Institute of Naval Architects, London
Shipbuilder and Marine Engine Builder Ltd., London
Shipbuilding and Shipping Record Ltd., London
State Library of New South Wales, Sydney
State Library of South Australia, Adelaide
State Library of Tasmania, Hobart
Supreme Court Library, Hong Kong
University of Singapore Library, Singapore
World Ship Society Central Record and journal *Marine News*

SHIPPING COMPANIES/ SHIP AND ENGINE BUILDERS/SHIPBREAKERS

Broken Hill Proprietory Ltd., Melbourne
Carmichael and Clarke Co. Ltd., Hong Kong
Century Shipping Agencies, Port Moresby
Chinese Maritime Trust, Hong Kong
David Rowan and Co. Ltd.
J.T. Duncan and Co. Ltd., Cardiff
Fearnley and Eger Ltd., Oslo
Grangemouth Dockyard Co. Ltd., Grangemouth
Greenock Dockyard Co. Ltd., Greenock
Guan Guan Shipping Pte. Ltd., Singapore
H.C. Sleigh Ltd., Melbourne
Henderson and Macfarlane Ltd., Auckland
Holm and Co. Ltd., Wellington
Wm Holyman and Sons Pty Ltd., Launceston
Hong Kong Chiap Hua Manufactory Co. Ltd., Hong Kong
Hong Kong and Whampoa Dockyard Co. Ltd., Hong Kong
Howard Smith Industries Ltd., Sydney
Jardine Matheson & Co. Ltd., Hong Kong
John Swire and Sons Ltd., London
John G Kincaid Ltd., Greenock
Lambert Bros.Limited, London
Leung Yau Shipbreaking Co., Hong Kong
Lithgows Limited, Port Glasgow
Mediterranea Marittima di Nav., Genoa
Miyachi Steamship Co. Ltd., Kobe
Richardsons Westgarth (Hartlepool) Ltd., Hartlepool
Swan Hunter Shipbuilders, Wallsend on Tyne
Uni-Ocean Lines Pte. Ltd., Singapore
Union Oil Company of California, San Luis Obispo
Wallem and Co. Ltd., Hong Kong

BOOKS

Broxam, Graeme, *Shipwrecks of Tasmania's Wild West Coast*, Navarine Publishing, Hobart, 1993

Bruce, A.B., *The Life of William Denny, Shipbuilder, Dumbarton*, Hodder and Stoughton, London, 1888

Burrell, D.C.E., *Furness Withy 1871–1991*,World Ship Society & Furness Withy & Co. Ltd., London 1992

Cowden, J.E. & J.O.C. Duffy, *The Elder Dempster Fleet History 1852–1985*, Mallet & Bell Publications, London, 1986

Credland, A.G., *The Wilson Line of Hull 1831–1981*, Hutton Press, Beverley, Yorkshire, 1994

Denny, Wm. & Bros. Ltd., *Denny of Dumbarton 1844 -1932,* Wm. Denny & Bros Ltd., Glasgow, 1932

Dick, H.W. & S.A. Kentwell, *Sold East, Traders and Tramps in Chinese Waters*, Nautical Assn of Australia, Melbourne, 1991

Driscoll, I.H., *Flightpath South Pacific,* Whitcombe & Tombs Ltd., Wellington, 1972

Falkensteen, Jorgen, Dampskibsselskabet "NORDEN" 1871–1996, Norden A/S, Copenhagen, 1996

Furniss, C., *Servants of the North(Northern Steam Ship Co)*, A.H. & A.W. Reed Ltd., Wellington, 1977

Gill, G. Hermon, *Royal Australian Navy 1939–1942*, Australian War Memorial, Canberra, 1957

Gill, G. Hermon, *Royal Australian Navy 1942–1945,* Australian War Memorial, Canberra, 1968

Grady, Don, *The Perano Whalers of Cook Strait 1911–1964,* A.H. & A.W. Reed Ltd., Wellington, 1982

Gregory, C. Dickson, *Australian Steamships Past and Present,* The Rochards Press, London, 1928

Hamilton, J.H., *The All Red Route 1853–1973*, British Columbia Historical Society, Vancouver, 1956

Hocking, C., *Dictionary of Disasters at Sea during the Age of Steam 1824–1962*, Lloyd's Register, London, 1969

Hubbard, Geo. C., *Leith Built Ships on War Service,* Henry Robb Ltd., Leith, 1946

Huddart, Parker Ltd., *Brief History of the Company 1876–1926,* Huddart Parker Ltd., Melbourne, 1926

Ingram, C.W.N., *New Zealand Shipwrecks 1795–1982,* 7th Ed, A.H. & A.W. Reed Ltd., Wellington, 1984

Johnson, J.W., *Union Airways,* Aviation Historical Society of New Zealand Inc., Christchurch, 1985

Jose, Arthur W., *The Royal Australian Navy 1914–18, Vol 1X,* Angus & Robertson, Sydney, 1928

King, John, David Phillips & Richard Waugh, *Early Risers – Pioneering story of Gisborne and Hawke's Bay Aviation,* Waugh, Manukau City, 1997

Lawson, Will, *Steam in the Southern Pacific,* Gordon & Gotch, Wellington, 1909

Lawson, Will, *Pacific Steamers,* Brown Son & Ferguson Ltd., Glasgow, 1927

Laxon, W.A. & F.W. Perry, *B.I. – The British India Steam Navigation Co. Ltd,* World Ship Society, London, 1994

Laxon, W.A., *Davey of the Awatea,* The Dunmore Press Ltd., Palmerston North, 1996

Loney, J., *Australian Shipwrecks Vol 3 1871–1900,* List Publishing Ltd., Geelong, 1982

Loney, J., *Australian Shipwrecks Vol 4 1901–1986,* Marine History Publications, Victoria, 1987

Lyon, David J., *The Denny List Vols 1 to 4,* National Maritime Museum, Greenwich, 1975

Maber, John M., *North Star to Southern Cross,* T. Stephenson & Sons Ltd., Prescott, U.K., 1967

Maude, W., *Antony Gibbs & Sons Ltd., Merchants & Bankers 1808–1958,* Millbrook Press, Soton, 1958

McDougall, R.J., *New Zealand Naval Vessels,* G.P. Books Ltd., Wellington, 1989

McKellar, N.L., *From Derby Round to Burketown – The A.U.S.N. Story,* University of Queensland Press, St. Lucia, 1958

McLauchlan, G., *The Line that Dared – A history of the U.S.S.Co.,* Four Star Books Ltd., Auckland, 1987

McLean, Gavin, *The Southern Octopus – The Rise of a Shipping Empire,* N.Z. Ship & Marine Society, Wellington, 1990

McLean, Gavin, *Canterbury Coasters,* N.Z. Ship & Marine Society, Wellington, 1987

McLean, Gavin, *Richardsons of Napier,* N.Z. Ship & Marine Society, Wellington, 1989

Mitchell, W.H. & L.A. Sawyer., *British Standard Ships of World War 1,* Journal of Commerce, Liverpool, 1968

Murray, Marischal, *Ships and South Africa,* Oxford University Press, Oxford, 1934

Page, Michael, *Fitted for the Voyage – Adelaide Steam Ship Co Ltd. 1875–1975,* Rigby Ltd., Adelaide, 1975

Rabson, Stephen, & Kevin O'Donoghue, *P & O – A Fleet History,* World Ship Society & P & O, London, 1989

Rhodes, Captain F., *Pageant of the Pacific,* 2 Vols, F.J. Thwaites Pty. Ltd., Sydney, 1936

Tregonning, K.G., *Home Port Singapore (Straits Steamship Co.1890–1965)* Oxford University Press Ltd., 1967

Waters, S.D., *German Raiders of the Pacific,* Dept. of Internal Affairs, Wellington, 1949

Waters, S.D., *The Royal New Zealand Navy,* Whitcombe & Tombs Ltd., Wellington, 1956

Waters, S.D., *Union Line 1875–1951,* Union Steam Ship Co. of N.Z. Ltd., Wellington, 1951

Shipping Index

A year in brackets after a name denotes the year the vessel entered the Union Company fleet.
Coal and Oil Storage hulks and launches are enumerated separately on pages 262–267

Abel Tasman (1933) 213
Abel Tasman (1957) 213
Adderley xx
Albion xviii, 12, 13
Amokura 231
Aorangi (1910) xix, xx, 88, 89
Aorangi (1924) x, xxi, xxiii, 120, 121, 122, 214, 253
Aotearoa 102, 103
Aparima 68, 69
Arahura 74, 75
Aramoana xxiii, 231
Aranui 231
Arawa 233
Arawata xviii, 10, 11, 247
Armagh 104, 105
Athelviscount 232, 233
Atua 78, 79, 84
Australia 32, 33
Awahou 233
Awatea x, xiii, xxi, xxii, 138, 139

Balls Head 232, 233
Baltannic 232, 233
Baltraffic 233
Banks Peninsula xviii, xix, 40, 41
Beautiful Star viii, x, xvii, 2, 3
Bellinger xiv, xix, 52, 53
Boojum 17
Bruce ix, x, xvii, 2, 3, 86
Brunner xviii, 36, 37
Bundhara xix

Canada Cape (*Waihemo*) xx
Corinna xix, 46, 47

Dartford xx, 228, 229
Dingadee 40, 41
Direct Condor 227
Direct Currawong 227
Direct Eagle 227
Direct Falcon 227
Direct Kea 227
Direct Kiwi 227
Direct Kookaburra 227
Dunedin 233

Edwin Bassett 228, 229
Erne 234
Euro 2

Fijian 38, 39
Flinders xix, 46, 47
Flora xix, 46, 47
Frederick Brown (*Karamea*) xxvii, 222

Gabriella xxi, 130, 131
Gawler 222
Genevie M Tucker 228, 229
Gladbrook 228, 229
Glenelg xix, 52, 53
Golden Age 234
Grafton xviii, 30, 31

Hamilton 234
Haupiri 54, 55
Hauraki xxi, 116, 117
Hauroto 20, 21
Hawea (1875) x, xvii, 4, 5
Hawea (1897) 54, 55

Hawea (1967) xxiii, 194, 195, 197
Herald 62, 63
Hero xviii, 16, 17
Himitangi 235
Hinemoa 150, 151, 172
Holmburn 218
Holmdale 204, 205, 216, 218, 253
Holmlea 218
Holmpark 218
Holmwood 219

Ilma 228, 230

James Cook 213
Janet Nicoll 42, 43

Kahika (1915) xx, 100, 101
Kahika (1938) 142, 143
Kaiapoi (1906) 78, 79
Kaiapoi (1949) 162, 163
Kaikorai 110, 111
Kaimai (1924) 118, 119
Kaimai (1956) 178, 179, 181
Kaimanawa (1920) 114, 115
Kaimanawa (1944) 148, 149
Kaimiro (1929) 128, 129
Kaimiro (1956) 174, 175
Kairanga 118, 119
Kaitangata (1908) 84, 85
Kaitangata (1948) 160, 161
Kaitawa 162, 163
Kaitoa 176, 177, 185
Kaitoke (1920) 96, 108, 109, 110
Kaitoke (1948) 160, 161
Kaituna (1905) 72, 73

263

Kaituna (1956) 176, 177
Kaiwarra 106, 107
Kakapo (1900) 64, 65
Kakapo (1903) 70, 71
Kakapo (1937) 140, 141
Kakariki 126, 127, 142
Kalingo xxi, 130, 131
Kamo (1913) 98, 99
Kamo (1947) 154, 155, 159
Kamona (1901) 68, 69
Kamona (1949) 164, 165
Kanieri 32, 33
Kanna (1911) 90, 91, 141
Kanna (1946) 148, 149, 150
Kaponga (1925) 124, 125
Kaponga (1955) 172, 173
Karamea 222
Karamu (1912) 92, 93
Karamu (1953) 170, 171
Karepo (1929) 128, 129
Karepo (1964) 188, 189, 191, 253
Karetu (1924) 120, 121
Karetu (1964) 190, 191, 253
Karitane (1905) 74, 75
Karitane (1939) 146, 147, 148
Karoon 166, 167, 169
Karori 70, 71
Kartigi 122, 123, 125
Karu (1915) xx, 102, 103
Karu (1935) 136, 137
Katea 182, 183
Katoa 92, 93
Katui 150, 151
Kauri (1912) 92, 93
Kauri (1936) 138, 139
Kawaroa 164, 165
Kawatiri (1887) xviii, 32, 33
Kawatiri (1920) 110, 111
Kawatiri (1950) 164, 165
Kawerau 174, 175
Kekerangu 110, 111
Kia Ora 58, 59
Kini (1898) 56, 57
Kini (1930) xxi, 134, 135
Kittawa 62, 63
Kiwitea 124, 125
Kokiri (1915) xx, 100, 101
Kokiri (1951) 166, 167
Komata (1907) 80, 81
Komata (1938) 144, 145
Komata (1947) 156, 157, 169, 170, 175, 179

Konini (1924) 118, 119
Konini (1957) 180, 181
Konui 162, 163
Koonya (1899) xx, 60, 61
Koonya (1957) 180, 181
Kootara 168, 169
Kopua 158, 159
Koputai 235
Koraki 180, 181, 183
Koranui (1885) xviii, 28, 29
Koranui (1920) 112, 113
Koranui (1956) 178, 179
Koromiko (1907) 82, 83
Koromiko (1947) 158, 159
Korowai 142, 143
Kotuku xxvii, 235
Kotuku (1900) 64, 65
Kowhai (1910) 88, 89, 92
Kowhai (1953) 170, 171
Kuaka xxvii, 236
Kumalla 178, 179, 181
Kurow (1909) 88, 89
Kurow (1939) 144, 145
Kurutai 168, 169

Ladybird xvii, 7
Leitrim 104, 105, 215
Limerick (1912) xx, 94, 95
Limerick (1925) 122, 123, 215
Loch Lomond 228, 229
Loongana x, xix, 72, 73, 224
Luhesand 236

Maheno (1905) 76, 77
Maheno (1969) xxiv, 194, 195, 196
Mahinapua 18, 19
Maitai (1885) xviii, 28, 29
Maitai (1908) 84, 85, 253
Makura xxii, 86, 87
Manapouri x, xviii, xx, 18, 19, 253
Manawatu xviii, 28, 29
Mangana xix, 44, 45
Manuka 70, 71
Maori (1875) viii, x, xvii, xviii, 2, 3
Maori (1907) 82, 83, 151
Maori (1953) xxiii, 172, 173, 193, 252
Mapourika 58, 59
Marama (1907) 82, 83
Marama (1969) xxiv, 196, 197
Mararoa xviii, xix, 30, 31, 253

Margaret W 215
Marrawah 236
Mary Holyman 214
Matthew Flinders 213
Matua xiii, 136, 137, 195, 253
Maui Pomare 236
Maunganui 90, 91
Mawhera xviii, 26, 27, 253
Melbourne xxi
Moa xix, 50, 51
Moana xix, 56, 57
Moana Roa 236
Moeraki 68, 69, 253, 254
Mokoia 60, 61
Monowai (1890) 40, 41, 253
Monowai (1930) xxiii, 134, 135, 171, 253
Moreton xix, 48, 49
Moura 62, 63, 253

Nairana 224, 225
Narbada 104, 105, 215
Natone 66, 67, 253
Navua (1904) 72, 73
Navua (1955) 174, 175, 179, 181, 253
Nelson 18
Ngahere (1922) xxi, 236, 237
Ngahere (1966) 192, 193, 253
Ngakuta (1942) xxi, 146, 147
Ngatuka (1962) xxiii, 186, 187, 193, 253
Ngapara 192, 193, 253
Ngatoro (1942) xxi, 148, 149
Ngatoro (1962) 186, 187, 193, 253
Niagara xx, 96, 97, 214
Nimrod xx

Ocean Bulk 1 xxvii, 222
Ohau 25
Omana xxi, 130, 131
Omapere 20, 21
Oonah xix, 48, 49, 224
Opihi 116, 117, 137
Opouri xx, 116
Oreti xix, xviii, 36, 37
Orowaiti (1887) xviii, xix, 34, 35
Orowaiti (1921) xxi, 114, 115, 122, 253
Otokia 122, 123, 253
Ovalau 44, 45, 253

Paloona 86, 87, 253
Pamir 236, 237
Parera 219
Pateena (1891) xix, 48, 49, 253
Pateena (1958) 184, 185
Pateke 219
Penguin xix, 12, 13
Phoebe xvii, 4, 5
Pilot 71
Pioneer 53
Plucky 236
Poherua 44, 45
Poolta (1925) xxi, 120, 121
Poolta (1959) 184, 185
Port Tauranga (Kopua) xxiii, 159, 216
Port Underwood (Underwood) 216
Port Waikato xxiii, 158, 159, 216
Port Whangarei 216
Pretty Jane viii
Pukaki 36, 37, 253
Pukeko 219
Puriri 216

Rakanoa 52, 53
Rangatira (1931) x, xxi, xxii, 134, 135, 172
Rangatira (1972) xxiv, 196, 197, 227
Rapuhia 238
Rarawa xx
Red Pine 238
Richmond (Haupiri) xix
Ringarooma xviii, 10, 11
Risdon 186, 187
Rosamond 38, 39, 247
Roscommon xx, 94, 95
Rotoiti xx, 58, 59
Rotokino 42, 43
Rotomahana x, xviii, xix, 14, 15, 16, 253
Rotorua xvii, 8, 9

Samson xvii, 238
Searoad Mersey xxvii
Searoad Tamar xxvii
Seaway Hobart 206, 207
Seaway King xxiii, 190, 191
Seaway Melbourne 206, 207
Seaway Prince x, xxiv, 198, 199, 201, 213, 227
Seaway Princess x, 200, 201, 213, 227

Seaway Queen xxiii, 188, 189, 198
Snark 22, 23
Sophia R Luhrs 228, 229
Southern Cross xviii, 16, 17, 253
Spirit of Competition 223
Spirit of Free Enterprise 223
Squall (1912) xx, 78, 79
Squall (1972) 217
St.. Kilda xviii
Storm 218
Sussex 116, 117
Suva xviii, 22, 23

Tahiti xx, 90, 91
Taiaroa xvii, 8, 9
Taieri 38, 39
Taiko xvi, xviii, 204, 205, 253
Taioma xxi, 156, 157, 253
Takapuna xviii, 24, 25
Talune (1891) xix, 50, 51, 253
Talune (1930) 132, 133
Tamahine xxiii, 124, 125
Tapuhi 156, 157, 253
Taranaki xvii, 6, 7
Tararua xviii, 12, 13
Tarawera (1882) 22, 23, 257
Tarawera (1958) 182, 183
Taroona 224, 225
Tasman Enterprise xxvi, 238
Tasman Venture xxvi, 238
Tatana 226
Taupo (1875) x, xvii, 4, 5
Taupo (1884) xix, 27
Taveuni (1968) 194, 195
Taviuni (1890) xix, 42, 43, 195
Te Anau 16, 17
Tekapo xviii, xxiv, 26, 27
Terawhiti 80, 81, 101, 157, 253
Titoki 204, 217
Tofua (1908) 84, 85
Tofua (1951) 168, 169
Tolten 140, 141
Totara (1926) 216
Totara (1972) 217
Totara (1982) xxv, 238
Tuatea 76, 77
Turihaua 216
Tyrone xx, 94, 95, 104

Underwood 146, 147
Union Aotearoa xxiv, 202, 203, 239
Union Auckland 206, 207, 239, 253

Union Australia 239
Union Dunedin 239, 240
Union Endeavour 208, 209, 253
Union Hobart 206, 207, 241
Union Lyttelton 207, 241
Union Melbourne 201, 241
Union Nelson 204, 205
Union New Zealand 239, 240
Union Rotoiti x, xvi, xxvii, 201, 202, 203, 253
Union Rotoma xvi, xxvii, 208, 209, 253
Union Rotorua xxiv, xxvii, 200, 201, 253
Union South Pacific 227, 242
Union Sydney (1974) 242
Union Sydney (1983) 242, 243
Union Trans Tasman 239, 240
Union Wellington 198, 199
Upolu 50, 51

Wahine (1913) 98, 99, 151
Wahine (1966) xxiii, 192, 193, 196
Waiana 140, 141
Waihemo (1914) xx, 100, 101
Waihemo (1919) 108, 109
Waihemo (1946) 154, 155, 214
Waihi 18, 19
Waihora (1883) 24, 25
Waihora (1907) 80, 81
Waikare (1897) 56, 57, 60
Waikare (1958) 182, 183
Waikawa (1915) 102, 103
Waikawa (1919) 108, 109
Waikawa (1946) 152, 153, 214
Waikouaiti 112, 113
Waimarino (1915) 98, 99
Waimarino (1930) 132, 133
Waimate 74, 166, 167
Waimea (1928) 128, 129
Waimea (1953) 170, 171, 183
Wainui (1887) 34, 35, 253
Wainui (1930) 123, 133, 137
Wainui (1965) xxiv, 190, 191
Waiotapu 112, 113
Waipahi 126, 127, 253
Waipiata 126, 127, 132
Waipori (1901) 67
Waipori (1938) 144, 145
Wairarapa xviii, 20, 21
Wairata 154, 155, 160, 183
Wairimu 160, 161, 183

Wairuna (1905) 74, 75
Wairuna (1919) 106, 107
Wairuna (1946) 152, 153, 214
Waitaki (1879) xviii, 14, 15
Waitaki (1934) 136, 137
Waitaki (1964) 188, 189, 190
Waitaki (1983) xxv, 239
Waitemata (1908) 86, 87, 253
Waitemata (1919) 106, 107
Waitemata (1946) xxiii, 150, 151

Waitomo (1913) 96, 97
Waitomo (1946) 152, 153, 214
Waitotara 104, 105
Wakatipu xvii, 10, 11, 253
Wanaka (1876) xvii, 6, 7
Wanaka (1897) 54, 55
Wanaka (1938) 142, 143
Wanaka (1970) xxiii, xxiv, 196, 197
Wareatea xviii, 34, 35, 214
Warrimoo 66, 67, 84

Wellington xvii, xviii, 6, 7
Westmeath xx, 96, 97
Whangape 64, 65
William Holyman 214
Willochra 243
Wingatui 114, 115, 140

Yolla 60, 61

Zealandia 243

General Index

Abel Tasman Shipping Co. Pty. Ltd. 213
Abeles, E.H.P. xv, xvi
Adelaide Steam Ship Company xi, 243
Air New Zealand xiv
Albion Shipping Company xvii, 8, 9
Anchor Dorman Limited 216
Anchor Shipping & Foundry Co. Ltd. 58, 59, 74, 75, 128, 129, 215, 216
Associated Steamships Pty. Ltd. xxiv, 227
Auckland Steam Ship Co. Ltd. xviii, 16, 17
Australasian Shipping xxvi
Australasian Steam Navigation Company Ltd. xvii, xviii
Australasian United Steam Navigation Co xi, 40, 41, 254
Australian & New Zealand Direct Line (ANZDL) xvi, xxvii, 227
Australian Consolidated Industries Ltd. xvi, xxvii, 227
Australian National Airways vii, xiv, xxi
Australian National Line xxv, xxvi, xxvii
Australian Offshore Services xxiv, 220

B.P. New Zealand Limited xxi, 231, 233, 234, 235, 236
Beswick, H.J. 215
BIL Maritime Holdings Limited 227
Black Diamond Line (W.R. Williams) xviii, 28-31, 34, 35, 228, 253
Blackball Coal Company Limited xxi, 146-149, 237, 253
Brierley Investments Limited xvi, xxv, xxvii, 226, 227
Bright Bros. & Company ix, 16, 17
British India Steam Navigation Co. Ltd. xix
Brunner Coal Company Limited xviii, 36-39
Bulkships xxvi, 214, 227
Burns Philp & Co. xi

Canadian Australasian Line xxi, xxiii, 120, 121, 214
Canadian Australian Royal Mail Line xix, 66, 67, 84, 85, 88, 89
Canadian Pacific Airlines xxiii

Canadian Pacific Railway Company 214
Canadian Union Line Limited xxiii, 152-155
Canterbury Shipping Company Limited 92, 93, 214, 223
Canterbury Steam Shipping Co.Ltd. 215, 216, 217
Cargills xiii
Coal & Bunkering Co. Ltd. 233
Coastal Express Line Pty.Ltd. xxvi, xxvii
Coastal Tankers Limited 204, 205, 235, 236, 253
Conifor Consultants Limited xxv, xxvi, xxxvi
Consort Shipping Line 223
Cook Islands Trading Corp. Ltd. xxv
Cook Strait Airways Limited xxi
Cook, Thos & Company Limited xxv, xxvi
Cory, Wm & Sons Limited 114, 115, 122, 123, 253
CP Ships of Canada xvi, xxvii, 227
Crossocean Forwarding Services xxvii
Crowley Maritime Corp. Ltd 222
Cruising xvii, xviii, 8, 22, 56

Darling, John viii, ix
Denholm, J & J Limited xi
Denny, Peter ix, x, xii, xiii
Denny, Wm & Bros. ix, x, xii
Diver Services International Limited xxv
Donald & Edinborough xix, 54, 55
Dorman Engineering Company Ltd. 216

East Coast Airways Limited xxi, xxii
Eastern & Australian Steamship Co. Ltd. xxiii
Eckford, Captain Thomas xix
Erikson, Gustaf 236, 237
Executive Printing (1977) Limited xxiv

Falla, N.S. xiii, xiv, xv
Fell Brothers xix
Fletcher Holdings Limited 226
Freightways Holdings Limited 215

General Motors Corporation xii

Gisborne Sheepfarmers Frozen Meat Co 215
Grand Pacific Hotel, Suva xx
Grey Valley Coal Company Limited xviii
Grice Sumner & Company xviii
Group Bollore Technologies of Paris xxvii, 227

H.C.S. Coasters Pty. Ltd. 213
Harbour Steam Company vii, viii, ix, x, xvii, 2, 234, 238
Holm Shipping Co. Ltd. 204, 205, 216, 218, 236, 253
Holm, Ferdinand 100-103, 215
Holyman Air vii, xiv
Holyman Limited xvi, xxvii, 227
Holyman, James Pty. Ltd. 214
Holyman, Wm & Sons Pty. Ltd. xxi, 214, 236
Houlder Bros Limited xx, 94-97
Howard Smith (N.Z.) Limited xxvi
Howard Smith Limited xi, xxvi
Huddart Parker Limited xi, 86, 87, 214, 224, 243

Imperial Airways xiv, xxii
Indian service xviii, xix, xxi. xxiv, 26, 104, 116, 140, 154, 160, 189, 190
Indo-Pacific Shipping Company Ltd. xxi, 104, 105, 122, 123, 140, 141, 215
Inter Ports Shipping Corporation Limited 223
Inter-Island Express Ltd. xxv
Inter-Island Services x, xiii, xix, xxi, xxiii, xxiv, 12, 48, 83, 98, 124, 134, 150, 172, 192, 196
Invercargill Shipping Company Limited xix, 215
Isaac, William viii

Johnson & Company Limited xix
Jones, J.R. viii
Jones, John vii, viii

K.P.N. Group xxvii, 227
Kaipara Steam Ship Company Limited 226
Keegan, John xv, xvi

Lamb, R.S. & Company Limited xxi, 130, 131, 134, 135, 253
Land & Mortgage Securities Limited 215
Levin & Co. Ltd. 233, 235
Livestock International Limited 215
Lloyd Triestino xxii

Macfarlane, Captain James viii
Malcolm, Captain James viii
Mann, George & Co. Ltd. 146-149, 236
Maoriland Steamship Company Limited xx, 38, 39, 100-103, 215

Maritime Carriers (N.Z.) Limited xxv, 233, 239
McEwan, J & Company Limited xviii, 22, 23
McIlwraith, McEacharn Limited xi
McKay Shipping Limited xxvii
McKenzie, R. Brooke 223
McLatchie, G. & Co. Ltd. 215, 224
McLean, Dr Gavin xii
McMeckan, Blackwood & Co. x, xvii, 10-13
Melbourne Steamship Company xi
Mercantile Investments Limited 215, 216
Milburn New Zealand Limited 222
Mill, John & Co. Limited 220
Mills, James viii, ix, x, xii, xiii, xiv, xv, xvii, xxi, 215
Mitsui O.S.K. Lines xxvi

N.Z. Maritime Holdings Limited xxiv, xxv, xxvi, 214, 226, 227
N.Z. Stevedoring Co. Ltd. xvi, xxv, xxvi
N.Z.Stevedoring & Wharfingering Co. Ltd. xxv, xxvi
New Zealand Government (Railways Dept.) xxiii, 231
New Zealand Govt. (Dept of Scientific Research) 238
New Zealand Govt. (Island Territories Dept) 236
New Zealand Line xxvi
New Zealand National Airways Corp. xiv, xxiii
New Zealand Offshore Services Limited xxiv, 220
New Zealand Oil Consortium 231, 233, 234, 236
New Zealand Shipping Co. Ltd. xx, 66, 67, 84, 85, 88, 89, 188-191, 220
New Zealand Steam Shipping Co. Ltd. xvii
North American services xviii, xix, xx, xxi, xxiii, 30, 40, 56, 86, 90, 96, 120, 152, 154, 253
Northern Steam Ship Company Limited xviii, xix, xx, 32, 33, 58, 59

Oamaru & Dunedin Steam Company Limited xviii, 14, 15
Ocean Bulk Limited xxvii, 221, 222
Ocean Towing & Salvage (Cook Island) Limited xxvii, 221, 222
Oceanic Steamship Company xviii, xx
Opouri Shipping Company Limited xx
Orient Line xvii
Otago Towing Company 235, 236
Owens Group Limited xxvii

P & O S. N. Co. xi, xiii, xiv, xix, xv, xx, xxiii, xxiv, xxvi, xxvii, 214, 220, 226, 234, 241
Pacific & World Travel Limited xxi
Pacific Forum Line xxvi
Pacific Islands services xiii, xviii, xix, xx, xxvi, 16, 44, 72, 78, 84, 126, 136, 168, 253
Pacifica Shipping Company Limited xxv, 214, 223

General Index

Peninsula & Akaroa Steam Navigation Co. Ltd. xviii, 40, 41
Perry Dines Corporation Limited 216
Piesse Transport Limited 227
Pine Steamship Co. of Westland Limited 238

QANTAS Airways xxii

Railroader xi
Reynolds, T.A. & Company Limited xix, 52, 53
Richardson & Company Limited xx, 78, 79, 215, 216, 219, 253
Royal Interocean Lines xxiv, xviii

Saturday Sunny Swinging Holidays Ltd. xxv
Sea Containers Chartering Limited 242
Seafreighter xi, xvi
Seaport Operations Limited xxv
Shaw Savill & Albion Co. Ltd. 233
Shipping Corporation of New Zealand Limited xxv
Skeggs Foods Limited xxv, 223
Skeggs, C.G. 223
Sleigh, H.C. Limited 213
Sloan, Alfred P xii
Smokeless Fuel & Briquettes (Canterbury) Ltd. 224
Smokeless Fuel Company Limited 224
SOFE Shipping Enterprises Limited 223
Solid Energy Limited 221, 222
South Pacific Passenger Services Limited xxvi, 226, 227
South Seas Shipping Limited xxv, 223
Stevedoring Services of America Limited xxvi
Super Luggage Stores Limited 216

T.N.T. Shipping N.Z. Limited xxiv, xxvi, 226, 227
Tasman Empire Airways vii, xiv, xxii, xxiii
Tasman Express Line Limited xxvi, xxvii
Tasman Pulp & Paper Co. Ltd. xxvi, 238
Tasman Union Limited xv, xxiv, 226
Tasmanian Government xxi, 120, 121
Tasmanian Steam Navigation Co. Ltd. xix, 44-51
Tasmanian Steamers Proprietory Limited xxi, 48, 49, 72, 73, 224
Thomas Nationwide Transport (T.N.T.) xv, xvi, xxiv, xxv, xxvii, 227
Timaru Stevedoring Company Limited xxv
Trans Pacific Passenger Agency Ltd. xxi
Trans Tasman trades x, xiii, xv, xvi, xvii, xviii, xxi, xxii, xxiii, xxiv, xxv, xxvi, xxvii, 9, 10, 134, 138, 214
Trucape Pty. Ltd. 214

Union Airways vii, xiv, xxi, xxiii
Union Bulkships Pty. Ltd. xxiv, xxv, xxvi, xxvii
Union Citco Travel Limited xxv
Union Corporate Services Limited xxvi, 227
Union Direct Line xxvii, 227
Union Engineering Limited xxv
Union Industrial & Marine Limited xxv
Union Industries Limited xxv
Union Maritime Services Limited xxiv, xxv, xxvi, xxvii
Union Merchants Limited xxv
Union Royal Mail Line xxii
Union Shipping Australia Pty. Ltd. xxvi, xxvii
Union Shipping Bulk Limited xxvii, 221, 222
Union Shipping Group Limited xi, xxiv, xxv, xxvi, xxvii, 226, 227
Union Shipping New Zealand Limited xxvi, xxvii, 221, 222
Union Steam Ship Company (U.K.) Limited 227
Union Steam Ship Company of Australia Pty. Ltd. xxiv, xxvi, 213
Union Stevedoring Services Limited xxiv, xxv, xxvii
Union Travel Limited xvi, xxv
United Baltic Corporation Limited 233

Wairau Steam Ship Company Limited xix, 18, 19, 215
Waitaki Container Line xxv, 238
Wallcott, James A. ix
Watchlin, Captain A.F. xxiii, 146, 147, 158, 159, 216
Waterfront Industry Commission xxvi
Weir, Andrew & Co. xi
Wellington Marine Repair Works Ltd. xx
Wellington Patent Slip Co. Ltd. xx
Wellington Steam Packet Co. Ltd. xix, 50, 51
Westport Coal Company Limited xviii, 32-35
Wong Shipping Company Limited 223